Facilitating
Shared
Success

A *Practical Guide* for
Leading Collaborative
School Improvement

Deb Page   Jean Quigg
Judith Hale   Kayla Duncan

Foreword by Michael Duncan

Solution Tree | Press
a division of
Solution Tree

555 North Morton Street
Bloomington, IN 47404
800.733.6786 (toll free) / 812.336.7700
FAX: 812.336.7790

email: info@SolutionTree.com
SolutionTree.com

Visit **go.SolutionTree.com/schoolimprovement** to download the free reproducibles in this book.

Printed in the United States of America

FSC
www.fsc.org
MIX
Paper | Supporting
responsible forestry
FSC® C008955

Library of Congress Control Number: 2025022108

ISBN: 979-8-89374-025-7

Solution Tree
Cameron L. Rains, CEO
Edmund M. Ackerman, President

Solution Tree Press
Publisher: Kendra Slayton
Associate Publisher: Todd Brakke
Acquisitions Director: Hilary Goff
Editorial Director: Laurel Hecker
Art Director: Rian Anderson
Managing Editor: Sarah Ludwig
Copy Chief: Jessi Finn
Developmental Editor: Gabriella Jones-Monserrate
Senior Production Editor: Christine Hood
Copy Editor: Jessi Finn
Proofreader: Elijah Oates
Text and Cover Designer: Fabiana Cochran
Content Development Specialist: Amy Rubenstein
Associate Editor: Elijah Oates
Editorial Assistant: Madison Chartier

Acknowledgments

Thanks to all of those who believed in us and supported us.

—Deb, Judy, Jean, and Kayla

❧

We are so very grateful for the mentoring and wisdom of Dr. Judith Hale. She has impacted countless organizations and professionals, and we are thankful that we are among the many. Thank you!

—Deb, Jean, and Kayla

❧

Solution Tree Press would like to thank the following reviewers:

Lindsey Bingley
Literacy and Numeracy Strategist
Foothills Academy Society
Calgary, Alberta, Canada

Doug Crowley
Assistant Principal
DeForest Area High School
DeForest, Wisconsin

Janet Gilbert
Principal
Mountain Shadows
Elementary School
Glendale, Arizona

Janet Nuzzie
Intervention Specialist,
K–12 Mathematics
Pasadena ISD
Pasadena, Texas

Visit **go.SolutionTree.com/schoolimprovement** to
download the free reproducibles in this book.

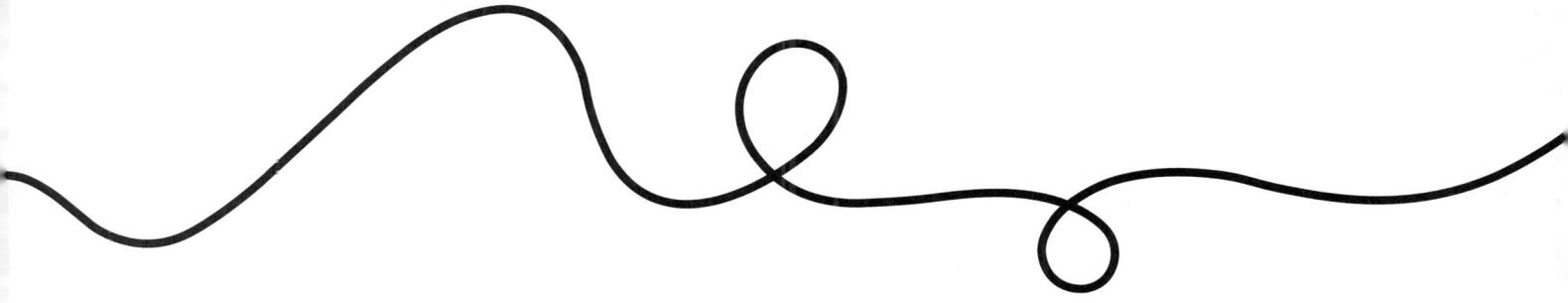

Table of Contents

Reproducibles are in italics.

About the Authors

Deb Page is owner and president of The Institute for Performance Improvement, which trains and certifies school-improvement specialists, performance-improvement specialists across all sectors, and adult-development and performance-support professionals. She is a former senior executive director of the Georgia Leadership Institute for School Improvement and senior vice president for Citibank. She began her career as a high school language arts teacher. Her purpose and passion are to develop professionals to facilitate learning and performance journeys for collaborative improvement, innovation, and implementation.

Page is a Certified Performance Technologist and longtime member of the International Society for Performance Improvement (ISPI) and has collaborated with former ISPI president Judith Hale to develop and validate standards and certifications for professionals who guide collaborative performance improvement. Page is a lifelong, self-directed learner who has studied under international performance-improvement experts such as Judith Hale, Gloria Gery, and Robert Brinkerhoff, the leading expert in adult learning transfer to practice. She completed her High Performance Learning Journeys® certification in 2018 and her Certified Performance Improvement Facilitator™ certification in 2019.

Her coauthored books include *The School Improvement Specialist Field Guide, First Edition* and *Second Edition*. She has contributed chapters to *Fundamentals of Performance Improvement* and *Improving Performance Through Learning*. She has also published numerous *Performance Improvement Journal* articles.

Page holds a bachelor of science in education from the University of Georgia.

To learn more about Deb Page's work, visit The Institute for Performance Improvement website (www.TIFPIedu.org), or follow her at www.linkedin.com/in/deb-page-cpt-cpif-a5 403737 on LinkedIn. You may contact her at www.TIFPIedu.org/contact.

*J*udith Hale, PhD, CPT, CFT, AIM, is an International Board of Standards for Training, Performance and Instruction (IBSTPI) fellow and the president of Hale Associates. Since starting her firm in 1974, Dr. Hale has worked with the public and private sectors across all industries, specializing in performance improvement, certification, and assessment. Her professional focus has been and continues to be the development of performance-based and portfolio-based assessments.

Dr. Hale taught speech for seven years at Wright College and taught graduate courses in management for fourteen years for the Insurance School of Chicago, where she received the school's Outstanding Educator award. Currently, she advises clients on how to be good stewards of generative AI when leveraging it to develop training, instructional tactics, and exams. Her firm offers certificates in test and assessment design, qualitative and quantitative data-gathering methods, analytics, and psychometrics.

Dr. Hale is a past president of the International Society for Performance Improvement, IBSTPI, and the Chicago Chapter of the Industrial Relations Research Association. She served on the Illinois Occupational Skill Standards and Credentialing Council and was a commercial arbitrator with the American Arbitration Association.

She is a coauthor of the award-winning *School Improvement Specialist Field Guide* and the author of the award-winning book *Performance-Based Certification, Second Edition*. She is the author of the popular *Performance Consultant's Fieldbook, Second Edition*; *Performance-Based Evaluation*; *Performance-Based Management*; and *Outsourcing Training and Development*.

Dr. Hale received a bachelor's degree in communication from Ohio State University, a master's degree in communication from Miami University, and a doctorate in instructional design from Purdue University. Her research was on controlling bias in competency studies.

To learn more about Judith Hale's work, visit the Hale Center website (www.HaleCenter .org), or follow her at www.linkedin.com/in/judith-hale-b7b3aa on LinkedIn and at www .facebook.com/judith.hale.50 on Facebook.

*J*ean Quigg, EdD, is a performance-improvement consultant. She also serves as national director of certification for The Institute for Performance Improvement and develops and teaches courses for educators about the facilitation of collaborative and sustainable improvement.

Dr. Quigg is a retired school system superintendent in Georgia, where she was an innovative and recognized leader of excellence in school improvement. As superintendent, she led the alignment of curriculum, instruction, and assessment; the implementation of standards-based instruction and grading; and the planning and implementation of a career academy. Dr. Quigg began her career as an educator in 1978 and has also served as a teacher, reading specialist, assistant principal, principal, and assistant superintendent of curriculum and instruction for grades preK–12. Her experience includes working in rural, urban, and low- and high-performing schools.

As a principal in Texas, Dr. Quigg led her school to earn the U.S. Department of Education Blue Ribbon Award for National Exemplary School and the National Endowment for the Arts Commendation. She believes a collaborative and consistent process for school improvement is critical for success. She has presented at conferences around the United States on topics including leadership for school improvement, instructional coaching, and the Certified School Improvement Specialist™ (CSIS) standards and certification. Dr. Quigg is coauthor of the training courses *LAUNCH!*™ and *Elevate*™ *Learning and Performance Journeys*. She is coauthor of *The School Improvement Specialist Field Guide, Second Edition*.

Dr. Quigg's academic journey set the foundation for her deep commitment to teaching and leading for learning. She earned a bachelor's degree in elementary education from the University of Georgia, a master's degree in reading from the University of Georgia, a specialist degree in reading from Valdosta State University, and a doctorate in education mid-management from the University of Houston. She is a Certified School Improvement Specialist and has Instructional Design and High Performance Learning Journeys certifications.

To learn more about Jean Quigg's work, visit The Institute for Performance Improvement website (www.TIFPIedu.org), or follow her at www.linkedin.com/in/jean-quigg-ed-d on LinkedIn. You may contact her at www.TIFPIedu.org/contact.

Kayla Duncan, EdD, is the coordinator of continuous improvement for Forsyth County Schools in Georgia and a professor of human performance improvement at the University of West Georgia. With expertise in instructional design, professional learning, and systemic school improvement, she supports schools in developing sustainable, data-driven strategies that enhance student performance and educator effectiveness.

Previously, Dr. Duncan served as a professional learning specialist; she designed and implemented strategic professional learning initiatives, led districtwide innovation efforts, and supported schools in building capacity for continuous improvement. She began her career in the classroom, where she remains grounded in her practice. She has had the opportunity to support a diverse range of schools, including Title I schools, International Baccalaureate programs, and international schools. Her purpose in education is to empower and support teams to reach their goals by fostering collaborative and innovative approaches to improvement.

Dr. Duncan is actively engaged in professional organizations and leadership programs, including the Learning Forward Academy and The Institute for Performance Improvement. She is also a board member of the Learning Forward Georgia affiliate. Dr. Duncan has presented at national and international conferences, such as the Association for Educational Communications and Technology (AECT) National Research Conference and the American International Schools in the Americas (AMISA) Science of Learning Conference in Brazil. She has contributed her research on learning transfer and school improvement to publications such as *Learning That Transfers: Designing Curriculum for a Changing World* and her dissertation, *Examining Students' Approaches to Transfer in Mathematics*.

Dr. Duncan holds a bachelor of science in health and physical education from the University of Georgia; a master of arts in mathematics education from Western Governors University; and an education specialist degree in learning, design, and technology from the University of Georgia. She earned her doctor of education in school improvement, with a concentration in learning, design, and technology, from the University of West Georgia.

To learn more about Kayla Duncan's work, follow her @MrsKaylaDuncan on X and www.linkedin.com/in/kaylabduncan on LinkedIn.

To book Deb Page, Judith Hale, Jean Quigg, or Kayla Duncan for professional development, contact pd@SolutionTree.com.

Foreword

By *Michael Duncan*,
Founder, NorthStarK12

As educators and leaders, we continually seek ways to ensure students are prepared to meet the challenges of our rapidly changing world. For decades, we have known what works to improve student outcomes, yet execution has too often been lacking—perhaps simply due to a scarcity of will.

In *Facilitating Shared Success*, you will find a gold mine of practical wisdom and actionable advice that is sorely needed in today's K–12 education landscape. This handbook provides a comprehensive guide to navigating the complexities of school improvement, emphasizing the importance of systemic collaboration, critical analysis, and sustained engagement.

One of this book's key strengths is its emphasis on helping readers understand the profound systemic issues that create the current state of education before jumping to solutions. Leaders must reflect on previous work to inform the analysis and consideration of future endeavors. Jumping to solutions can be a fatal flaw in school-improvement efforts despite the widespread availability of training and resources.

The book also underscores the value of people and partnerships as vital components of school improvement. Collaborative inquiry promotes collective efficacy and creates the conditions for motivation, value, and joy in the learning process.

How motivated are students to achieve a goal they had no hand in creating? We know that students perform better if what they're learning matters to them. Engaging with students to understand what they want from their education is an essential part of the educational process. We must give students a voice in their own journey.

This book offers a compelling vision for the future of education by emphasizing the value of learner-centered environments that cultivate student agency and autonomy. These environments promote the acquisition of durable skills such as critical thinking, problem solving, communication, and collaboration—cornerstones of effective school improvement and a path to deeper learning for all students.

Deeper learning occurs when rigorous academic content is integrated with experiences that cultivate durable skills. The outcome of this is authentic, student-led inquiry. Students apply their knowledge and skills to real-world challenges, bridging the gaps between content, durable skills, and application.

Often, though, we fall short of the mark when attempting to create meaningful and engaging learning experiences for students. Our relentless focus on test scores leaves students struggling to find personal relevance and joy in their education. If we broaden our view of student success to include durable skills and deeper learning, we can create an ecosystem of education that expands beyond the walls of the school and honors the learning that occurs in all facets of life.

Facilitating Shared Success is a valuable resource that equips leaders with the tools and processes necessary to make meaningful, lasting change in education. It promotes the creation of instructional environments characterized by inquiry, self-direction, and authenticity, ensuring all students are ready for the challenges and opportunities of the future.

It is my hope that this handbook will inspire and guide educators to transform their schools, ultimately preparing all students to succeed in our rapidly changing world.

Introduction

*E*ducation is the foundation of progress, and at its heart lies the relentless pursuit of growth. For educators, improvement sharpens methods, innovation transforms classrooms, and implementation ensures ideas impact learners' lives. In an era when education faces unprecedented obstacles—ranging from socioeconomic disparities and mental health crises to the rapid pace of technological and cultural change—hope and resilience are not merely desirable; they are essential. These qualities equip educators to navigate complexity, sustain their passion for teaching, and inspire their students to thrive.

Hope and resilience are the foundation of educational excellence. Hope propels educators to envision brighter futures for their students, even in the face of adversity. It fuels resilience, empowering both teachers and learners to rise above challenges and persist in the pursuit of meaningful growth. By embracing hope and resilience as driving forces, schools can shift from reactive change to proactive innovation, and they can ensure that students develop not just academic knowledge but the adaptability and problem-solving skills critical for success.

Schools exist within a dynamic ecosystem where student success is influenced by an intricate web of factors—shifting workforce demands, economic conditions, social inequities, evolving family structures, mental health challenges, and rapid technological advancements. The traditional siloed approaches to school improvement are no longer sufficient. To drive meaningful, sustainable change, schools must embrace collaborative improvement, innovation, and disciplined implementation.

Improvement efforts often fail not because schools and communities lack good intentions but because they lack a structured, shared process for working together to address challenges. When school-improvement programs fail to engage the people who can impact the outcomes, they are a waste of time and a source of frustration. Sustainable school improvement requires collaboration among stakeholders. The work also requires taking a systemic view while staying focused on results.

The stakes have never been higher. Many students, particularly those from historically underserved backgrounds, continue to face barriers to academic success. Schools are on the front lines of supporting students in a time of rising anxiety, trauma, and social-emotional challenges. Educators face increasing burnout, leading to staffing shortages and declining morale. Schools must prepare students for an unpredictable future, yet many struggle to align instruction with workforce and economic needs. Without a systematic, collaborative approach, the best ideas remain unimplemented, resources are underutilized, and improvement efforts stall before real impact can be realized.

Done well, school improvement is an engaging, empowering process that shifts people from independent work to authentic collaboration on shared goals. Collaboration creates a cycle of growth and adaptation, fostering a resilient and forward-thinking educational environment. It is how to engage stakeholders in authentic collaboration that makes this book unique.

To address pressing challenges and transform school-improvement efforts, this book provides a road map for educators committed to the three aforementioned essential pillars: (1) improvement, (2) innovation, and (3) implementation. The ten national Certified School Improvement Specialist (CSIS) standards provide the framework for the information shared in this book. Each chapter aligns to one of them. These standards, researched and developed by Judith Hale and Deb Page for The Institute for Performance Improvement, are validated every five years and reflect the work that practicing educators identify as most effective in their improvement work (Page & Hale, 2013). They are the foundation for the CSIS project-based certification offered by The Institute for Performance Improvement (www.TIFPIedu.org). The ten standards are as follows.

1. Analyze and apply critical judgment.
2. Facilitate deriving meaning and engagement.
3. Focus on systemic factors.
4. Plan and record.
5. Organize and manage efforts and resources.
6. Guide and focus collaborative improvement.
7. Build capacity.
8. Demonstrate organizational sensitivity.
9. Monitor accountability and adoption.
10. Implement for sustainability.

In addition to being a guidebook for these actionable, research-based strategies, this book is an invitation to explore how to cultivate hope as a cornerstone of educational practice and strengthen resilience to weather both personal and professional challenges. Drawing from real-life stories, evidence-based insights, and actionable strategies, this book offers educators a compass for fostering environments where growth, connection, and possibility flourish through the following elements.

- **A framework for collaborative problem solving:** Schools, districts, and community partners must work together to address root causes rather than surface-level symptoms.

- **Proven processes for innovation and implementation:** Improvement requires more than good ideas; it demands disciplined execution, iteration, and adaptation.
- **Scalability across contexts:** Whether they are improving literacy rates, reducing absenteeism, or fostering career pathways, this book equips teams with tools to tackle both local and systemwide challenges.

Teachers, principals, superintendents, academic coaches, other school and district staff, and lifelong learners hold the power to inspire change, not only in students but also in themselves. The work of school improvement is difficult as educators juggle their other responsibilities while trying to maintain the engagement of stakeholders. This book is your guide to easier and more productive team-based improvement and avoiding common pitfalls. The work is never finished and requires continuous learning and iteration. This book prepares you to facilitate the journey required for sustainable improvement.

Schools are focused on every aspect of their students' diverse needs, from literacy and numeracy to attendance and deeper learning that prepares them for future opportunities. Educators are working together to develop themselves and their peers while navigating social, demographic, economic, political, and workplace changes and factors. Those who are leading school-improvement initiatives play a critical role in shaping future educational success. Your leadership and collaboration make a meaningful impact on students and communities. The tools, rules, and guidelines apply whether you are working with leadership teams, school-improvement teams, a professional learning community (PLC), staff, or other stakeholders and teams whose efforts can contribute to collaborative improvement and innovation.

Years have gone into crafting the processes and tools in this book, which have been used by thousands of educators to support their improvement efforts. Effective school improvement is an ongoing and iterative process. When approached collaboratively, it can empower educators to achieve their goals while creating a positive impact on students. While federal, state, provincial, and local models outline the *what* of school improvement, this book focuses on the *how*—providing practical strategies for successful implementation. It is designed to be a practical companion as you navigate school improvement.

Whether you are a teacher, administrator, counselor, or other educator invested in the transformative power of education, this book equips you with the mindset and skills to persevere, inspire, and lead with heart. Together, we will embark on this journey to nurture hope, foster resilience, and build the kinds of educational experiences that change lives—not only for our students but also for ourselves as educators.

How to Use This Book to Succeed

This book is about facilitating shared success. For the purposes of this book, the definition of *facilitator* is the person who makes an action or process easier. A teacher serves as a facilitator of learning. The goal of a teacher is to make learning easier and more effective for students. Facilitators of improvement projects may be administrators, teacher leaders, teachers, instructional coaches, school-improvement team members, or others within the school. Whatever position they hold, facilitators of improvement projects guide groups in how to work together more easily and effectively. Facilitators support formal and informal teams, departments, guiding coalitions, and other groups formed to develop and implement an improvement initiative. As a school-improvement team member, you can use the processes and tools in this book to guide your improvement efforts.

The *what* of school improvement is well documented from the body of research about effective schools since 2002. Educators can easily research evidence-based practices for what should be done to improve schools and school systems. It is the *how* or the guidance of that process that holds the key to successful improvement. Using the ten CSIS standards (Page & Hale, 2013), we outline how a team can systemically analyze and plan for school improvement. This book guides you through practical, proven processes that result in more productive team-based collaborative improvement. It is unique, as it focuses on how to engage and guide teams assigned to school-improvement projects, not how to execute compliance-focused projects that are unsustainable or ineffective.

As you work through this book, treat it as a trusted coach who is committed to your success. Mark it up, write in it, and use it daily to guide your work, reflections, decisions, and actions. Designed to support your day-to-day collaborative efforts, this book is also the text used by The Institute for Performance Improvement for training and certifying school-improvement specialists.

When using this book with your team, work through it chapter by chapter. Each of the first five chapters supports and prepares you for the work in the following chapter, especially if you are just beginning the process of school or district improvement. As you complete the work aligned with the first five chapters and need support for enhancing collaboration, chapter 6 dives deeper into supporting that collaboration—the heart of the work. For deeper guidance in building the capacity of collaborators, chapter 7 is there to support you. Through the years of developing educators in the work of the ten standards, the order of standard 8, demonstrating organizational sensitivity, has been a source of healthy debate. Half of educators typically say that it should be the first standard, as they consider it foundational for succeeding collaboratively and critical for avoiding pitfalls. Chapters 9 and 10 support the monitoring and discipline needed to implement the plans you developed and to iterate as you go. The following sections describe various elements you will find in the book.

Your Team

Schools typically designate a diverse group of staff members to serve as a core or lead school-improvement team. They work together to facilitate the improvement process, gathering input from all stakeholders. This group is usually representative of different content areas, grade levels, departments, job positions, and levels of the organizational chart.

In addition to this core group that becomes the hub of input regarding the development or revision of a school-improvement plan, there are other teams within the school or school system that serve as the spokes of this hub. These teams provide ongoing input to the core school-improvement team. Examples of these teams are entire grade levels, departments, all content-area teachers, guiding coalitions, job-role groups, teacher leaders, leadership teams, implementation teams, family representatives, community business partners, and others.

The groups of people involved in the overall process of school improvement have different names; however, independent of what the group supporting your initiative is called, we will refer to the group as *your team*. The content of this book applies to all teams working toward improvement, innovation, and implementation.

The Big Rock Analogy

Throughout the book, your team will be asked to focus on a single challenge, which we refer to as the *big rock*. Some teams choose to focus on multiple big rocks or have team members focus on their individual big rocks. What you and your team will experience is that the big rock will shift and change as you uncover information and gain insight from your collaboration. You may decide to narrow your focus to a *priority pebble*—a smaller challenge within the big rock. We will help you stay focused on the complex challenges you want to address collaboratively. As you apply the ideas in these pages, you will gradually break down, carve, and craft those big rocks into achievable outcomes.

Most importantly, your team will get the most out of this book by immediately applying its guidance and tools while working together. You might be familiar with leadership expert Simon Sinek's (2009a) popular TED Talk *How Great Leaders Inspire Action*. In this presentation, Sinek explains how leaders can inspire cooperation, trust, and change based on his research into how the most successful organizations think, act, and communicate by starting with *why*. You will use the challenge represented by your big rock as your *why* to engage your team and implement proven practices. Your big rock will be your learning and performance focus (Sinek, 2009b).

Rocks have been used throughout human history to mark the way and to celebrate an accomplishment, victory, or turning point. Even in the 21st century, stacks of rocks called *cairns* sometimes point the way for hikers. Over the course of your team's journey, guided by the practices in this book, you will support the team in breaking down the big rock by focusing on the many systemic factors that have created it and crafting sets of solutions that engage all the members of the school. Your facilitation will coordinate all team members' efforts as they focus on the parts of the big rock that they can impact. These become their smaller rocks to address.

Your view into the systemic nature of the challenge and the work of your big rock helps guide and support the order of the work and its interdependencies. Think of this as guiding the difficult work of stacking team members' completed rocks until they fit together, are stable, and become guides for the continuous journey of improvement. This collaborative effort of stacking the rocks results in a celebratory cairn of collaborative accomplishments.

The work of building an actual trail cairn is hard; it is creative and can be frustrating to those who want to do it quickly without the needed collaborative thinking, planning, testing, and balancing. Creating a solid foundation together is the key to success. Once it is built, it can be appreciated by all who participated in its creation, as well as those who have the opportunity to observe it and learn from it.

Look carefully at the image of a cairn in figure I.1. Imagine the collaborative efforts and skills needed to craft it and have it endure. Imagine what those who built it were celebrating. If you encountered cairns along a trail, you might wonder why people who traveled before you made the effort to leave these for your guidance and assurance. As you collaborate on your big rock, you will understand why you are reshaping that massive challenge into work that produces enduring results worthy of celebration. This book supports you and your team in *how* you fulfill your *why* together.

FIGURE I.1: Cairn.

Performance Improvement

We share proven practices drawn from the discipline of *human performance improvement* (*HPI*), also referred to as *human performance technology* (*HPT*). The International Society for Performance Improvement defines *HPI* as a systematic, data-driven approach to improving individual and organizational performance in the workplace (Hampton Roads International Society for Performance Improvement, n.d.). It focuses on enhancing performance by identifying and addressing underlying problems.

HPI is used in sectors where the risk of human errors is high, like nuclear power, medicine, engineering, and other settings where what someone does or does not do well really matters. Education leaders, academic coaches, and school-improvement teams know that what educators do matters as much as jobs in those other sectors because their performance impacts the course of millions of lives for generations.

Performance improvement takes a systematic approach to enhancing the performance of individuals and the organization—such as a school or group of schools. It is grounded in both behavioral science principles, which focus on when and how people act and interact, and organizational development, a systematic, long-term effort to make an organization more effective. Both disciplines seek to enhance the effectiveness, efficiency, and satisfaction of individuals within an organization, while recognizing that the organization is under the direction of its leaders, who are central to creating the conditions for change and improvement.

The education context is impacted by a powerful confluence of economic, demographic, political, technical, and social forces. HPI principles and tools provide useful frameworks for analyzing the complex work of school improvement. This book introduces strategies that educators have found effective in applying these concepts. For example, HPI refers to the people who perform the work of schools as the "workers." They include all the people who show up with or without the will, skill, and readiness to do what needs to be done. Leaders at all levels are responsible for building workers' capacity and efficacy while guiding them through constant changes and challenges.

Education leaders must lead the organization's workers in executing the systematic processes required for improvement and be willing to make the hard decisions necessary to improve student achievement and close achievement gaps. If leaders are going to guide successful performance improvement, consistent processes and daily decisions are required. Leaders cannot be afraid to lead. To be effective, leaders must always be listening, learning, building the capacity of their teachers, and improving their own capacity for collaborative improvement (Meyer, Hartung-Beck, Gronostaj, Krüger, & Richter, 2023).

Collaboration with and between teachers who are in classrooms every day is critical (García-Martínez, Montenegro-Rueda, Molina-Fernández, & Fernández-Batanero, 2021). However, sometimes leaders must make decisions that are *non-negotiable* to move the work forward. When a leader knows the work and earns the respect and trust of staff, the non-negotiable decisions, as well as the collaborative decisions, are understood as being the decisions that will improve performance.

Likewise, school leaders and the school-improvement team must work hard to earn the trust and respect of everyone in the school who must work together and agree on shared goals if they are to achieve better outcomes for educators and students. The school-improvement team may not have the authority to make all needed decisions, so leaders are key to the improvement process; however, sustainable success requires the collective effort and collaboration of teachers, administrators, staff, students, and the wider school community.

Many educators have found that taking a thoughtful, step-by-step approach leads to long-term success. A structured process can build momentum for meaningful, sustainable improvement. You will be able to show the results you have achieved and your progress toward your goals. Most importantly, you will be able to celebrate your collaborative work and its positive impact on educators, students, and your community.

How This Book Is Organized

This book offers insights into improvement, innovation, and implementation, highlighting strategies to navigate common challenges and avoid potential pitfalls. The chapters are organized around proven processes and tools based on The Institute for Performance Improvement's research. The ten chapters parallel the validated CSIS standards (Hale, Page, & Quigg, 2024).

This book is divided into two parts. Part 1, "Systematic Processes," covers CSIS standards 1–5. Chapters 1–5 reflect the typical workflow of improvement teams, beginning with discovery, analysis, goal setting, intervention selection and planning, organization, and resource management for implementation and evaluation. Part 2, "Systemic Perspectives," covers CSIS standards 6–10. Chapters 6–10 consider critical systemic practices necessary for doing this work.

The systematic processes and the systemic perspectives are shown in figure I.2. The systematic process standards in the outer area with the arrows between them illustrate that these processes occur in a linear order but are cyclical and iterative. The systemic perspectives are listed in the center of the cycle because they are applied throughout the improvement process.

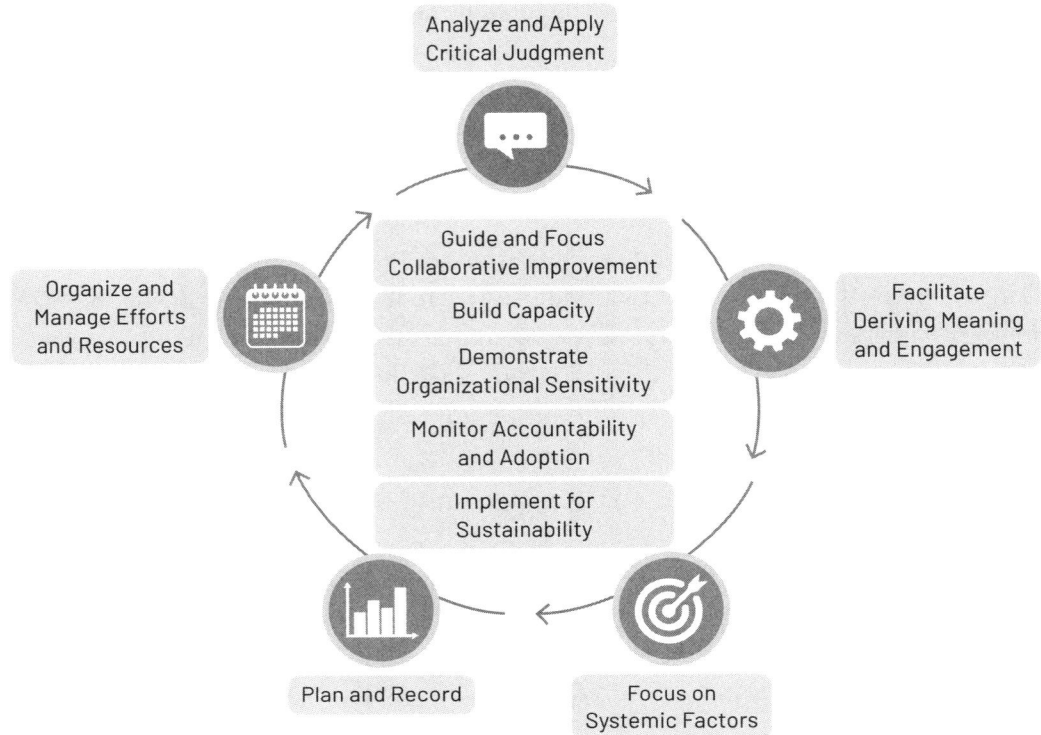

FIGURE I.2: Certified School Improvement Specialist standards.

Systematic Processes: Chapters 1–5

In the first five chapters of this book, you will learn how to discover, analyze, set goals, select sets of solutions, plan, organize, and manage resources for implementation and evaluation.

- In chapter 1, "Analyze and Apply Critical Judgment," you will refine your improvement priority—your big rock. As you and your team advance through the systematic processes, you will shape your big rock into something that is both worthy of doing and feasible. You will do an initial analysis of your big rock. In that analysis, you will begin to understand the gap between the current level of performance and the level you want. You will also think about the factors that may be impacting that gap before you engage others outside your team.

- In chapter 2, "Facilitate Deriving Meaning and Engagement," you will engage others who can impact results. You will facilitate their exploration and analysis while building trust and credibility, earning their respect, and gaining their commitment to shared goals.

- In chapter 3, "Focus on Systemic Factors," you will guide your team to collaborate in the processes of identifying and analyzing the causes and factors impacting results. Collectively, you will select a set of solutions along with the actions, decisions, resources, and support needed to implement those solutions.
- In chapter 4, "Plan and Record," you will develop a project plan for implementing solutions. The plan will include what to do, who will do it, by when it will be done, and how the work will be monitored.
- In chapter 5, "Organize and Manage Efforts and Resources," you will identify the main tasks in the project plan and break them into steps and actions so that the work can be distributed among the team and performance support can be provided.

Systemic Perspectives: Chapters 6–10

We recognize that school improvement is complex, and the performance of educators and students is impacted by a broad range of systemic factors. Those factors include the adequacy of the school's infrastructure, the skills of the school's teachers and leaders, a culture that fosters learning and accountability instead of blame and buck passing, and a willingness to recognize and celebrate everyone's contributions to progress. Chapters 6–10 explain how to nurture collaboration, build your team's capacity to do the work, demonstrate the organizational sensitivity necessary to make collaborative improvement possible, monitor progress in a way that encourages accountability and long-term sustainability, and implement not only the plan but also the processes needed for successful goal achievement. These practices are applied throughout the school-improvement process.

- In chapter 6, "Guide and Focus Collaborative Improvement," you will apply proven processes and tools to achieve and sustain needed engagement, commitment, and support.
- In chapter 7, "Build Capacity," you will build the capacity of those doing the work so they can do it effectively and independently when you are no longer guiding them.
- In chapter 8, "Demonstrate Organizational Sensitivity," you will demonstrate organizational sensitivity to increase and sustain the trust, engagement, inclusion, and commitment required for setting and meeting shared goals.
- In chapter 9, "Monitor Accountability and Adoption," you will choose and implement monitoring practices that support accountability, progress, and continuous improvement as needed.
- In chapter 10, "Implement for Sustainability," you will apply practices for successful implementation of the solutions and celebration of progress and results.

Unique Features of the Book

Each chapter has structures designed to support you and your team as you work through the improvement process. These structures are also designed to support your learning.

- 💡 **Idea hubs:** These unique features provide an opportunity for reflection and purposeful conversation. Idea hubs appear in various spots throughout each chapter. Our intent is for you to pause and reflect on what you are experiencing and learning. You will ask yourself questions such as "How does what I am discovering match with what I anticipated?" Just before the conclusion of every chapter, an idea hub encourages your team to pause, reflect, and engage in purposeful conversation. A purposeful conversation begins with taking the time to ask a series of questions and reflect on the answers. Use the insights gained to adjust and have an authentic exchange of ideas. Visit **go.SolutionTree.com /schoolimprovement** to find the *Facilitating Shared Success* Reflection and Application Journal where you can record your responses, thoughts, and reflections for the idea hubs.
- ⏳ **Success tools:** These tools include instructions, facilitation tips, and worksheets. Collectively, the tools and tactics guide you in making decisions, choosing actions, and calibrating your thinking. Depending on your school's context, your school-improvement team might not use every suggested tool or tactic. Select the ones that are best for your team's goals! Again, the focus is on how to do the work, not just what the work of school improvement is. Where appropriate, we have included examples of what worksheets might look like to capture ideas.
- **An effective example of the standard:** This recurring chapter section includes a story that demonstrates how the focus of the chapter was performed well in a school and how its application produced the intended progress and outcomes.
- **A less effective example of the standard:** The effective application in each chapter is followed by another story that demonstrates how the work in the chapter was *not* performed well. Comparing this example of what to avoid with the previous example of what to do ensures the clearest guidance on how to enact each chapter's standard.
- **Do and avoid chart:** The do and avoid chart is an opportunity for your team to calibrate, troubleshoot, adjust, and commit to actions that facilitate future success while purposefully avoiding common pitfalls.
- **Plan-ahead chart:** The intent of this chart is to encourage your team to think about the next steps and who will do the work. The goal is to keep your team moving forward with your school-improvement planning and monitoring.

How to Begin Your Learning Journey

Whether you are new to school improvement or seeking to enhance your current approach, these initial actions will guide your path forward. First, you will learn how to form a diverse, credible team that brings collective wisdom to address complex challenges. Next, you will discover methods for establishing a shared purpose that aligns your team's efforts with meaningful outcomes. Then, you will identify your big rock—that significant challenge worth addressing—to focus your collective energy. Finally, you will explore common pitfalls to avoid and practical planning tools to sustain momentum.

By thoughtfully engaging with each of these steps—team formation, purpose alignment, challenge selection, and strategic planning—you establish the conditions for improvement that will flourish throughout your school community and create a lasting positive impact for students, educators, and stakeholders alike.

Step 1: Forming Your Team

It is beneficial for school administrators to consider selecting a diverse team that has credibility and a strong work ethic, as perceptions of experience and expertise can foster engagement in the process of improvement. Successful improvement facilitators stress that the beginning of the engagement process is not the time to share expertise concerning improvement solutions; rather, demonstrate expertise in facilitating others to work together effectively. For school improvement to be truly collaborative, teams, coaches, and educators benefit from facilitating the process rather than simply directing it. A focus on capacity building ensures all stakeholders are empowered to contribute meaningfully.

Step 2: Agreeing on a Shared Purpose

The next step is to facilitate conversations with your team members on what they expect, what they hope to achieve, what they want as their big rock, and what systemic factors they think they will face while undertaking this initiative. Figure I.3 can help with this step.

Instructions: Facilitate a discussion with your team members about what they want to accomplish and why. Use the following questions to guide the conversation.

1. Why is our team interested in using the processes outlined in the book? What is in it for us?
2. How will we maintain the discipline to follow the processes and practices and apply them immediately to day-to-day efforts to guide collaborative improvement?
3. Think about our past school-improvement efforts. What data did we review? Do we have an improvement plan in place? How valid is the plan?

Capture and summarize the main points. Use the concerns, doubts, and answers as the team advances through the book to discuss if there has been a change in sentiment and why. Record what the team members see as their shared purpose, as it will help later as they decide on the team's big rock.

FIGURE I.3: Success tool—Agreement on our shared purpose.

*Visit **go.SolutionTree.com/schoolimprovement** for a free reproducible version of this figure.*

As described previously, HPI is a discipline that recognizes that organizations get things done through people. The discipline recognizes that those who guide and support other people's improvement efforts can be successful if they are systematic *and* systemic in how they work. HPI follows five principles referred to as *RSVPS* (Van Tiem, Moseley, & Dessinger, 2012).

1. *R* represents focusing on *results*.
2. *S* is for taking a *systemic* view.
3. *V* reminds us to be adding *value*.
4. *P* is for *partnering* or collaborating.
5. The last *S* means being *systematic*.

These principles remind us to be purposeful in what we do and how we do it by using proven processes and tools. The principles also remind us to have a systemic focus on the work people are expected to do and the factors that support or impede how well they can do it.

Systemic factors include local social, economic, political, and environmental variables that affect people's ability to be successful (for example, how well the local economy attracts businesses that provide employment opportunities). These, in turn, affect the community's ability to attract and retain medical personnel, teachers, and school administrators. Ultimately, access to qualified professionals and resources affects nutrition, health, job readiness, and more. Use figure I.4 to introduce and discuss the RSVPS principles.

Instructions: Show the team the questions in the chart. Decide if you want members to brainstorm answers as a team or individually. Next, use the questions to facilitate discussion about the principles and come to a consensus.

Facilitation tip: Consider the following tips as you conduct the conversation.

1. Allow time for individual brainstorming (two to five minutes, depending on whether you brainstorm individually or collectively).

2. Engage in a discussion protocol to come to consensus (five to ten minutes per step). The use of sticky notes or a virtual tool like FigJam (www.figma.com) can help you collect ideas from all members of the team.

3. Document and save the team's collective wisdom.

Your team might not have answers to *all* the questions at first. That's OK! The chapters that follow offer further guidance.

Principle	Questions
1. Focus on results.	What are the results we must focus on achieving? Which are the highest priorities? What mindsets and skills are critical to reaching those results? Consider all data types—achievement, process, and perception—when answering this question.
2. Take a systemic view.	What systemic factors impact results? What systemic factors impact our ability to choose and implement solutions that produce the right results? What systemic factors allow us to sustain solutions over time?
3. Add value.	What will we do, and what are we committed to learning to do well, to create value for the school, educators, students, and stakeholders? How will we add value by using proven processes and tools to effectively guide others to collaboratively set and meet goals?
4. Work in partnership.	Who must we partner with at every level across the school, school system, and school community?
5. Follow a systematic process.	What is our continuous improvement process? Who knows it and follows it? How do we know? Is it a compliance effort, a true commitment to doing and getting better continuously, or something in between? Why?

FIGURE I.4: Success tool—RSVPS principles.

*Visit **go.SolutionTree.com/schoolimprovement** for a free reproducible version of this figure.*

Step 3: Selecting Your Big Rock

Once the right people are on the team and the group is united in its shared purpose of enhancing the school, it is time to select your big rock. Think about and decide on a school-improvement challenge you and your team want to use to practice the proven processes described in the book. Be forewarned—the challenge you select will most likely evolve as you uncover information and come to new insights.

Idea Hub: Your Big Rock

Ask yourself the following questions, and then discuss them with your team.

» What might be a challenge or big rock you want to work on?

» Why do you think this is a priority?

Remember: What you think may be your big rock right now might shift as you dig into your data and analyze needs based on that data. Just record your choice of big rock for now. The important thing is to record the team's decision so you can reference and most likely amend it as you progress through the book.

Step 4: Watching Out for Pitfalls

Discussing common pitfalls and how your team can avoid them will guide you in taking steps to make your school-improvement process as strong as possible. Figure I.5 features a list of common pitfalls. After all of them, there are explanations and questions you can use to facilitate conversations with your team. Also included are references to the chapters where each pitfall is discussed in greater detail.

Instructions: Use this list of pitfalls as a checklist to help your team members recognize if or when they, or the school, are in or near pitfalls. Consider the guidance and questions after each pitfall. Discuss the likelihood that your team can avoid the pitfall.

Facilitation tip: Display or post the fifteen pitfalls for easy reference during the conversation.

☐ 1. A small number of people are involved in the development of the school-improvement plan.

+ The goal is for the team to be composed of a diverse group of people, including administrators, teachers, support staff, and other stakeholders.

+ What is the makeup of your team? (See chapters 2, 4, 6, and 8.)

☐ 2. The plan is communicated to a limited number of people.

+ Everyone who can contribute is engaged in planning, giving feedback, and contributing to the process so that you gain commitment from those closest to the work ahead.

+ How engaged are your team members? Are they sharing the work? (See chapters 2, 4, 5, 6, and 8.)

☐ 3. Limited analysis is conducted, so the factors causing gaps in performance are not adequately examined.

+ The team conducts a deep, thorough analysis to identify factors causing gaps in performance rather than superficial symptoms.

+ Is the analysis thorough enough? Do you skip over any factors? (See chapters 1 and 3.)

FIGURE I.5: Success tool—Common pitfalls.

continued ▶

Success Tool Notes:

☐ 4. Cause analysis is limited to a few issues and does not lead to identification of the factors impacting improvement, innovation, and implementation.

+ The team applies a systemic lens when doing the cause analysis to uncover factors impacting improvement, innovation, and implementation.

+ Does your team consider factors at multiple levels, such as in the school or the school district? (See chapter 3.)

☐ 5. When selecting interventions, the team focuses on solutions rather than the sets of interventions needed to successfully explore, install, and implement those solutions.

+ The team focuses on selecting the best sets of interventions to solve identified problems and carefully considers how to install and implement them.

+ Does your team think about or consider a combination of solutions? (See chapter 3.)

☐ 6. Periodic checks meet compliance requirements, but the team might not use them to inform iteration, make decisions, and drive celebrations of progress.

+ Benchmarks or periodic checks are built into the plan, and the team uses them to inform iteration, make decisions, and drive celebrations of progress.

+ Does your team set key dates, benchmarks, and periodic checks? Do you plan time to check progress against goals? (See chapter 9.)

☐ 7. The school-improvement plan is not broken down into action plans that engage all the stakeholders who can make a difference.

+ The school-improvement plan has corresponding action plans that clearly engage all stakeholders in making a difference.

+ Does your team have action plans that engage others? (See chapters 4 and 5.)

☐ 8. A few people are working hard to drive improvement rather than building the capacity of the whole school to engage, improve, innovate, and implement.

+ The school-improvement plan and goals are shared by all and lead to improvement, innovation, and implementation.

+ Do you have evidence that the responsibility for the work is shared? (See chapter 7.)

☐ 9. Meetings do not focus on the work to be done or products and outputs that will be created in the meeting or afterward according to deadlines.

+ Meetings focus on the work to do, including products and outputs to create by set deadlines.

+ Do your meetings stay focused on the work? (See chapters 5, 6, 7, 9, and 10.)

☐ 10. Professional learning is prescribed without determining and addressing other factors impacting educator performance.

+ Professional learning is relevant to the adults in the building and addresses the factors impacting educator performance.

+ Does your team participate in learning that is relevant to accomplishing the goals you have agreed on? (See chapters 1, 3, 4, and 5.)

☐ 11. Capacity building is focused on what people should know rather than what they must do. Educators lack the support to transfer their learning to effective performance on the job. Without sufficient practice of the tasks and feedback against clear criteria, they fail to reach proficiency.

+ Professional learning builds educators' capacity by supporting the transfer of learning to the job and providing sufficient practice of the tasks with feedback against clear criteria to reach proficiency.

+ Is your team making sure that training is effective? (See chapter 7.)

☐ 12. The school jumps to full implementation without taking time to explore and ensure that sufficient infrastructure and resources are in place.

+ Teams take the time to explore and ensure sufficient infrastructure and resources are in place before moving to full implementation.

+ Does your team make sure that what is required to implement changes exists? (See chapters 5 and 10.)

☐	13. Change is seen as an organizational process rather than a people process, and the process of change is not understood or considered during work with stakeholders. + The school views change as a people process that is understood when working with stakeholders. + Does your team talk about change as a people process, and does your team take responsibility for engaging the people who are expected to change? (See chapter 8.)
☐	14. There is a disconnect between vision and action. + There is clear alignment among the school's vision, goals, and actions. + Are you and your team checking that what you are doing is aligned with your goals? (See chapter 6.)
☐	15. School improvement is an event to check off. + School improvement is a systemic, systematic, engaging process where everyone works to set and meet shared goals for the success of students, educators, and the community. + How committed is your team to following a systematic process while maintaining a systemic view? (See chapters 1–10.)

*Visit **go.SolutionTree.com/schoolimprovement** for a free reproducible version of this figure.*

Even though there are pitfalls, the good news is that there are more opportunities to succeed than there are to stall or get off the path. We are going to help your team mark these opportunities and celebrate them.

The Importance of Planning Ahead

Planning ahead is not simply about scheduling tasks; it is about developing a shared course of action that increases the likelihood of success for every stakeholder involved. Thoughtful planning creates clarity, alignment, and momentum, particularly when navigating the complex challenges of school improvement. It helps you help collaborators understand their roles, timelines, and interdependencies.

Figure I.6 (page 16) offers a simple but powerful tool to begin organizing your next steps. While it may appear straightforward, tools like this are grounded in proven practices of effective team performance. They prompt reflection, foster shared ownership, and reduce ambiguity. When used intentionally, they ensure important actions do not fall through the cracks and the right people are engaged at the right time.

Our philosophy is that practical tools should make your work easier, not more complicated. The success tool in figure I.6, as well as the others throughout this book, does just that—it guides your team to focus on what matters and needs to be done.

We hope we have helped prepare you to guide your team by acting as a catalyst for change and following proven school-improvement processes. This introduction opened the door to the journey of school improvement. Our intent is to show you the map and what is ahead as you learn how to introduce and guide changes that lead to and support students' success and achievement. The following chapters will take your team through each stage of the planning process with a variety of tools and strategies to aid in your efforts.

Success Tool Notes:

Success Tool Notes:

Instructions: This tool is meant to remind you to plan and take the necessary steps to facilitate success. Think about each step, who is needed and responsible for it, and when the work is to be completed.

Action Step	Person or People Responsible	Due Date
1. Agree on when the team will meet next and send a calendar invitation to all team members.		
2. Read chapter 1 and jot down your initial thinking related to the idea hubs and success tools. Come prepared to discuss.		
3. If you are reflecting on a current improvement process, print or distribute the current improvement plan and a succinct summary of the process used to develop the plan so the team may reflect on current practices and those recommended throughout the chapters.		

FIGURE I.6: Success tool—Document for planning ahead.

*Visit **go.SolutionTree.com/schoolimprovement** for a free reproducible version of this figure.*

Part 1

Systematic Processes

In the introduction, we pointed to the analogy of collaboratively breaking down a big rock and working to select, develop, align, and implement sustainable solutions as a team. In part 1 (chapters 1–5), you will learn how to guide your team in uncovering the underlying factors that cause gaps between what teachers, administrators, and students can do and what they need to do. You will focus on ensuring that the resources you need are organized and managed effectively for the successful implementation of solutions and evaluation of their impact.

Chapter 1

Standard 1: Analyze and Apply Critical Judgment

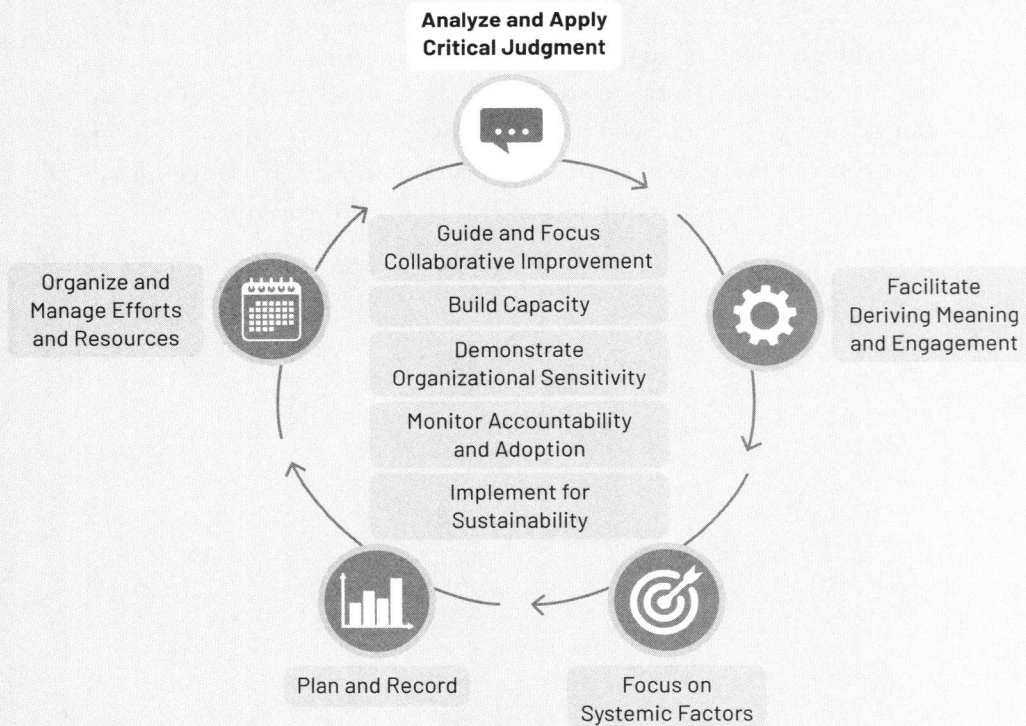

Analyze and Apply Critical Judgment

Organize and Manage Efforts and Resources

Guide and Focus Collaborative Improvement

Build Capacity

Demonstrate Organizational Sensitivity

Monitor Accountability and Adoption

Implement for Sustainability

Facilitate Deriving Meaning and Engagement

Plan and Record

Focus on Systemic Factors

*B*efore engaging and guiding others in systemic improvement efforts, you must do preparatory assessments—analyzing data to uncover gaps in performance and then thinking critically about what factors impact performance. Critical judgment is the connective tissue among improvement, innovation, and implementation. It identifies areas for improvement by analyzing current systems. By fostering a culture of critical thinking in education, schools can continuously transform, ensuring that teaching and learning remain relevant, impactful, and inclusive.

What comes to mind when thinking of school improvement? Typically, responses to this question fit into one of two categories: (1) "It is an essential component to guiding our school's work," or (2) "It is a compliance check we must complete for the district or state." We hope that you are in the first category but understand that you may be in the second. When school improvement is focused on compliance, educators may perceive it as an effort to blame educators or a rigid, time-wasting event that does not promote innovation or flexibility (DeMatthews & Wang, 2023).

The social-emotional aspect of improvement is an important focus. Educators have many responsibilities, and the demands of their job are increasing, which is why it is imperative to approach the work of standard 1 with empathy, care, and attention so people feel supported rather than blamed or judged. Change models like Kurt Lewin's (1958) Unfreeze-Change-Refreeze, John Kotter's 8 Steps (Kotter International, n.d.), Jeffrey M. Hiatt's (2006) ADKAR model, or the W. Edwards Deming Institute's (n.d.) Plan-Do-Study-Act all provide systematic ways to view and approach change in an organization. While reviewing these models, we identified five common principles shared by all of them that are essential for implementing successful change.

1. Create a sense of urgency or awareness about the need for change.
2. Maintain open communication.
3. Approach changes systematically.
4. Focus on continuous improvement.
5. Reinforce change to embed it in the culture.

The process outlined in this chapter enables your team to understand what is currently happening in and outside of school that impacts the enhancements that should be made. However, do *not* jump to solutions or immediately act on changes. While team members are actively collecting and analyzing data, take your time, make no judgments, and ensure you trust each other to focus on what can help everyone succeed. Take the time to understand before you begin conversations with others.

This chapter will guide you in using a series of tactics to grasp the work ahead as you begin the school-improvement journey. First, you will learn what types of data to collect, how to create a data profile, and how to analyze that profile. Second, you will learn how to conduct performance-gap and performance-factors analyses using the data. Finally, you will identify the expertise required of your team to do the work ahead.

Collecting and Analyzing Data

School leaders, academic coaches, and school-improvement teams do standard 1 work all the time. This is why we focus first on collecting and analyzing data and then on thinking critically about what the data means. We also propose thinking through an asset-based lens or an enhancement mindset. In her renowned TED Talk *Every Kid Needs a Champion*, the late Rita Pierson (2013) exhibits this when she shares a story about a student failing an assessment and says, "Minus eighteen sucks all the life out of you. Plus two says, 'I ain't all bad.'" Finding that glimmer of hope is the essence of an enhancement mindset. Anytime *improve*, *transform*, or *innovate* appears in this book, ask yourself, "What will I enhance?" Enhancement comes with the understanding that a school must commit to what needs to be done to get from where it currently is to where it wants to be.

Just as critical thinking, problem solving, communication, and collaboration are priorities for student success, they are the cornerstones of school improvement. Those working together to guide the enhancement process must think critically together. Understandably, those guiding the work will have strong feelings about which solutions are needed and the urgency to make progress, and frustrations about the time it takes to see meaningful change. Successful and sustainable improvement is not just about "getting the doing done." It is about doing the work that allows the people in the education system to be efficacious and successful, and that allows the improvements and breakthroughs to be sustainable. This requires a focus on both people and processes, and you cannot identify areas to enhance without good data and a thorough analysis.

Using valid data takes opinions out of the equation. You must have a clear picture of your current reality and be open to discussing this with your team. Data, especially in an area that needs deep enhancement, can often feel like a judgment. You must shift this narrative. There is no judgment. Data is data. Gathering multiple data points and conducting a thorough analysis presents a view of your current reality. This is your jumping-off point to move forward! Ask, "Where are we currently? Where do we want to be? What do we need to do to get there? What is currently keeping us from getting there?"

Later in this chapter, we offer a success tool to help you build a comprehensive data profile inclusive of demographic data, student learning or achievement data, program data, and perception data. Good data and analysis help you answer the preceding questions at a deep level, rather than a superficial one. This is an initial analysis to determine the gap between the current level of performance and what you believe it can be to achieve sustainable performance improvement.

The work of this standard is needed to prevent missteps and frustrations. Determining solutions without thorough data collection and analysis is only assuming, and we know what happens when we assume: Assumptions mislead. Data directs. Engaging in a continuous cycle of data collection and analysis allows the team to embrace and model a learner's mindset. This formative (rather than summative) approach means you can adjust and get incrementally closer to your goals instead of waiting until the end of the year to review data and hoping your efforts have paid off. As we interviewed school, district, regional, and state professionals across the United States when researching and codifying the CSIS standards, they consistently agreed on the importance of devoting time to analyzing and seeking to understand data before engaging others. This means you must work with your improvement team or guiding coalition before you jump into pilot or schoolwide initiatives.

Vangie Altman, a school-improvement facilitator and highly successful academic coach in Kentucky, shares her best advice for starting the school-improvement process: "I have learned over my career that when beginning the process of supporting and guiding others to improve and change, I must first 'lay low and mosey'" (V. Altman, personal communication, June 13, 2024). This means keeping the focus off you and, instead, focusing on the data.

Pausing to first conduct a systemic analysis may feel counterintuitive, especially in environments where the needs are urgent and outcomes matter. Educators and stakeholders often feel immense pressure to act quickly in response to challenges, driven by a deep commitment to student success and external accountability demands. The instinct is to do something, anything, immediately, but not every school-improvement effort benefits from immediate action.

While urgency is real and valid, those who are successful in guiding school improvement, change, and innovation understand that deep analysis must come before action. Rushing into solutions without a clear understanding of current conditions can undermine trust, waste resources, and miss root causes. Systemic analysis of data, processes, and performance gaps equips you and all collaborators with the insight needed to guide meaningful improvement. It ensures the team is working on the right problems, not just the most visible ones. Trust and commitment grow when people see that decisions are informed, intentional, and grounded in evidence.

Idea Hub: Past Practices

Reflect on the paragraphs you have just read and consider how your prior improvement practices helped or hindered progress.

» What stakeholders were involved in the planning?

» How was communication handled about beginning the improvement process and following steps to ensure a thorough analysis?

» Was all relevant data collected and analyzed before you jumped to solutions?

Improvement efforts that skip or rush analysis risk becoming performative or reactive. Pitfalls often arise not from lack of effort but from actions based on assumptions rather than evidence. Leaders and teams that invest time in creating a comprehensive data profile, conducting performance-gap analyses, and exploring the human performance factors at play are far more likely to develop strategies that stick. Analysis is not a delay; it is a strategic move that sets the foundation for sustainable, targeted improvement. Think of this as the critical foundation for later purposefully crafting and stacking those rocks for your cairn!

Comprehensive Data Profile

Building a comprehensive data profile can help you understand and eventually communicate to others the gaps in performance and what is causing them. These gaps may be in student achievement, teacher performance, or the school's overall performance. Often in education, we might be "data-rich but information-poor," meaning we have a ton of data points but do not connect the dots that lead to deep insights or action (Wilson, 2016). There are several overarching ways to categorize data for analysis.

- **Demographic data:** Who are the students we are serving? Are we meeting the needs of these students?
- **Achievement data:** What is our current level of academic performance? How are our students performing across key content areas? To what extent are students demonstrating higher-order thinking or critical thinking skills?
- **Program data:** What programs have we implemented with students or staff to achieve our goals?
- **Perception data:** How satisfied are our "customers" with our efforts?

These different categories provide a systematic way of grouping and going through all the data at your disposal. Therefore, we compiled possible data points for each category in table 1.1. These lists are not comprehensive, and other systems may have data points unique to their context or may categorize certain data points differently. That is OK! These lists are a starting point for data collection and analysis to encourage fruitful discussion.

TABLE 1.1: Types of Data to Collect by Category

Demographic Data	Achievement Data	Program Data	Perception Data
• Total enrollment • Student mobility • Attendance • Socioeconomic status • Discipline • Gender • Ethnicity • Differing abilities • English proficiency • Graduation and dropout rates	• End-of-year standardized assessments • District benchmark, diagnostic, or formative assessments • Performance-based assessments • Student growth percentiles	• Teacher evaluation system • Professional learning • Academic programs • Title I programs • Curricular documents • Staff experience • School schedule • Behavior trends or PBIS data	• Student, parent, teacher, and community feedback • Surveys • Observations • Focus groups or empathy interviews

Many systems and states now have data dashboards or statewide longitudinal data systems for storing this information in a central location. If not, the school or district should consider these options to make data collection and storage easier. Use the graphic in figure 1.1 and the data-collection planning tool in figure 1.2 (page 24) to work through the data-collection process.

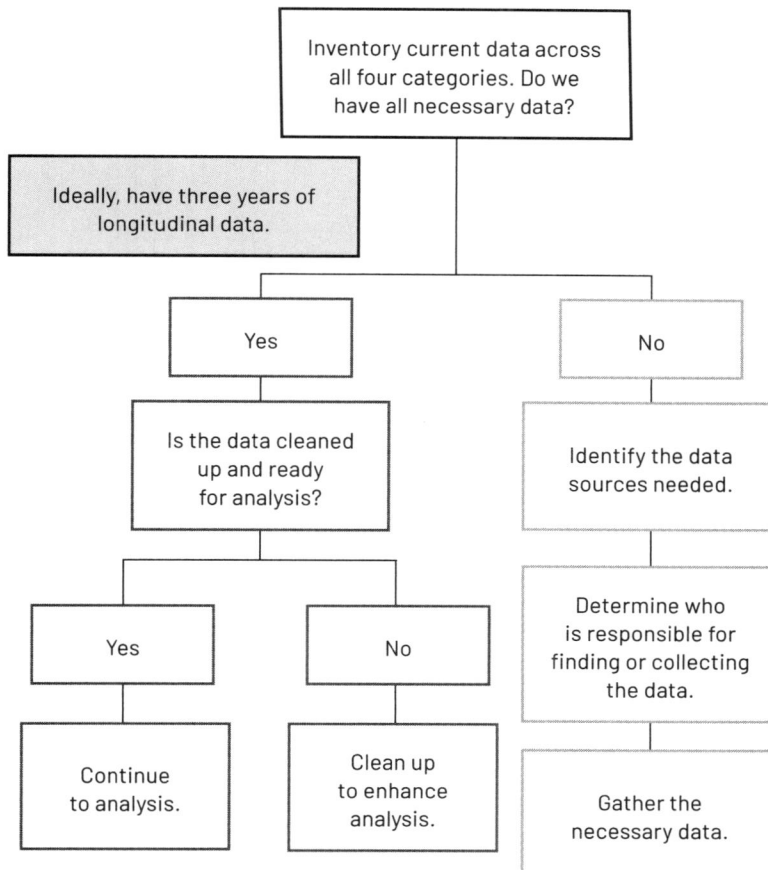

FIGURE 1.1: Data profile creation flowchart.

Instructions: Read the information in each box of the data profile creation flowchart (figure 1.1, page 23). Then take the following steps.

1. Identify what data is currently available and ready for analysis. This means the data is not raw but summarized in easy-to-interpret dashboards, charts, tables, or other visuals. If possible, collect longitudinal data (three years of it) to look for trends during analysis.

2. Identify what data is missing or will enhance your analysis.

3. Assign tasks to team members for any data collection or data cleanup.

4. Use the following data-collection planning tool to record what data you have, what data you need, and what you need to do.

Data Type	What Data Do We Have? *Check the box if the data is ready for analysis.*	What Data Do We Need?	What Do We Need to Do? *Identify the person or people responsible for collecting or cleaning up the data to prepare for analysis.*
Demographic data	☐		
Achievement data	☐		
Program data	☐		
Perception data	☐		

FIGURE 1.2: Success tool—Data-collection planning tool.

*Visit **go.SolutionTree.com/schoolimprovement** for a free reproducible version of this figure.*

Next, use the comprehensive data profile analysis tool in figure 1.3 to analyze the data.

Instructions: Use the following information and questions to aid you in analyzing your student data. Ideally, you have three years of longitudinal data to build out a robust profile.

Demographic data: This data is never viewed as "bad" or "good." It provides information about the population you serve.

1. What is the profile of your student base?
   - The percentages of students grouped by ethnicity, gender, or subgroup
   - Graduation, dropout, or retention rates for all students and by subgroups
   - Attendance for all students and by subgroups
   - Discipline rates or incidences—a total count and breakdown by subgroup (During what time of the year are these incidences happening?)
2. Look for trends and ask:
   - Are there any shifts in the makeup of the school population?
   - Are there noticeable trends in attendance or behavior?

For behavior, look at the data compared to the timing of breaks, timing during the day (if possible), location in the school, or timing of before- and after-school bus routes.

Achievement data: This data includes standardized tests, benchmarks, local diagnostics, and so on.

1. What percentage of students is at each performance level or score as a whole student body and by subgroup (grade level, gender, race, special education, gifted, English for speakers of other languages [ESOL], early intervention program, Title I, and so on)?
2. Look for trends and ask:
   - Are there performance increases or decreases for certain content areas or grade levels among all students or only certain populations?
   - Where have students demonstrated mastery or a need for improvement?
   - Do the results of local assessments at the school or district level align with the results of standardized assessments?

Program data: This data might not be easily quantifiable but is worthy of discussion.

1. What is the profile of your teacher base?
   - Teachers' total years of experience or length of time working in the school or system, by content area or grade level
   - The prior foci of their professional learning, curricular documents (scope and sequence), priority standards, discipline management, instructional strategies, assessment, evaluation, and more
   - Pathway completion
   - Students served in gifted, early intervention, Title I, or English learner programs; mentoring; extracurriculars; and so on
2. Look for trends and ask: How well do your programs support your students' performance?

Perception data: This data is derived from empathy interviews, focus groups, observations, and surveys.

1. What perception data do you collect? Who is the audience?
2. How do stakeholders feel about the school climate, expectations for achievement, instruction, family and community engagement, and instructional leadership?

Intersections: Where are there intersections of certain data points? Are there any possible connections or relationships between data points analyzed across different categories?

Success Tool Notes:

FIGURE 1.3: Success tool—Comprehensive data profile analysis.

*Visit **go.SolutionTree.com/schoolimprovement** for a free reproducible version of this figure.*

Your team has undertaken an important first step in the improvement process. You have established a comprehensive data profile consisting of a variety of data sources that can be triangulated to identify trends and patterns. And you have begun to make meaning of your data by cleaning it up for deep analysis. Now that your team has had a chance to analyze the data, it is time to reflect and engage in discussion so you can select the most essential priorities, or big rocks, for the focus of your improvement efforts.

Idea Hub: Big Rocks, Intersections, and Priorities

Individually reflect on your data analysis from figure 1.3 (page 25), and then discuss your findings as a team. Review the trends in the comprehensive data profile.

» What are the noticeable findings and possible intersections?

» Do they line up with the big rocks (if already defined)?

» What has emerged as a priority to be addressed?

Remember, everything *cannot* be a priority. Take time to talk. If needed, use a prioritization protocol to focus the discussion.

Your findings prepare you to engage others in data analysis later on. However, first, you will use the data to determine the current state of student and school performance and define the desired state.

Performance-Gap Analysis

You are now ready to move on to performance-gap analysis. Analysis is not new for school-improvement teams. However, the tactics presented here with their concepts, terms, and tools may be new or different from what you have experienced because you will now focus on gaps in performance. We borrowed performance-gap analysis methods from nonacademic organizations and industries to provide new ways to assess strengths and areas needing improvement and transform performance from the current state to the desired state. Now, you'll begin to compare the current findings to your ideal. As we walk you through this next success tactic, ask yourself, "What is the ideal performance? How does our current performance compare?" Think about what is causing the gap between current levels of performance and where performance can be. (In chapter 3, we will guide you on how to repeat this process with your team.)

Begin your performance-gap analysis using your comprehensive data profile. The profile usually focuses on student data first. You need to understand how your students currently are performing in their academic learning and critical behaviors that support learning, such as attendance and engagement. From this data, you can set target outcomes or goals.

Your school-improvement team is then ready to analyze administration and staff performance and look for connections between this and the big rocks identified from the student data. Gaps do not necessarily have to be problems. Take the opportunity to state the desired performance for all workers involved with the identified priorities. Then celebrate where performance exceeds these expectations and identify where performance could be improved toward the desired goals. The performance-gap analysis tool in figure 1.4 walks your team through this process. Use this tactic to help your team work through the performance-gap analysis for teachers and leaders as it relates to each priority area or big rock.

Success Tool Notes:

Instructions: Answer the questions in this worksheet. Then, guide a discussion with your team members about how these questions relate to their big rocks.

Facilitation tip: Document the discussion on chart paper or in a digital file. Refer to the chart or file as you learn more and your understanding increases.

Big Rock

List each priority individually.

Desired Performance

- What are the goals or expectations for desired performance for each priority?
- What are the metrics to measure performance?

Areas to Celebrate	**Areas to Enhance or Improve**
• Where does performance exceed expectations?	• Where does performance fall short of expectations, indicating a need for improvement? • What is working but may need to be enhanced?
• What will happen to the organization if this behavior continues? Doesn't continue?	• What will happen to the organization if this behavior continues? Doesn't continue?

Performances to Prioritize

- What is most essential to achieving desired results?

After the team has listed the areas to enhance or improve, engage in a protocol, such as a priority matrix, to come to consensus on which performance gaps should be given priority.

FIGURE 1.4: Success tool—Performance-gap analysis.

*Visit **go.SolutionTree.com/schoolimprovement** for a free reproducible version of this figure.*

Once the team has defined areas to enhance or improve, prioritize the performance gaps because it is impossible to improve everything all at once. For the prioritization phase, your improvement team must include a variety of stakeholders and not just the administrators in the building. This improves discussion and belief in the results.

After they consider the gaps described for the groups, those you are guiding could be tempted to say, "If these [name the people] would just do what is needed and expected, this big rock could be moved and overcome." Hearing this is your cue to prevent team members from jumping to solutions or blaming others.

For example, this type of thinking could lead team members to immediately prescribe learning and development for educators. For decades, training has been one of the most common interventions used by organizations (Dirksen, 2024). Although valuable, training may not be the best or only solution. (Chapter 7 provides more guidance and tools for determining when development is the right intervention or part of an aligned "suite of solutions.") It is important *not* to jump to any solutions after the gap analysis because there are more analyses to complete before the most valid solutions can be determined. It is vital to now analyze the factors that impact educator and student performance.

Performance-Factors Identification

We describe school improvement as "taking a view through new lenses." Successful school improvement is a process of continuously viewing the current and desired states and the performance gaps using a variety of lenses. Those lenses help you identify factors that create the gaps between what exists and where you envision performance to be. Because the factors impacting schools are constantly changing, you can rely on four lenses that are commonly used in the field of human performance improvement to identify and analyze performance factors: (1) the marketplace, (2) the workplace, (3) the work, and (4) the workers (Rothwell, 2005; Van Tiem et al., 2012). Each lens helps uncover factors that are impacting the performance of students and the school. The lenses go from a broad to a more nuanced view, as shown in figure 1.5.

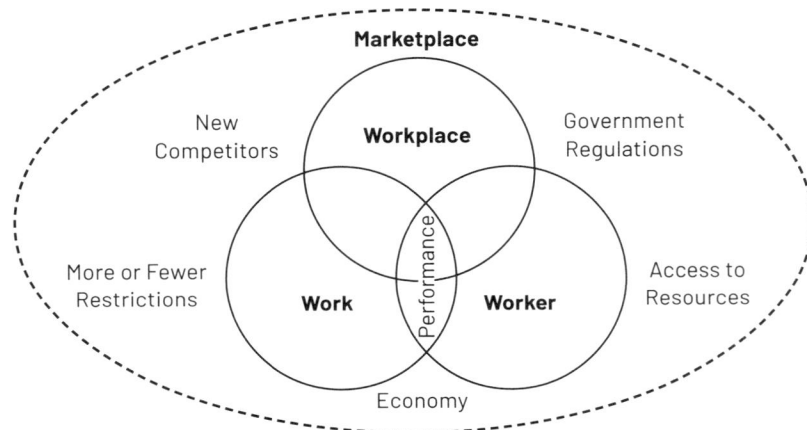

Source: Adapted from Rothwell, 2005; Van Tiem et al., 2012.

FIGURE 1.5: Four lenses to view and evaluate factors impacting school and student performance.

The following is an overview of the four lenses and what they mean.

1. The *marketplace* includes external factors that impact the school but are outside its direct control, while the workplace, work, and worker are all internal factors. Some examples of marketplace factors are government policies, community support, economic conditions, family culture and involvement, and external assessments. Although you do not have control over the marketplace factors, they are important to consider during your analysis and, later, your identification of solutions, as there may be interventions that can mitigate the impact of these factors.

2. The *workplace* is the school. Look at the infrastructure, policies, tools, and resources in place and ask, "Are they designed to support school staff (workers) in being successful?"

3. The *work* is what must happen on the job for the school to be successful. The work is what educators do, including processes and procedures.

4. The *workers* are those who carry out the work. Factors influencing their performance include knowledge, skill, capacity, and motivation.

Analyzing and applying critical judgments through these lenses allows you to holistically and systemically approach school improvement so that you avoid piecemeal or fractured initiatives and solutions. The purpose of the varying lenses is to "identify and prioritize the realities that support actual performance" (Van Tiem et al., 2012, p. 145). Again, this is not to pass judgment but to critically view external and internal factors impacting the school to explain why stakeholders perform or behave the way they do (Rothwell, 2015).

Facilitating school-improvement discussions requires the team to take a step back and look through these lenses, among others, to truly appreciate and understand what is happening. When the analysis of student, staff, and school data begins, keep in mind the varying external or marketplace factors that might influence these trends.

You have analyzed data and defined performance and outcome gaps that need to be closed. Before identifying the specific factors impacting your big rock, you can use the information you have gathered from the data analyses thus far to brainstorm areas of strength (pluses) and areas for change (deltas). The chart in figure 1.6 can be useful for compiling this information.

Instructions: In this plus-delta chart, list the factors affecting performance. List the positive factors in the Plus column and the negative or limiting factors in the Delta column. If possible, create this chart in a file that the entire team can access.

Plus +	Delta Δ

FIGURE 1.6: Success tool—Plus-delta chart.

*Visit **go.SolutionTree.com/schoolimprovement** for a free reproducible version of this figure.*

After collecting your team's responses on the plus-delta chart, work with the team to label each strength and each opportunity for improvement as being a *marketplace* (*MP*), *workplace* (*WP*), *work* (*W*), or *worker* (*WR*) issue. Labeling the items on your plus-delta chart will assist your team with the next analysis—the performance-factors analysis.

Performance-Factors Analysis

The plus-delta chart is complete, and you have categorized every factor as rooted in the marketplace, workplace, work, or workers. You can now begin to zoom in on each of the factors to prioritize them for deeper analysis. This ensures you thoroughly embrace standard 1, analyze and apply critical judgment. It is important only to think about factors impacting performance and *not* to jump to solutions yet, as more analysis is necessary before your team is equipped to determine the most valid solutions.

For example, a worker factor may be stated as "Teachers are not teaching the reading curriculum standards." This is a worker factor that would be stated in the performance-factors analysis. At this stage, it's best to avoid solution statements such as "Teachers need professional learning about teaching the curriculum standards." Professional learning in the reading standards may not be the best or most valid solution for the performance factor identified. After further analysis, you might find that teachers just do not have the reading materials needed to teach the reading curriculum standards. They may not need professional learning; they may just need material resources. Therefore, make statements about the factors impacting performance and avoid jumping to solutions at this point in the process. You may use the tool in figure 1.7 to conduct your performance-factors analysis.

Instructions: Think about the current state of performance, the desired state of performance, and the data you have collected and analyzed related to your potential big rock. Answer the questions under each lens. Note where you do not have the needed data and where or how you might find that data. Think about how you might later facilitate discussions with your team once you have a better understanding of insights gained from using the different lenses.

Marketplace: External Factors

- What external factors are affecting school, educator, and student performance? Consider factors such as new governmental policies, relationships between the school and community partners and families, economics, demographic shifts, workforce shortages, and more.

- Can these factors be changed by local efforts, or must interventions be determined within the school to mitigate their impact on performance?

Workplace: The Organization and Work Environment

- What in the school is impacting the desired performance, such as culture, climate, schedules, leadership changes, policies, expectations, and more?

- Who has responsibility for impacting each factor?

Work: Tasks, Activities, Deliverables, and Services Performed

- What is happening with the work of the school, such as changes in the curriculum, instructional strategies implemented, technology, complexity, and more?

- Who has responsibility for impacting each factor?

Worker: Those Who Perform the Work

- Do workers have the will, skills, knowledge, and readiness to support the needs of the student population?

- Who has responsibility for impacting each factor?

FIGURE 1.7: Success tool—Performance-factors analysis.

*Visit **go.SolutionTree.com/schoolimprovement** for a free reproducible version of this figure.*

Data analysis and critical judgment cannot be based on opinion or assumption. For each statement or data point given in the performance-factors analysis, answer the question "How do you know?" If this is not based on concrete data sources like interviews, observations, or document analyses, determine what is the most appropriate way to collect the information needed to answer these questions. Factors analysis will provide you, and later your team, with a chance to reflect on all the work that has taken place, respect those past attempts, and begin to analyze the current reality.

As you focus on how to guide others to complete their collaborative analysis without jumping to solutions, you must overcome what is rooted in good intentions: sharing your expertise about improvement solutions, telling those you are guiding what the solutions should be, or directing them. To nurture collaborative efforts and gain the trust and credibility needed to do so, concentrate on how you can facilitate setting goals with your team and working together to achieve them. Avoid the seductive trap of taking on the work rather than building the capacity of others to do it.

However, you should first develop your own understanding of the situation to better prepare yourself for guiding others. How others perceive your intentions and credibility during this process impacts your ability to guide and support others' engagement in your improvement efforts.

Success Tool Notes:

Analyzing the Expertise of the Team

Now that you have collected and analyzed data using a performance-gap analysis and a performance-factors analysis, it is time for your core school-improvement team or guiding coalition to review the expertise of the team members. Expertise matters for successful improvement work. You may use figure 1.8 to review the skills and expertise of each team member and identify what additional expertise may be needed as you prepare to engage other stakeholders in the work.

Instructions: Record the name of each team member and their job. Then, have each team member share the areas of expertise to which they can contribute. Next, determine what other expertise is needed and who you might ask to support the team. You may want to ask each team member to complete this in advance and summarize the input as a team.

Team Member	Job	Expertise
Other Expertise Needed	**Who Can Help**	**Who Can Gain Their Support**

FIGURE 1.8: Success tool—Expertise analysis.

*Visit **go.SolutionTree.com/schoolimprovement** for a free reproducible version of this figure.*

Looking back at the performance-gap analysis and performance-factors analysis can help you scan for who needs to be involved because the work of their job will impact the intended results. Once you determine who needs to be engaged, consider what expertise or perspectives they can lend to the collaborative work ahead. When you spot a gap and factors that no team member can address, determine what expertise or authority is needed and decide who to tap from outside your team to support the work ahead.

Reviewing Examples of Standard 1

To help you use what you have learned in chapter 1, we have included an example of an effective practice and an example of a less effective practice. Comparing these examples will help you determine what to do and what to avoid when applying the work of standard 1.

An Effective Example

Luna Alvarez was a new assistant principal in an elementary school of 820 students. The school was remarkably diverse with more than fifty-four nationalities represented and a poverty rate of 67 percent. She had worked in the school for more than fourteen years as a mathematics teacher, including five years as a mathematics coach. She had also been active in professional learning teams.

The year before she was selected as one of five assistant principals, Alvarez participated in her school district's assistant principal development program. The program covered aspects of school leadership, including school improvement. When the principal hired her as assistant principal, she told Alvarez that in the coming year, she was to lead the improvement of disciplinary practices for prevention and better outcomes. Alvarez decided to apply what she knew about analysis; this included finding and testing practices that worked, iterating, and working as teams to improve what both the adults and the students were accomplishing.

Before the school year began, Alvarez analyzed the previous three years of discipline, climate, attendance, and achievement data. She recognized that external factors, such as shifting economic conditions and other external variables, were impacting the school. Having been a mathematics teacher and coach, she could see the challenging factors inside the school and opportunities to improve, including how discipline was managed at all levels. She recognized a need to better support leaders, teachers, and staff, as the frequency and intensity of discipline infractions had risen sharply. She knew teachers were feeling overwhelmed and how she engaged them and guided them would be critical.

Alvarez dug into recent research and reached out to other assistant principals in the school and school district to see what they were experiencing and what was working. She found that many were focusing on proactive ways to build positive student engagement and support the social-emotional well-being of both teachers and their students.

Before school began, Alvarez developed some questions that she placed on the school's internal website to allow teachers and staff to look back on the previous year and anonymously share what they saw as strengths in the disciplinary practices, why those practices had seemed to work, and what they felt needed to improve and why. She offered opportunities for volunteers to join a team that would do the analysis and support the coming year's planning and improvement process for discipline, student engagement, and social-emotional well-being.

As she worked on this improvement focus for the coming year, Alvarez realized she needed others with expertise to support the effort. She began compiling a list of what she thought she might need to know more about or have support for and reviewed the list with the principal, who recommended people in the school and at the system office who could help. As she looked at the list of those in the school whom the principal suggested, she thought of the teachers, leaders, and staff who would be influential in getting everyone to commit to addressing the improvement needs.

Alvarez made a private list to help her remember who to engage first and consider how to engage them. Reflecting on her learning in the assistant principal development program the previous year, she made notes of what she needed to do to gain the trust of those who could make a difference and to gently enter the process, since she was new to the role. She wanted to avoid looking like the new boss and to be accepted as a guide to success for all.

A Less Effective Example

Leon Ward was excited about his new role as high school principal in the town where he grew up and lived. He had served for several years in a large, high-performing high school in the county school system and eagerly anticipated leading the high school in the city school system. The city school system was ranked in the top-ten school districts in the state, after having experienced a five-year transformation from ranking as one of the lowest-performing districts. Ward began the school year with challenges to the faculty and staff to rise even higher. He shared his vision for what they would do and encouraged them to embrace the changes.

Three months into the school year, things were not going as smoothly as Ward had envisioned. He had focused on needs, including student tardiness to school and to classes. He also wanted to change the approach that the school was using for project- and problem-based learning. The faculty and staff were not warming up to his ideas or guidance. One veteran teacher told him, "Frankly, we don't care how you did it in the county schools. Things here are different. We know what we need to do here."

One day when Ward pulled into the school parking lot, he saw groups of teachers forming outside the school. He could not imagine what was going on so early. Within thirty minutes, the group had surrounded the front of the school to protest his changes. Teachers had dyed streaks in their hair in the school colors, representing their commitment to the school and their ways of teaching and working together.

Two weeks later, Ward was moved to a district operational role and replaced as principal by a long-term assistant principal. He told the superintendent, who knew Ward was talented but made the wrong initial impressions, that he had learned a valuable lesson. Ward then became a successful leader in a large school district, having learned what to do and avoid doing when guiding change and improvement.

Idea Hub: Reflection

Reflect individually on what you learned in this chapter, and record your thoughts. Then use your individual reflections to collaboratively answer the following questions with your team.

> » What did Alvarez do that aligns with the guidance in this chapter?
> » What did Ward do that misaligns with the guidance in this chapter?
> » What are your and your team's biggest takeaways?
> » How will you embrace the work of chapter 1?
> » How will you engage in the work of chapter 1?

Conclusion

The work of standard 1 requires you to develop your own understanding of the work ahead. Once this analysis is complete, you will be prepared to guide your team in gaining a deeper and wider view of the gap between the current state of performance of the chosen big rock and what that performance can be.

This chapter introduced you to the importance of creating and using a comprehensive set of data to determine your school's current situation, including demographic, achievement, program, and perception data. It walked you through a decision flowchart to help you identify the data you have, the data you still need, and whom to engage to get the data you need. The performance-gap analysis tool guided you in how to derive meaning from your data. The performance-factors analysis tool walked you through the process of applying different lenses to more thoroughly analyze your data. Using multiple lenses that consider the external environment, the school as a workplace, the work that people do, and the people who do the work enables you to identify factors that impede learning. It might provide ever-greater insight into why performance has not yet reached the desired expectation. Hopefully, during your discovery and analysis, you practiced a mindset where you ask yourself, "What performance will we enhance or improve?"

In chapter 2, you will engage others in discussing the data while you calibrate your team's understanding to ensure everyone is on the same page as you move forward. Throughout the process, you will see opportunities to adjust your thinking as you collect and analyze the data.

Now you are better prepared to engage more members of the school in analyzing, understanding, and breaking down their big rock based on what was found in doing these analyses. When school personnel see that your team is trying to understand and is coming from a place of care, you can build trust and increase belief in the process. You will have created shared ownership!

Before moving on to chapter 2, complete the "Standard 1: Do and Avoid Chart" and "Standard 1: Plan-Ahead Chart" reproducibles (pages 36 and 37) with your team to reflect on and process the work you accomplished for standard 1 and plan ahead for next steps.

Standard 1: Do and Avoid Chart

As you move through the standards for improvement, you will find things to do and things to avoid. After reading the effective and less effective practice examples and reflecting on them and the work of standard 1, complete the following do and avoid chart to help you record your thoughts about the work of this standard.

Instructions: Record what you plan to do and avoid. Consider the following questions.

1. How will you introduce your team to the processes introduced in this chapter?
2. How will you encourage your team to examine data without judgment?
3. How will you facilitate discussions about how to bring an enhanced mindset to the processes?
4. How will you support identifying gaps in performance without jumping to solutions?
5. How will you facilitate analyzing the systemic factors impacting performance without jumping to solutions?

Do	Avoid

Standard 1: Plan-Ahead Chart

To get a clearer perspective on the next steps, consider your do and avoid chart as you complete the following plan-ahead chart. In addition to conducting initial analysis, the work of standard 1 prepares you to build the trust and credibility needed to begin collaborative analysis.

Instructions: Use the information from chapter 1 to identify your and your team's next steps to complete each action.		
Actions	**Person or People Responsible**	**Due Date**
Use the comprehensive data profile analysis (see figure 1.3, page 25) as a starting point for data collection and analysis to encourage fruitful discussion.		
Conduct a performance-gap analysis (see figure 1.4, page 27) to assess strengths and areas needing improvement to transform performance from the current state to the desired state.		
Conduct a performance-factors analysis (see figure 1.7, page 30) to identify factors in the marketplace, workplace, work, and workers that are impacting the performance gap.		
Use the expertise analysis (see figure 1.8, page 32) to identify the expertise of team members.		
Explain how all these analyses inform your choice of a big rock.		

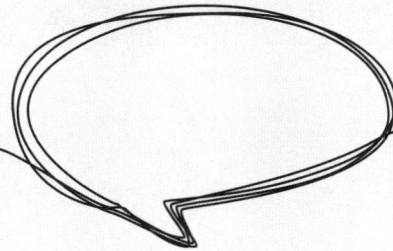

Chapter 2

Standard 2: Facilitate Deriving Meaning and Engagement

Analyze and Apply
Critical Judgment

Organize and
Manage Efforts
and Resources

Guide and Focus
Collaborative Improvement

Build Capacity

Demonstrate
Organizational Sensitivity

Monitor Accountability
and Adoption

Implement for
Sustainability

**Facilitate
Deriving Meaning
and Engagement**

Plan and Record

Focus on
Systemic Factors

$\mathscr{S}$tandard 2 is about guiding others in creating meaning from data while building supportive and collaborative relationships. The intent is to help all stakeholders comprehend the implications of their actions and to gain their commitment so that they feel engaged. This standard directly supports improvement, innovation, implementation, and further progress by fostering educators' deeper learning, creativity, and adaptability. When you emphasize meaning and engagement, you inspire students and educators to improve, innovate, and pursue excellence. This also transforms school improvement into a process that is not only effective but also enjoyable and impactful.

Doing the analysis and planning for how best to apply what you learn on your own can feel a bit like trying to cut your own hair. It is challenging, lacks the needed perspectives and expertise, and may take time and growth to correct a botched attempt. During the research that led to the development of the CSIS standards (Page & Hale, 2013), we had the opportunity to identify less effective practices, one of which is exemplified in the following anecdote about a new principal.

A newly appointed school principal devoted her summer to analyzing her new school and developing the school-improvement plan. At the start of the school year, she shared the 114-page document with the leadership team (including administrators, support staff, and teacher leaders) and charged them with implementing portions of the plan. As the weeks passed, she grew frustrated with the lack of interest from teachers and the lack of progress in implementation. Her analysis and planning were well intentioned, but she had not engaged those who must do the work. Therefore, the leadership team did not understand what was impacting results or why team members should do the planned work.

As this principal participated in a focus group discussing the selected standards, she heard her peers share their experiences and practices for engaging those who do the work in analysis and planning. She shared what she had done and her frustration. Some peers commented that they or others they had observed had similar experiences, so they took a more purposeful approach to engagement and inclusion in analysis and planning. Looking back, the principal realized that her urgency to get the school moving in the right direction caused her to fail to help others understand why changes were needed. She learned that facilitating those who must make changes and take actions to find and implement solutions through the analysis phase was required to produce what she, and they, could envision for the school.

There is a saying that goes, "When the student is ready, the teacher will appear." This applies to the second phase of the school-improvement process. In this chapter, you will guide others in deriving meaning from the gathered data, make new meaning through emotional connection and asset-based foci, review example applications of standard 2, and plan to apply the standard so the team is ready to do the work ahead.

Facilitating Deriving Meaning and Engagement

To *facilitate* means to make it easier for something to happen. To *derive meaning* means to think in ways that extract or obtain significance, understanding, or an interpretation of something. It can involve making connections, drawing conclusions, and synthesizing information to create a deeper understanding or insight. Making sense of what is happening to navigate complex ideas and experiences is a fundamental aspect of human cognition.

Engagement is achieved by nurturing active participation through the processes and tools that you use to gain the needed levels of emotional commitment, motivation, and dedication. Everyone you engage with has their own unique thoughts, feelings, and perspectives about the work, whether they are novices, experts, or fall somewhere in between on a continuum of experience and proficiency. Keep in mind how adults think and make decisions so you can successfully engage them in collaborative work.

Adults have had prior experiences and have existing knowledge and points of view (Chuang, 2021). They may have well-constructed mental models about how things are and should be. They may not yet have the experience to independently recognize needs and how to meet them. What they think is grounded in what they feel, believe, and have or have not experienced. Skillful facilitation capitalizes on these prior experiences, or lack thereof, as resources that will enhance the improvement process. Skillful facilitation also provides opportunities for adults to see the current reality of their school's performance and the factors impacting it. The effort can hook their curiosity and help them understand the implications of continuing the same performance. It prepares them to set and meet shared goals and shift from working together to truly collaborating.

Since understanding, learning, and committing require attaching a feeling to what someone is experiencing, it is not counterproductive when adults become emotional (Shackleton-Jones, 2023). This is part of the process. People's initial feelings about collaboration can shape their engagement. Building trust and fostering a positive environment enhance the likelihood of success. Anticipating reactions to change is necessary to successfully facilitate the improvement process. Change can bring a mix of reactions. Pausing to ask, "What are your thoughts?" or "What insights do you have?" can encourage meaningful engagement. Through facilitation efforts and the following four steps, you can help your team members examine their beliefs and prior knowledge so that they are updated and informed by the team's analysis.

Step 1: Identify the Critical Mass

Engaging others in analysis and knowledge sharing fosters commitment to shared goals. While urgency is important, thoughtful planning ensures long-term success. Building a strong foundation helps sustain meaningful school improvement. Research on organizational change suggests that reaching a critical mass of innovators and early adopters—approximately 16 percent of a group—can help drive meaningful change (LaMorte, 2022; Rogers, 1962). These are the opinion leaders who embrace new ideas and change. Within this group, Hale (2012) finds that you do not have to elicit all the change makers, just 51 percent of the *right* people. Who comprises the 51 percent required to advance the work of the big rock and bring others with them? They are the people whose influence is needed to get everyone moving in the right direction and sustain progress. Once you have identified the right group of people to help your school or team find success, we recommend using the next three steps to structure your meetings and work to be more effective.

School leadership plays a crucial role in the success of improvement efforts. However, we recognize that teams and schools vary. If you are not the supervisor of the team members, you must secure their supervisors' permission for them to participate. Team members and their supervisors need to know the purpose of the team, why their support is important to its efforts, and what will be expected of them, including the amount of time they will need to dedicate and when the team will meet. Team members must know their responsibilities, what authority they will have for actions and decisions, and who will be leading the team.

Step 2: Develop a Team Charter

After you identify your critical mass, the core group of individuals who are ready and willing to engage in the improvement effort, the next essential step is to unify that group around a common direction. A team charter helps you do just that. This simple tool creates a shared purpose and collaborative vision for the team. It transforms a group of individuals into a team by clarifying purpose, priorities, expectations, and commitments. It also identifies supporters and establishes target timelines, all of which are essential for coordinated action.

Establishing a charter early builds ownership and trust. It ensures everyone understands not only why the team exists but also what it is committed to achieve. This shared clarity reduces confusion, supports accountability, and keeps the team focused as the work progresses. The charter becomes a living document, a guide that grounds your team in its collective *why* and helps you navigate challenges along the way.

Figure 2.1 (page 42) shows a team charter tool you can use with your team.

Instructions: Facilitate one or more discussions with your team to create a team charter. The charter will be a living document that you and your team use as a guide. Begin by responding to the following prompts.

Our purpose is:
Our members are:
Our supporters are:
We are committed to achieve:
Our dates for reaching our needed results are:

FIGURE 2.1: Success tool—Team charter.

Visit **go.SolutionTree.com/schoolimprovement** *for a free reproducible version of this figure.*

Step 3: Establish Team Norms

Once you complete the team charter, which establishes a shared purpose and collaborative vision for the team, it's time to set or revisit norms for the team. Developing or revisiting norms is important because norms create the foundation for effective collaboration and a healthy team culture. Effective norms do not just help teams function—they help them thrive. Revisiting them ensures they stay relevant and supportive of continuous school improvement.

Norms establish clear expectations by setting ground rules for how team members will work together—how they will communicate, make decisions, handle disagreements, and stay accountable. When expectations are clear, meetings are more focused and productive. Everyone knows what respectful and professional behavior looks like.

Norms build trust and psychological safety. When norms prioritize listening, equity of voice, and respectful dialogue, team members feel safer to share ideas, take risks, and express concerns. This trust leads to deeper collaboration, stronger innovation, and shared leadership. Norms also improve consistency and accountability. They help teams stay consistent in their behavior over time—even as members or circumstances change. They provide a shared reference point when conflict arises, someone strays from agreed-on expectations, or decisions need to be revisited.

Regularly revisiting norms supports the process of ongoing improvement because it allows team members to reflect on what is working and what needs to change as the team evolves. It models a growth mindset and keeps team functioning aligned with goals, especially when new initiatives or challenges arise or when the team dynamics shift.

When norms are cocreated and regularly revisited, team members feel ownership over how they work together. Their commitment to the work is strengthened. This increases engagement, collaboration toward shared goals, and alignment with schoolwide improvement efforts.

Figure 2.2 shows a tool your team can use to establish or revisit team norms.

Instructions: Guide your team in setting its own rules of engagement. You can add steps as needed.

1. Schedule a team meeting to discuss the importance of agreeing on norms or how they will work together.
2. During the meeting, emphasize the need for mutual respect, open communication, and the setting and achievement of shared goals.
3. Brainstorm beneficial norms using collaboration protocols and techniques.
4. Vote or otherwise agree on each norm.
5. Compile a document of agreed-on norms.
6. Make sure the norms are posted and visible during meetings.
7. Revisit the norms periodically and update them as needed.

FIGURE 2.2: Success tool—Establishment of team norms.

*Visit **go.SolutionTree.com/schoolimprovement** for a free reproducible version of this figure.*

Step 4: Create a Team Meeting Agenda

As you plan your team meetings, remember to create an agenda. Missing this step can lead to inefficient or confusing meetings. Agendas are easy, effective tools to keep the team on track and focused on your shared goals and purpose. Agendas also give you a document trail of what happened, when it happened, and who participated. We recommend bookmarking the tool in figure 2.3 and revisiting it after reading the chapter.

Instructions: Create an agenda template or use this one. Record when meetings are held, who facilitates them, who attends them, the decisions that are made, and the agreed-on action steps and who is responsible for them.

Date:	Time (start and end):
Meeting facilitator:	
Participants:	
Norms (list):	
Prereading or preparation for members:	

FIGURE 2.3: Success tool—Team meeting agenda.

continued ▶

Success Tool Notes:

Agenda Items	Decisions Made

Next steps:

Who is responsible for next steps:

*Visit **go.SolutionTree.com/schoolimprovement** for a free reproducible version of this figure.*

Idea Hub: Sustained Momentum With a Shared Purpose and Team Norms

Individual reflection:

How has developing a shared purpose and team norms changed the way you view your role on the team? In what ways might this clarity impact how your team makes decisions and navigates challenges going forward?

Team discussion:

Now that your team has established a foundation (critical mass, charter, norms, and meeting structures), what specific behaviors or routines will help you sustain momentum and ensure the work remains purposeful over time?

Now that you have reviewed key facilitation tips, identified the critical mass to get the work done, and reflected on how to sustain your momentum, it is time to move into the meat of the chapter—making meaning!

Making Meaning

Successfully guiding the school-improvement process requires revisiting your initial analysis and conducting similar analyses with stakeholders. The adages "In God we trust, all others bring data" (Fischer, 2008, p. 179) and "Facts often kill a good argument" (Joiner, 1985, p. 224) support the importance of having valid data to analyze. The point of these quotes is that you must set aside time for your larger group to dig deeply into the data collected in chapter 1. When performed well, the collaborative analysis process helps those who will make improvements understand what is needed and why it matters.

How you facilitate this analysis matters as much as what gets analyzed. Guiding your team through this process can help members develop a shared understanding of the data and uncover meaningful insights. You cannot rush this effort or assume understanding. As your team moves through analysis, keep in mind the humans behind these data points. Begin by looking for ways to help your team form an emotional connection with the data. Maintain this connection by employing an asset-based focus and engage stakeholders in performance-factors analysis to refine your big rocks.

Emotional Connection

Data analysis is a key part of school improvement, but it is equally important to connect the data to the people it represents. Helping your team see beyond the numbers can deepen their commitment and engagement. Activities that tap into emotions are powerful tools for capturing stakeholder attention and building commitment. Creating personal connections to data—such as by sharing stories that illustrate real-world impact—enhances engagement in ways that raw numbers alone cannot.

Research shows that *data storytelling*, which blends narrative with evidence, engages both the rational and emotional parts of the brain, making information more memorable and motivating action. Author and communication expert Carmine Gallo (2019) highlights how this approach activates the amygdala (emotion center) and the hippocampus (memory center), and thereby increases the likelihood that messages stick and drive behavior. Storytelling-based engagement has consistently led to higher buy-in from diverse stakeholders, from community members to staff, by making the data feel personally relevant (Heath & Heath, 2007).

One way to create connections is to associate student names or stories with key data points to make the information more meaningful. For example, if the graduation rate is 70 percent, share a composite picture of a group of students at the school. Then delete 30 percent of the students from the picture. You can also list students by performance level at the end of course assessments. Seeing students' names in writing humanizes the data and makes it more than numbers. We encourage creating more personal connections with the data and reminding team members that students are more than the numbers or levels of these data points.

Another way to show team members how lives are impacted is to engage in *design thinking*. This is an iterative, five-step process—(1) empathize, (2) define, (3) ideate, (4) prototype, and (5) create—that places the users (or stakeholders) of an organization at the center of the improvement initiative. The process begins with *empathy interviews*. Empathy interviews are common with organizations such as IDEO, High Tech High's Graduate School, and Stanford University's Hasso Plattner Institute of Design, which promote human-centered design. Each organization might have a slightly different approach, but overall, the interview process helps them gain a deeper understanding of each stakeholder's experience. Stanford's *Empathy Fieldguide* explains that empathy is the cornerstone of human-centered design and that we must deeply understand the people we serve to improve their experiences (Hasso Plattner Institute of Design, n.d.). This applies to students, staff, and parents.

It's important to stress to team members that conducting these interviews is a great first step, but they cannot stop there. They must engage in the rest of the design-thinking process to truly benefit from the interviews. The process includes spending time analyzing interview data for themes and root causes before moving into action planning and intervention selection. The steps and tips outlined in figure 2.4 can help you conduct an empathy interview.

Instructions: Use the guiding questions to accomplish the corresponding action in each step.

Step	Guiding Questions
1. Identify the stakeholder groups to interview.	Will you interview students, teachers, staff, parents, or community members? Sometimes, interviewing different groups at different times is beneficial.

2.	Plan a schedule for the interviews.	Will interviews happen face-to-face or online using a platform such as Microsoft Teams or Zoom? Will you schedule interviews during one school day or across multiple days?	**Success Tool Notes:**
3.	Craft your questions.	What questions do you want to ask? Ask open-ended questions that can elicit stories. These questions should be neutral or balanced so you are not skewing a group's responses in a certain direction.	
4.	Invite your participants.	How will you notify and elicit participants? Will teachers nominate a representative sample of students? Will you allow all parents the opportunity to sign up or start with your parent-teacher organization?	
5.	Conduct the interviews.	How do you plan to capture the conversations? We recommend having a partner in the interviews, sharing the purpose of the interviews, and using a tool such as Otter AI to transcribe the conversations. This is key so you do not accidentally leave out important information.	
6.	Analyze the interviews.	When will you analyze the interviews? You should do this once the interviews are all complete. We recommend dedicating at least a half day to one whole day for a thorough analysis.	

FIGURE 2.4: Success tool—Empathy interview protocol.

*Visit **go.SolutionTree.com/schoolimprovement** for a free reproducible version of this figure.*

Once your team has conducted all the interviews, you will end up with an overwhelming amount of data. When this happens, decide on a plan for gleaning useful information from pages of notes or hours of recordings. Team members must deeply immerse themselves in this work. We recommend at least a half day for this part of the process. Figure 2.5 (page 48) lays out a process you can follow to capture key themes from your data.

Instructions: Follow the steps laid out for each of the three phases. When you are done, you will have captured the key themes from the interviews.

Phase	Steps
Preparation	1. Decide who will be part of the analysis and invite them to the meeting. We recommend a combination of teachers, support staff, and administrators. 2. If you used a transcription tool (such as Otter AI), clean up the interview transcripts so they are legible. 3. Print multiple copies of each transcript to distribute among individuals or small groups in the meeting. 4. Decide who will analyze which interviews. If there is a small number of transcripts, all team members can read all the transcripts. If there is a large number of transcripts, divide them into equal portions. Distribute them to groups of two or three team members. We recommend that at least two people review the same transcript so there are multiple perspectives. 5. Gather materials for the meeting: transcripts, chart paper and markers (or a digital platform if preferred), sticky notes, and pens.

Analysis	1. Provide copies of the transcripts to the team members who will conduct the analysis.
	2. Post chart paper on the wall to capture the team's thinking. Charts can be labeled by stakeholder group or by question asked.
	3. Have each team member engage in the following three-pass protocol.
	   a. **First pass:** Read or skim through the transcript to familiarize yourself with what is said.
	   b. **Second pass:** Annotate the transcript, identifying key words or phrases that stand out.
	   c. **Third pass:** Discuss the transcript with your partner or small group. On sticky notes, write key words, phrases, or ideas that emerged from the transcript—one idea per note—and then post them on the appropriate chart paper.
	
	Note: Do not write down solutions or assumptions. Write facts based on what was said in the interview.

Synthesis	1. For each sheet of chart paper, engage in affinity mapping by reading the listed sticky notes and grouping them by common themes, patterns, or priorities. 2. Write a short phrase or sentence that describes each grouping. 3. Review each chart and identify areas to celebrate and problems that should be explored as part of the school-improvement process.

FIGURE 2.5: Success tool—Interview theme definition process.

Visit go.SolutionTree.com/schoolimprovement for a free reproducible version of this figure.

In our work with schools, affinity mapping has many benefits for teams. Affinity mapping is a powerful tool for analyzing empathy interviews because it creates space for individuals to first process and share their thinking independently by capturing key insights on sticky notes. Then, as a team, members collaboratively group related ideas, which allows them to calibrate their interpretations and identify common themes grounded in the actual interview data. This process helps team members not only discover patterns but also build shared understanding and alignment across the team.

Once this process is complete, the team will have affinity maps that look similar to the image in figure 2.6. This affinity map illustrates themes a team identified related to its student interviews.

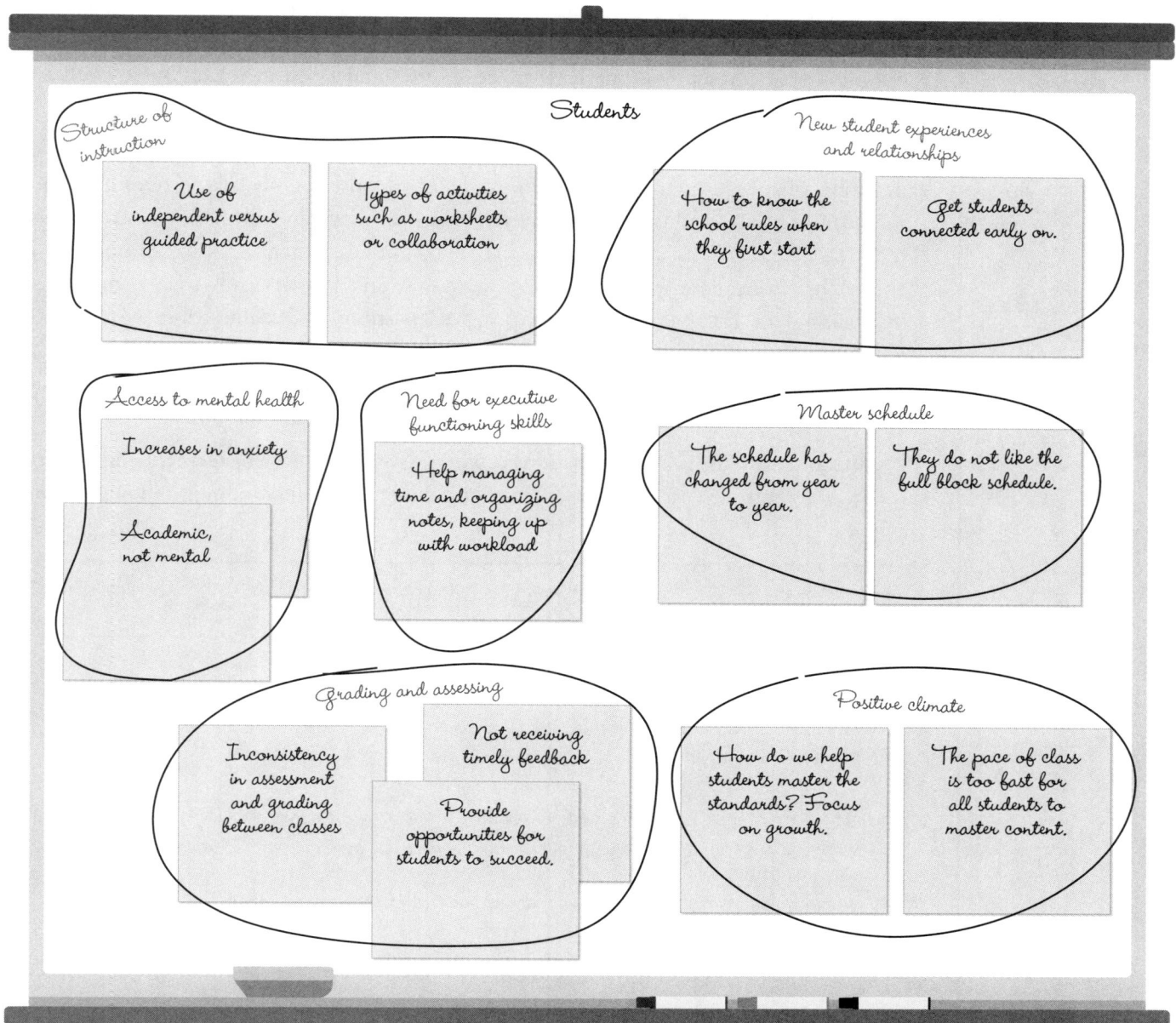

FIGURE 2.6: High school student affinity map.

As the team engages in this analysis, it is imperative to have established norms for applying candor while also not blaming any one group, such as teachers, students, or parents. These can be tough conversations, especially the first time that team members engage in the process. However, they often lead to valuable insights and stronger collaboration. The team may need to work through transcripts together before moving to smaller groups. If at any point it seems like the conversation is moving into making excuses for the data, blaming a group, or jumping to solutions, stop the conversation and navigate back to the purpose—unearthing insights to better understand the stakeholder experience.

**Success
Tool Notes:**

Asset-Based Focus

When analyzing data and identifying trends uncovered in empathy interviews (see figure 2.4, page 46), remember the asset-based mindset. It is easy to identify areas to improve, but what are your strengths or areas to celebrate? Communicate these back to the groups you have interviewed. This is a good time to use *appreciative inquiry*, a practice of asking positive questions that points to strengths and possibilities and helps organizations move past a deficit-based mindset (Armstrong, Holmes, & Henning, 2020).

Appreciative inquiry is based on the premise that groups and organizations move in the direction of the questions they continuously ask themselves. By asking questions about the positive efforts and outcomes they can point to, they can feel the joy of accomplishments, celebrate them, and focus on achieving more of them. Taking an appreciative approach before identifying specific gaps, causes, and barriers can balance the process by looking for the good to engage positive emotions and connections. Appreciative inquiry is a powerful practice for guiding collaborative school improvement. The Case Western Reserve University website has free resources for supporting appreciative inquiry (https://case.edu/weatherhead/fowler/areas-expertise/appreciative-inquiry).

Educators who use positive questions can increase the odds of engagement and commitment. Use figure 2.7 to guide your team in conducting positive inquiry about the work of the big rock.

Instructions: Start with the questions shown for each of the four Ds to examine the team's collective or individual big rock.

1. **Discovery:** What is working best now for us and for others in similar contexts?
2. **Dream:** What can we imagine could be?
3. **Design:** How can we collaboratively define and develop what can be?
4. **Destiny:** How will we achieve together what we designed?

Next, have the team ask, reflect on, and answer the three follow-up questions.

1. What is a wish you would make for our or your big rock if it were guaranteed to come true when worded positively?
2. What is happening or has happened that has positively impacted the school and has potential to help address the big rock?
3. What other positive questions can we ask those we guide as they look at data, performance gaps, and factors and imagine better outcomes?

Facilitation tip: A helpful question to ask when a person or group brings up a negative or a complaint is "We hear what you are saying. In your imagination, what would that look like if it were solved well?"

FIGURE 2.7: Success tool—Appreciative inquiry.

*Visit **go.SolutionTree.com/schoolimprovement** for a free reproducible version of this figure.*

A balanced approach to analysis highlights both strengths and areas for growth, which fosters engagement. With this foundation, your team can collaboratively explore performance gaps and opportunities for improvement. Figure 2.8 can guide this next step in facilitation.

Instructions: Begin by asking your team to read the questions in the following chart. After sharing everyone's answers, facilitate a discussion to come to consensus. Record your responses in the chart.

What results need to improve? Consider the gap between where you want to be and where you currently are.	How do you know this improvement is necessary?	Upon what strengths, assets, or past successes can we build?

FIGURE 2.8: Success tool—Inquiry chart.

Visit **go.SolutionTree.com/schoolimprovement** *for a free reproducible version of this figure.*

After analyzing data for overarching themes and trends, your team is ready to move into analyzing the factors that contributed to these findings. Use the tools and tips in the following section to assist you in these efforts.

Factors Analysis With Stakeholders

Recall the analogy presented in the introduction. Just as hikers build cairns by carefully placing individual stones to mark the path, stakeholders contribute to the larger improvement effort by focusing on their piece of the challenge. Your leadership or school-improvement team began this process in chapter 1, conducting an initial analysis of the big rock using a performance-factors analysis. Now it is time to guide other key stakeholders—such as faculty teams, department leaders, or community partners—through a similar analysis. Their work will focus on identifying which aspects of the challenge they can impact, what gaps exist, and what contributing factors need to be addressed. The goal is not only to deepen understanding but also to help stakeholders identify the specific areas they can directly influence. This turns the overwhelming challenge into smaller, actionable components, or smaller rocks for which teams and individuals can take ownership.

These stakeholders are not working on separate big rocks; they are contributing to solving the same overall challenge by addressing the specific elements they can influence. You may share the initial data profile and performance-gap analysis conducted by the leadership team, but do so intentionally. Frame it not as a final conclusion but as a starting point for shared sense making. Emphasize that the stakeholders' perspectives, knowledge, and engagement are essential to refining and validating understanding of the problem—and to crafting sustainable, actionable solutions. By engaging others in this way, you deepen the analysis, foster shared ownership, build trust, and lay the foundation for implementation that is both collaborative and effective.

Later, it may be helpful to compare each stakeholder group's analysis of what they believe they can impact—their smaller rocks—with the analyses conducted by other groups across the school, as well as with your team's original analysis of the big rock. Looking across these analyses can reveal important trends, patterns, and gaps in understanding that will inform next steps.

Success Tool Notes:

**Success
Tool Notes:**

The worksheet in figure 2.9 is designed to encourage a more in-depth look into stakeholders' beliefs about what is impacting performance. The intent is to focus their attention on a broad range of factors so they can identify all the performance drivers.

Instructions: Display each section of this worksheet for stakeholders on a whiteboard or flip chart, or project it from a computer. The information you collect will help you build on what you learned in your initial independent inquiry using the tools described in chapter 1. After group members answer each question, be sure to share and compare the data and findings from your research.

Section 1: The Workplace—The Environment in Which the Work of Education Occurs Within the School or School District

1. What impacts adults' work and their results in the workplace? Consider the culture, the capability of leadership, the adequacy of supervision, the availability of coaching and support, the incentives for teamwork, the adequacy of rewards and sanctions, and more. How do you know that these are impactful factors?
2. Of those workplace factors, which ones do the adults who work in the school or who support the work of the school have control over? Which ones do the adults lack control over but must still overcome or accommodate to effectively do their work and get the needed results?

Section 2: The Work—The Tasks and Responsibilities That Make Up the Jobs That People in Education Do

1. What impacts the effectiveness, quality, and value of the work of adults in the school (or school district)? Consider the complexity, design of the job or work, changing nature of the work, clarity of the processes of the work, and so on. How do you know these factors impact the ability of the adults to do the work?
2. Which impacts on the effectiveness, quality, and value of the work of the adults in the school (or school district) are within the adults' control? Which ones are outside their control but must be managed by them?

Section 3: The Workers—The Adults Who Work Within the School or School District Whose Performance Impacts the Outcomes

1. Do all workers have the knowledge and skills required to achieve the results? What (if any) knowledge and skills need to be enhanced or improved? For whom do they need to be enhanced or improved? How do you know?
2. Are the workers motivated to do what needs to be done?
3. What factors increase motivation to achieve the right results? What factors hinder motivation?
4. What would encourage the right behavior in this context?
5. How do you know whether motivation strategies are working?
6. Does every worker clearly understand what is expected of them?
7. How do you set performance expectations?
8. How do you communicate expectations to workers?
9. How do you monitor, inspect, and evaluate individual performance?
10. What happens when a worker is not meeting expectations?
11. What are you personally in control of that could make it possible to achieve the needed improvements and results?
12. What actions produce results that currently exceed what is required?
13. What actions contribute to a failure to produce the desired results?

Source: Adapted from © 2013 by Deb Page and Judith Hale. Used with permission.

FIGURE 2.9: Success tool—Performance-factors analysis worksheet.

*Visit **go.SolutionTree.com/schoolimprovement** for a free reproducible version of this figure.*

As you facilitate the performance-factors analysis with other stakeholders, help the group focus on what is within their control to impact and what they cannot impact but must keep in mind to be successful. As an educator, you have much to accomplish and cannot do everything at once. You must prioritize your work.

The success tool in figure 2.10 is designed to help teams focus their efforts. The nominal group technique was designed to control bias in decision making (Delbecq, Van de Ven, & Gustafson, 1975). It makes the outputs of the process easier to analyze qualitatively. This tool helps groups balance participation and reach consensus.

Instructions: Use the following protocol to guide a group meeting on making a decision, such as determining the highest-priority improvement need. What performance factors need to be prioritized?

1. Explain the purpose of the meeting and the goals of equal participation and active engagement for all. For example, to set norms for the group, explain that the purpose is to develop norms that have been co-created by all who will be following them.

2. Request that each participant silently write down their ideas. Encourage at least three or more ideas per person. Ask for short ideas in a verb-noun format, such as "Respect opinions."

3. Guide structured recording by having each participant verbally share one idea at a time, in a round-robin format, without repeating an idea that has already been shared. Post the ideas on a flip chart, whiteboard, or virtual tool. Do not allow discussion of the ideas, but allow participants to ask for clarification. Another option is for participants to write their ideas on separate sticky notes and add one idea at a time to chart paper. If one of their ideas is already there, they should pick another one. This option takes away any apprehension about sharing verbally in front of a group.

4. Facilitate the participants to combine any ideas they see as being similar enough to form a single idea.

5. Allow each participant to contribute three votes by placing check marks, stickers, or other marks by the ideas they rank as most important. They may distribute their votes among three ideas, give two votes to one idea and one vote to another, or give all three to one idea. Direct them to all vote at the same time so they are focused on their votes and not on how others are voting.

6. Tally the votes, posting the number of votes each idea received.

7. Vote again, allowing each participant two votes for the ideas that received two or more votes.

8. Tally the votes, capturing the ideas that received the most votes.

9. Allow one minute per person for anyone who wishes to advocate for an idea, if you desire.

10. Vote again, allowing each person to vote for the ideas on the list with the most votes.

11. Record the ideas with the most votes, eliminating those that received no votes in this round.

12. Present the list to the group, as well as any next steps to be taken.

Source: Adapted from Delbecq et al., 1975.

FIGURE 2.10: Success tool—Nominal group technique.

*Visit **go.SolutionTree.com/schoolimprovement** for a free reproducible version of this figure.*

At this point, you have guided those who can impact the work and outcomes through the modified nominal group process to reach consensus on priorities. But how do you know when your priorities are adequately finalized and it is time to move on?

You will know you are ready when there is clear agreement among team members about the top priorities and when each priority is defined with enough clarity that you can describe what it means and why it matters. A good check is to ask, "Can everyone articulate the selected priorities in their own words? Is there alignment between these priorities and the previously analyzed data and root causes?" If there is still significant disagreement or uncertainty, it may be necessary to revisit the criteria or engage in additional discussion.

Once there is shared understanding and buy-in, and the group is confident these priorities address the most critical needs, you are ready to move forward with planning actions aligned to those priorities.

Reviewing Examples of Standard 2

To help you use what you have learned in chapter 2, we have included an example of an effective practice and an example of a less effective practice. Comparing these examples will help you determine what to do and what to avoid when applying the work of standard 2.

An Effective Example

A large suburban school system was implementing new curriculum performance standards in mathematics. A great deal of time had been spent on training teachers in the new standards and coaching teachers in quality mathematics instruction aligned to the new standards. Teachers had collaboratively developed curriculum maps and modeled lessons for every standard. The curriculum director, Josh Newman, knew that benchmark tests were needed to monitor student growth and assess the instructional effectiveness of these new standards.

Benchmark tests for the old curriculum objectives had been developed about ten years earlier by three curriculum specialists in the system office. The tests were initially administered, but nothing was done with the test results. Many teachers said that the test items were not good, and no item analyses were ever conducted. They felt the tests were a waste of time. Slowly but surely, teachers had stopped administering the tests.

Newman, his curriculum team, a representative group of mathematics teachers, and the regional mathematics coordinator met to discuss the purpose of the new benchmark tests, how the tests could consistently be administered by all teachers, and how the results could be used to improve mathematics instruction. They also devised a plan to involve all mathematics teachers in developing the new benchmark tests to increase the chances that the tests would be quality assessments and all the teachers would commit to their successful implementation.

Teachers would be reviewing standards, researching test items, developing test items, piloting test items, giving feedback through item analyses, and revising test items. A representative group of teachers would then compile a draft test for all teachers to pilot, and revisions would be made again based on item analyses and reviews of results. Newman knew that successful implementation of the benchmark tests depended on engaging all staff in the process of developing the test items and understanding how they would use the tests to assess student progress on the new mathematics standards and guide future mathematics instruction.

A Less Effective Example

Mia Gomez was selected as the new superintendent of Grand Elmo Schools and took office on the first of July. She met with principals and told them she expected their finalized school-improvement plans to be sent to her before the first day of school in August. Ray McCuin, a middle school principal, had just received the previous year's data and had planned to meet with a few people on his school's leadership team to develop the final plan. The test data that McCuin received showed new areas of need. Because he did not want to make a bad impression on the new superintendent, he decided that he would review the data and write the final plan himself; that way, he could get it to the superintendent before anyone else. The plan had twenty goals and listed the people he had assigned to be responsible for each part.

When school started in August, McCuin told the staff that he had saved everyone work and written the final school-improvement plan. He instructed the grade-level teacher leader, subject-area teacher leader, and academic coaches to present the plan at grade-level meetings so people could get started. The grade-level and subject-area leaders and academic coaches were confused and overwhelmed by the twenty goals. They also had not seen the data that McCuin received in July and did not know how to explain to their peers why some of the goals had been selected. They just handed out copies of the plan and told their peers, "This is what we are supposed to do this year."

Idea Hub: Reflection

Reflect individually on what you learned in this chapter, and record your thoughts. Then use your individual reflections to collaboratively answer the following questions with your team.

- » What did Newman do that aligns with the guidance in this chapter?
- » What did McCuin do that misaligns with the guidance in this chapter?
- » What are your and your team's biggest takeaways?
- » How will you embrace the work of chapter 2?
- » Who will you engage in the work of chapter 2?

Conclusion

The work of standard 2 requires you to help others derive meaning from the data and understand the gap between the current state of performance of the chosen big rock and what it can be. This chapter introduced you to the importance of determining the team's expertise, additional expertise that is needed, and the people who can influence others to do the work well. You have determined what you can do and what you should avoid in completing the work of standard 2. You have a plan for the work of standard 2 to assist you in knowing what must be done, who will be responsible, and the desired completion dates.

Now you are ready for standard 3, which focuses on systemic factors impacting performance and determination of the root causes and causal factors of performance gaps that you have identified. This will lead to a suite of solutions that you can explore further to decide on the most valid interventions, the requirements for implementing each intervention, and what is needed to drive that work to reach your goals.

Before moving on to chapter 3, complete the "Standard 2: Do and Avoid Chart" and "Standard 2: Plan-Ahead Chart" reproducibles (pages 56 and 57) with your team to reflect on and process the work you accomplished for standard 2 and plan ahead for next steps.

Standard 2: Do and Avoid Chart

As you move through the standards for improvement, you will find things to do and things to avoid. After reading the effective and less effective practice examples and reflecting on them and the work of standard 2, complete the following do and avoid chart to help you record your thoughts about the work of this standard.

Instructions: Record what you plan to do and avoid. Consider the following questions.

1. How will you introduce your team to the processes introduced in this chapter?
2. How will you determine the expertise of the team, additional expertise needed, and the people who can influence others to support the work?
3. How will you facilitate so the team can be candid about areas to enhance or improve as well as celebrate strengths and positive accomplishments?

Do	Avoid

Facilitating Shared Success © 2026 Solution Tree Press • SolutionTree.com

Visit **go.SolutionTree.com/schoolimprovement** to download this free reproducible.

Standard 2: Plan-Ahead Chart

To get a clearer perspective on the next steps, consider your do and avoid chart as you complete the following plan-ahead chart. The work of standard 2 prepares you to facilitate meaning making about the data and engage team members in the work ahead.

Instructions: Use the information from chapter 2 to identify your and your team's next steps to complete each action.		
Actions	**Person or People Responsible**	**Due Date**
Engage a Larger Team • Identify the expertise and support needed to help your school reach success. • Create a team charter to establish a shared purpose, a collaborative vision, priorities, expectations, and commitments and set target timelines that facilitate coordinated action. • Establish team norms to set clear expectations and ground rules for how team members will work together—how they will communicate, make decisions, handle disagreements, and stay accountable.		
Create an Emotional Connection to the Data • Review your data analyses from the Collecting and Analyzing Data section in chapter 1 (see pages 20–31) and then help your team members see beyond the numbers to deepen their engagement and commitment. • Conduct empathy interviews (see figures 2.4 and 2.5, pages 46 and 48) to gain a deeper understanding of each stakeholder's experience. • Complete the appreciative inquiry chart (see figure 2.7, page 50) and the inquiry chart (see figure 2.8, page 51) to highlight both strengths and areas for growth and foster engagement.		
Synthesize the Data • Conduct a performance-factors analysis (see figure 2.9, page 52) to engage other stakeholders and get a more in-depth look into stakeholders' beliefs about what is impacting performance. • Use the nominal group technique (see figure 2.10, page 53) to balance participation and reach consensus in selecting priorities.		

Chapter 3

Standard 3: Focus on Systemic Factors

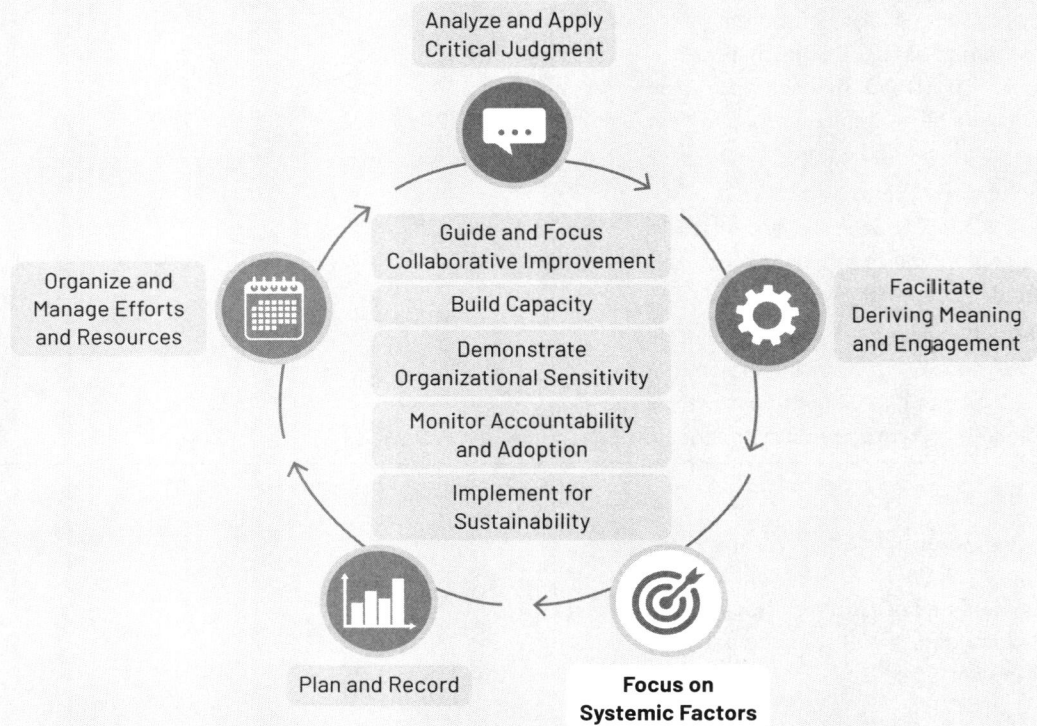

Analyze and Apply
Critical Judgment

Guide and Focus
Collaborative Improvement

Build Capacity

Demonstrate
Organizational Sensitivity

Monitor Accountability
and Adoption

Implement for
Sustainability

Organize and
Manage Efforts
and Resources

Facilitate
Deriving Meaning
and Engagement

Plan and Record

**Focus on
Systemic Factors**

*T*his chapter is based on standard 3, which addresses the systemic and often interdependent variables that affect student performance. By focusing systemically on the work that people do, their work environment, and their skills and motivation, you increase the likelihood of uncovering the real barriers to change. Systemic thinking considers all variables and ensures that improvement, innovation, and implementation are not static or siloed but interconnected processes. For example, a school that encourages innovation through pilot programs must also have mechanisms for scaling successful innovations through systemic improvements. A focus on systemic factors fosters a school culture where continuous improvement, experimentation, and learning are prioritized. It enables the school to adapt to new challenges and opportunities.

You can't fix a complicated problem with just one solution. If students aren't engaged in class, you can't solve it by only giving them a chance to share their opinions. To increase student engagement, you need to focus on all the reasons students are *not* engaged. This standard guides you to think carefully about what it will take to address the causes of the problem and avoid focusing on obvious or favorite solutions. This chapter will help your team take the steps needed to find solutions that work best for your specific situation and avoid the urge to rush into quick fixes.

First, you will explore how to do a root cause analysis and identify causal factors of your big rock challenge. There is a unique difference between these two terms, which we will guide you to focus on to find the best solutions. Next, you will prioritize the causes and use an intervention selection process to identify a suite or combination of possible solutions. You will assess the feasibility of your selected solutions and identify the implementation drivers required to change people's practices in the school system. Last, you will learn how to create goals that are specific, measurable, attainable, relevant, time bound, inclusive, and equitable.

Analyzing Root Causes and Causal Factors

Teams jump to picking solutions to problems if they have not looked at symptoms or dug deep enough into the causes. They must figure out what happened, how it happened, and why. Then they can focus on how to stop it from happening again (Woods, n.d.). It helps to know the differences among root causes, causal factors, and symptoms.

- **Root causes** are the starting point of a series of events. They are the main reasons that a problem happens. If you get rid of the root cause, the problem should never happen again (Okes, 2019). Getting to the root cause of a problem can be difficult because root causes are often hidden. In complex systems like education or health care, some root causes cannot be removed. For example, schools can't get rid of poverty, which can be a reason why some students struggle. But schools can offer extra support and services to help reduce the effects of poverty on student success. Similarly, hospitals can't eliminate cancer as a cause of poor health. They can, however, understand that it has many causes, choose the right treatments, and work to lessen its impact on patients' health.

- **Causal factors** are the various things that cause a problem. While George Maldonado and Sander Greenland (2002) offer a foundational understanding, contemporary research further clarifies the concept. For example, Liuyi Yao and colleagues (2021) describe causal factors within the *potential outcome framework*, defining them as variables whose manipulation leads to changes in an outcome. This means that causal inference often addresses complex interactions and uses modern statistical and machine-learning methods to identify these variables. For example, there may be several reasons that teachers are not planning lessons together. They may not have time set aside for planning together, or they may have to cover other classes during their planning time because there are not enough teachers. They may lack teamwork skills, or school leaders may not have provided them with the support or resources required to plan collaboratively. These are causal factors—specific conditions or barriers that contribute to the problem. However, they are not necessarily the root causes; deeper analysis is required to uncover the underlying systems, beliefs, or practices that give rise to these contributing factors. There can be many causal factors, and addressing them may lessen the issue but not eliminate it as when a root cause is addressed.

- **Symptoms** are signs of deeper issues. If students are having trouble understanding lessons, that is a symptom. Digging deeper, you might find that teachers haven't received enough training and coaching in the right teaching strategies. You might also find that teachers lack time to plan effective lessons together because of teacher shortages.

The tools and strategies in this chapter can help you better understand what is happening, why, and how.

Fishbone Diagram

The first tool to help you identify root causes is the fishbone, or Ishikawa, diagram. This tool is used to explore causes of problems and their effects (Suárez-Barraza & Rodríguez-González, 2019). The fishbone diagram allows your team to identify several potential causes, which you can then dig deeper into using the strategies in the following sections. Figure 3.1 is an example of a fishbone diagram that leaders may create to identify the reasons behind a student engagement problem.

Instructions: Follow these steps to complete the fishbone diagram.

1. **State the problem:** Write the problem or issue you want to analyze at the head of the fishbone diagram.
2. **Draw the backbone:** Draw a horizontal line extending from the head to the right. This is the backbone of the fish.
3. **Identify major categories:** Think about the big areas that contribute to the problem, and write them as branches coming off the backbone. Avoid blaming specific groups of people. For example, use categories like *school culture*, *instruction*, *social-emotional health*, and *family and community engagement* instead of just *family*.
4. **Brainstorm causes:** For each major category, list the causes that affect that category. Add these as smaller branches or bones coming off each major category. Some causes might fit into more than one category. These smaller causes can help you find important solutions.
5. **Organize the causes:** Once your fishbone diagram is complete, sort the branches into three groups: (1) symptoms (what you see happening), (2) causal factors (things that influence the problem), and (3) root causes (the main reasons behind the problem). Set aside the symptoms and focus on the causes. For example, under *instruction*, if you see "instruction lacking real-world applications of learning," analyze it further to find the real root causes or causal factors to improve student engagement. Most of the branches will be contributing factors, not root causes.

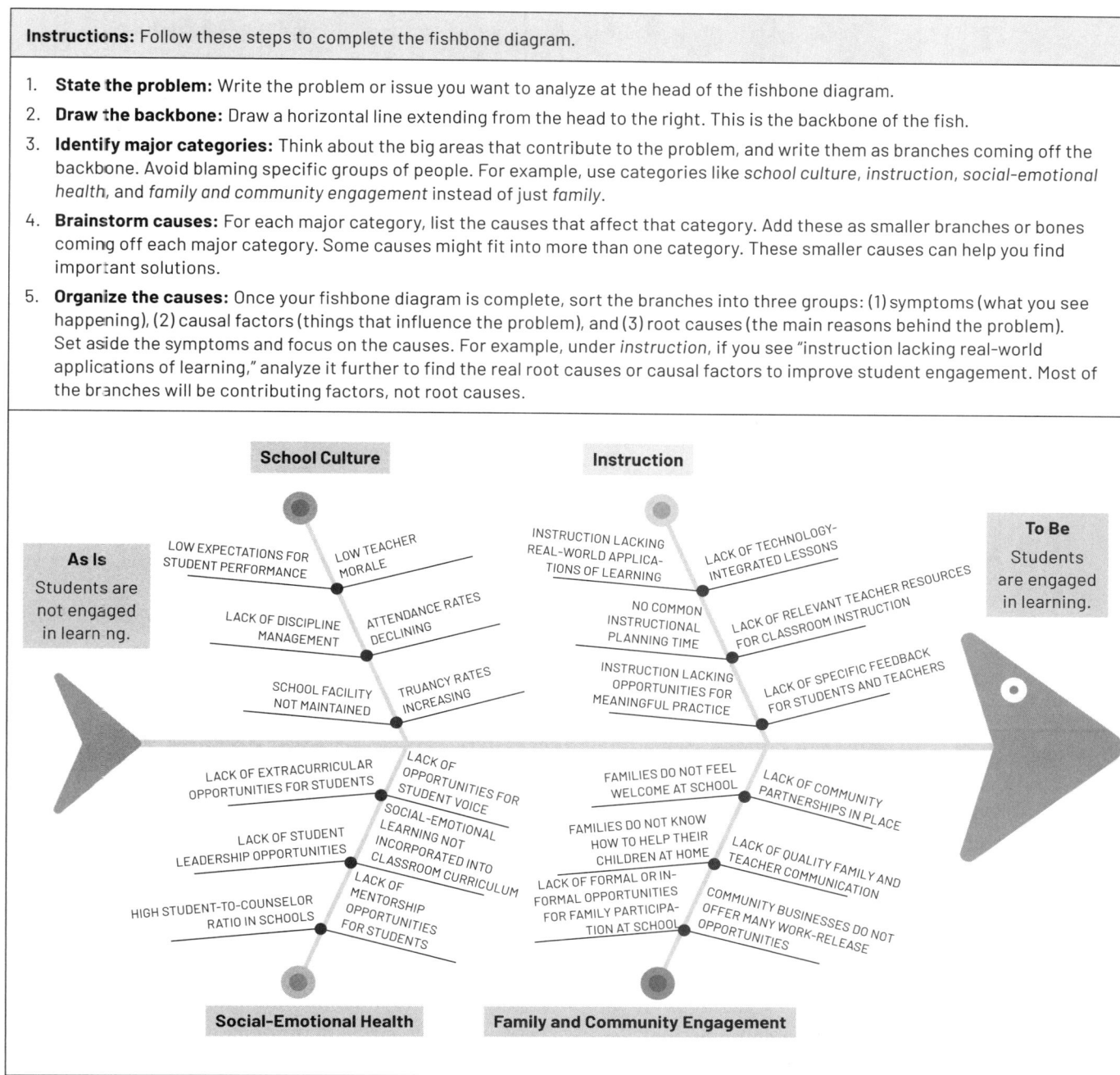

FIGURE 3.1: Fishbone diagram example.

Visit go.SolutionTree.com/schoolimprovement for a free blank reproducible version of this figure.

**Success
Tool Notes:**

Five Whys Protocol

The example five whys protocol shown in figure 3.2 is a process used to dig deeper into the potential causes identified using the fishbone diagram (Card, 2017). This protocol reveals multiple variables that may be contributing to each cause by encouraging the team to explore a chain of reasoning. Each *why* builds on the previous one, gradually peeling back the layers of the issue to uncover more foundational causes.

Instructions: Identify a cause from the fishbone diagram that your team feels significantly contributes to the current reality or problem. Then ask yourself, "Why is this happening?" Follow up with actual data or instances, not assumptions. Once it is hard to answer *why*, you likely have identified the root of the problem.	
Cause identified: Instruction lacks real-world applications of learning, as shown in the fishbone diagram about lack of student engagement.	
1. *Why* does instruction lack real-world applications of learning? 　　+ How do you know that?	*Teachers don't know how to plan lessons or projects with real-world applications to engage students.*
2. *Why* don't teachers know how to plan lessons or projects with real-world applications? 　　+ How do you know that?	*Teachers lack the know-how or skills to develop real-world examples in their lessons.*
3. *Why* don't teachers have the knowledge and skills for real-world lessons? 　　+ How do you know that?	*The school doesn't train or coach the teachers in how to develop or use real-world applications of learning and doesn't provide opportunities to learn.*
4. *Why* doesn't the school provide the needed professional learning and coaching? 　　+ How do you know that?	*The school doesn't have the resources or time for professional learning or on-the-job coaching. There is no common planning time, and there's no funding for these programs.*
5. *Why* do teachers not have common planning time, and *why* are funds not allocated for all schools? 　　+ How do you know that?	*Common planning time has not been a priority. Teacher shortages have impacted the ability to implement common planning time. Administrators claim the school district has not provided funding for development.*

FIGURE 3.2: Success tool—Five whys protocol and worksheet example.

*Visit **go.SolutionTree.com/schoolimprovement** for a free blank reproducible version of this figure.*

A word of caution: The five whys protocol can sometimes lead a team down a single line of thinking if not facilitated carefully. This may result in overlooking other contributing factors. For that reason, it may not be the best tool when addressing complex or "messy" problems, where multiple, interrelated root causes are likely at play (Pojasek, 2000).

The example in figure 3.3 illustrates the results of the five whys protocol when multiple groups within a team start with the same first *why* question. The collective ideas can be compiled and compared for a more comprehensive view of issues impacting performance. This process helps the team explore the problem using systemic lenses.

Group 1	Group 2	Group 3
Why does instruction lack real-world applications of learning? *Teachers do not know how to plan for real-world applications of learning.*	**Why does instruction lack real-world applications of learning?** *Lesson plans are primarily focused on acquisition of knowledge.*	**Why does instruction lack real-world applications of learning?** *Teachers are not incorporating practical examples into their instruction.*
Why do teachers lack the knowledge and skills to plan lessons that include real-world applications of learning? *They do not have collaborative planning time when they can discuss real-world applications.*	**Why are the lessons primarily focused on acquisition of knowledge?** *The curriculum guidelines emphasize mastery of knowledge and skills over practical application.*	**Why are teachers not incorporating practical applications into their instruction?** *They feel they don't know relevant applications related to their content or how their content relates to work outside the classroom.*
Why don't teachers have collaborative planning time? *The school has not implemented teacher teams or other collaborative planning structures into the schedule.*	**Why do the curriculum guidelines emphasize mastery of knowledge over practical application?** *The guidelines were developed based on academic standards that prioritize knowledge and skills as opposed to application of knowledge and skills.*	**Why don't teachers know relevant applications or how their content relates to work outside the classroom?** *They lack a deep understanding of their content outside an academic setting.*
Why has the school not implemented common planning into the school structure? *The administration is using the existing schedule that has worked in the past.*	**Why do the curriculum guidelines prioritize foundational knowledge and skills?** *The standards were designed to ensure students have a strong knowledge base before they apply concepts in a practical way.*	**Why do they lack a deep understanding of their content outside an academic setting?** *They don't have opportunities to collaborate with external stakeholders or participate in other learning opportunities.*
Why is the administration using the existing schedule? *The principal is new and does not want to implement major changes in their first year.*	**Why were the standards designed this way?** *The state education agency has advocated the need for a solid theoretical foundation over real-world or practical applications.*	**Why do teachers lack those opportunities?** *The environment (school) does not facilitate access to those opportunities.*

FIGURE 3.3: Five whys protocol example for multiple groups.

This series of *why* questions can continue to dig deeper and find high-leverage causes that, when addressed, will increase real-world applications of learning in instruction. You repeat the *why* question at least five times not just to dig deep into symptoms or causes but to help surface other variables. Even though this analysis tool is called the *five whys*, you may need more than five *why* questions to drive the analysis to valid and agreed-on root causes or causal factors. Notice in the previous questions that multiple variables may surface each time *why* is asked.

Idea Hub: Five Whys Protocol

Ask yourself the following questions, and then discuss them with your team.

» How are the answers to the *why* questions from the three groups in figure 3.3 (page 63) alike or different?

» How can this process help you identify systemic factors?

There are five things to remember in the five whys protocol.

1. Sometimes, identified causes are really symptoms of a problem.

2. There are usually multiple causal factors impacting a problem.

3. You may not be able to identify or address all root causes due to the systemic nature of the causes and factors impacting education outcomes.

4. Causes can be interdependent and may require deep and systemic analysis and more *why* questions.

5. Educators' performance can be impacted by multiple influences outside their control.

Environment and Worker Analysis

How well educators do their jobs is affected by what's going on around them. The environment and worker analysis tool leads to deep systemic analysis that does not place the blame or claim for success just on the "workers." This powerful tool combines two diagnostic models: (1) Thomas F. Gilbert's (2007) behavioral engineering model and (2) Carl Binder's (1998) Six Boxes™ model of behavior influences.

If you've already done the performance-factors analysis (see figure 2.9, page 52), look at the worker factors you found. Think about how things at work, like the school environment, might be affecting these factors. For example, if teachers aren't working together, check what's happening at school that might stop them from collaborating. Also, look at their daily work schedule to find any barriers to teamwork.

Motivation to do a good job can be affected by extrinsic things that an educator cannot control, like leadership's praise practices, or things that are intrinsic to themselves, like their ability to handle changes. If someone knows how to do something but isn't doing it, it's not a skills issue. Look for *why* they are not doing it. To decide whether they are ready to do their work, consider how they were prepared for it. A new teacher might need extra practice and support.

Figure 3.4 guides your team through the environment and worker analysis. You can use the results of the performance-factors analysis (figure 1.7, page 30) and performance-gap analysis (figure 1.4, page 27) to complete or adapt the tool because this tool is another way to help a school determine why a performance gap might exist. The questions provided represent only a few of those you might ask.

Instructions: Individually reflect and write notes on the questions in each cell. Then, as a team, find the causes impacting staff and student performance. First, focus on addressing causes in the work and workplace. Second, focus on those related to workers or educators. You may want to use your team's big rock to practice using this tool.

Big Rock

What's going on in the work and the workplace that affects how well educators perform? How do educators' knowledge, skills, abilities, and motivation affect their results?

Environment	Information	Resources	Motivation
The Work and the Workplace *What does the school administration or district office provide for workers to be successful?*	• Do staff know how their performance compares to the desired performance? • How often do workers receive feedback? Is it constructive? • Are procedures and policies clearly defined and explained?	• Do staff have the tools, facilities, or resources to achieve the desired performance? • Are materials, job aids, assistance, and coaching available to do the job well? • Does professional learning allow opportunities to practice and lead to the application of learning?	• What meaningful incentives are given to staff who perform well? • Do any school policies or procedures provide a hidden incentive to perform poorly? • Are there consequences for underperformance?
People	**Knowledge and Skills**	**Capacity**	**Motives**
The Worker *What does the person's experience and knowledge bring to the work?*	• Do staff have the necessary knowledge and skills to perform well?	• Do staff have the physical, emotional, and reasoning capabilities to succeed at meeting expectations in the current context?	• Do staff demonstrate a desire to perform well for the school and students? • Are staff willing to perform for the incentives or consequences?

FIGURE 3.4: Success tool—Environment and worker analysis.

*Visit **go.SolutionTree.com/schoolimprovement** for a free reproducible version of this figure.*

The results of this analysis should give the team a better understanding of what is causing performance challenges. You may also find it helpful to have teachers or staff involved in the performance related to the big rock complete this analysis. Compare their views with those of the improvement team. When school staff see that the team is trying to understand and genuinely cares, it helps build trust and increases their belief in the school-improvement process.

Success Tool Notes:

Success Tool Notes:

_____

_____

_____

_____

_____

_____

_____

_____

_____

_____

_____

_____

_____

_____

_____

_____

_____

_____

_____

_____

_____

Idea Hub: Causal Analysis

Review the fishbone diagram (see figure 3.1, page 61), five whys protocol (see figure 3.2, page 62), and environment and worker analysis (see figure 3.4, page 65).

» How do these tools help you get a broader perspective on what is really happening in the school?

» Do your team members have different perspectives on what is happening in the school? If so, what might contribute to these differing perspectives?

» How do these processes help you avoid the pitfall of jumping to solutions?

Prioritizing Causes

Finding multiple causes leads to the challenge of knowing what to address first. Research finds that each complex challenge usually has at least three causes and at least four solutions (Wile, 2012). Often, there is a need to build staff's knowledge and skills, but it is not the only need. Other needs exist. For instance, the example five whys protocol (see figure 3.2, page 62) finds that lack of development is a cause of instruction that is short on real-world applications of learning, but it is not the only cause. School structures like professional learning teams are missing. Teachers do not have common planning time. Lack of professional learning is not the root cause or the only causal factor. Identifying and prioritizing all the causal factors or the root causes helps you select the best set of solutions.

Once you identify the causes of a problem, you must prioritize them. Decide what causes will add the most value to solving the problem at hand and achieving the desired results. You may use figure 3.5 to decide which causes to prioritize.

Instructions: Answer the following questions with your team.

Factor	Questions
Frequency	1. How frequent is the problem? 2. Does it occur often, sporadically, or rarely?
Importance	1. From the point of view of those who do the work, what are the most important problems? 2. What are the problems that the analysis shows must be resolved?

Importance	3. Is there a critical path to solving a problem that requires stages or sequences of work?
	4. Are quick wins needed to achieve momentum?
Feasibility	1. How realistic is it that we can resolve the problem?
	2. Will it be easy or difficult?
Effect size	1. What is the impact of interventions on student achievement?
	2. How do we know?
	3. What evidence are we using?
Requirements	1. What regulations, policies, contracts, or other requirements make addressing this problem's causes a necessity?

FIGURE 3.5: Success tool—Causes priority protocol.

*Visit **go.SolutionTree.com/schoolimprovement** for a free reproducible version of this figure.*

You have identified and prioritized the causes that seem most important. Before you pick the best solutions, make sure you haven't missed any other causes or factors that might be affecting performance.

Identifying a Set of Solutions

Use the performance-factors solutions consideration list in figure 3.6 (page 68) with people who did not take part in the performance-factors analysis but whose insights and expertise can help with seeking the best solutions. These people might be stakeholders who are not directly involved in developing the school-improvement plan but who can impact the achievement of improvement goals. An example is regional, state, or provincial

Success Tool Notes:

Success Tool Notes:

education agency personnel who support the work of the school. The list uses the same three parts as the environment and worker analysis does: (1) workplace, (2) work, and (3) worker factors. This list can also help the team find causes and factors that might not have been talked about yet but that could be affecting performance.

Instructions: Use the following checklist to review performance factors that may or may not have been identified up to this point yet need to be addressed for your big rock. Check the factors needing improvement, and add any additional causal factors that you identified in the fishbone diagram (see figure 3.1, page 61), five whys protocol (see figure 3.2, page 62), or environment and worker analysis (see figure 3.4, page 65). Then for each checked or listed factor, list four possible solutions that need to be explored.

Workplace considerations: What needs to be addressed in the workplace to improve the effectiveness of your big rock?

Place a check mark beside the *workplace* factors that need to be improved.	List four possible solutions to be explored for the checked factors.
☐ Organizational culture or climate	
☐ Staffing and assignment practices	
☐ Lack of awareness of (or unclear criteria for) what good work is	
☐ Lack of organizational support, such as time, resources, opportunities, coaching, data, or information	
☐ Management of teacher turnover	
☐ Administrator experience	
☐ Board experience	
☐ Leadership	
☐ Expected work being defined	
☐ Compliance with applicable federal, state or provincial, and local rules, policies, laws, and regulations	
☐ Performance targets and individual goals	
☐ Performance standards	
☐ Work processes and measures of effectiveness	
☐ Documented and followed corrective action processes	
☐ Documented processes for comparing performance to standards of practice	
☐ Documented communication processes that are effectively managed and conducted	
☐ Documented policies and procedures that are effectively managed and conducted	
☐ Strategic school improvement and project planning	
☐ Equitable resource allocation and management	
☐ Consistent instructional design	

☐ Benefits and compensation systems	
☐ Leader, teacher, and organizational performance evaluation processes	
☐ Physical classrooms or workspaces	
☐ Scheduling practices	
☐ Team structures	
☐ Job designs	
☐ Professional learning	
☐ Rewards and sanctions	
☐ Organizational design	
☐ Alignment of plans, priorities, actions, and interventions	
☐ Coworker, team, and department behaviors	
☐ Technology design and management	
☐ School or system governance and oversight	
☐ Other	

Work considerations: What needs to be addressed in the design of the work to improve the effectiveness of your big rock?

Place a check mark beside the *work* factors that need to be improved.	List four possible solutions to be explored for the checked factors.
☐ Complexity of the work, curriculum, and content standards	
☐ Changes in the work	
☐ Routines of work	
☐ Alignment of work to expectations and demands	
☐ Identified knowledge, skills, and attitudes required for the work	
☐ Levels of knowledge and skill mastery required for the work	
☐ Alignment of work to student achievement needs	
☐ Work evaluation	
☐ Physical work requirements	
☐ Workload	
☐ Technology alignment with and support of work	
☐ Risks in the work	
☐ Contextual work variables	
☐ Other	

Worker considerations: What needs to be addressed to improve the effectiveness of the workers engaged in your big rock?

Success Tool Notes:

FIGURE 3.6: Success tool—Performance-factors solutions consideration list.

continued ▶

Success Tool Notes:

Place a check mark beside the *worker* factors that need to be improved.	List four possible solutions to be explored for the checked factors.
☐ Knowledge of what they are supposed to do, how to do the work, or why the work should be done	
☐ Obstacles beyond their control	
☐ Lack of skill or knowledge	
☐ Fear and motivational issues of anticipation of negative consequences	
☐ Lack of positive consequences	
☐ Negative consequences	
☐ Positive consequence for not performing	
☐ Lack of negative consequences for not performing	
☐ Personal problems	
☐ Belief that no one could do the work, they are already doing the work (lack of feedback), the work will not work, their way is better, or something else is more important	
☐ Lack of readiness to do the work	
☐ Other	

Visit **go.SolutionTree.com/schoolimprovement** *for a free reproducible version of this figure.*

Assessing Feasibility

Before moving forward with implementation, you need to consider *feasibility*—whether the solutions you have selected are practical, realistic, and achievable within your current context. Feasibility includes factors such as available resources, time, support, and the capacity of those involved. Can you implement the solutions you chose? Solutions are effective only if they can be implemented.

Figure 3.7 helps you think through what is necessary to get others to adopt new ways of working.

Instructions: Complete this worksheet with your team. Start by reading the following questions. Then, add any local factors that could have an impact on the project. Next, answer the questions with *yes* or *no*. Finally, list the evidence that supports each answer. If any question can't be answered with a *yes*, your team will need to plan how to fix or reduce the impact of that factor.	

Questions	Yes or No	Evidence
1. Does the culture of the school support the expected behaviors that the project supports?		

2. Is sponsorship for the project and its related initiatives ensured in the long term?			
3. Is oversight or governance of the planned project in place beyond the immediate launch or refocus?			
4. Is there evidence that you can get adequate funding over the time required for the project to be effective? (For example, if a grant is available so you can start the work, what funding source will keep the work going after the grant expires?)			
5. Are expected new behaviors for implementing the project integrated into jobs, performance measures, and evaluations? (If the new behaviors are seen as "outside the regular work," it will be difficult to sustain them.)			
6. Are resources being committed to support the adoption of new behaviors over the long term? (For example, will resources for retraining or coaching be available after the start-up?)			
7. Is the infrastructure in place to support the interventions? (For example, are people, time, working arrangements, and more available to get the proposed work done?)			
8. Do current leadership and administrative practices support the new behaviors necessary to implement the project? (For example, do job descriptions and roles and responsibilities support doing the work of the project?)			
9. Is there a planned process for monitoring outcomes and impacts and measuring progress and results that will give people feedback in time to adjust?			

Success Tool Notes:

continued ▶

Source: © 2013 by Deb Page and Judith Hale. Adapted with permission.

FIGURE 3.7: Success tool—Feasibility analysis worksheet.

Success Tool Notes:

Questions	Yes or No	Evidence
10. Will the change that each intervention produces be enough to outweigh the estimated cost and effort?		
11. Will the targeted results be accepted as achievement or success? (For example, is everyone in agreement on what effectiveness and success look like?)		
12. Are all proposed interventions aligned with each other so they will work together to achieve the desired state of performance and results? (For example, are improved recruiting processes aligned with the school's plans to enhance specific student outcomes?)		
13. Will there be a critical mass of internal stakeholders to support this effort? (A critical mass is 51 percent of the right people—those who can influence others to support the effort, who can offer resources or help, and who could stall progress or prevent the work from being sustainable.)		
14. Will there be a critical mass of external stakeholders to support this effort?		
15. Other questions:		

Visit **go.SolutionTree.com/schoolimprovement** *for a free reproducible version of this figure.*

This feasibility analysis might help you find other solutions. It will help the team think through what it takes for solutions to work. Investing time now to question the feasibility of a solution will save time later. It will also prevent the frustration of starting initiatives only to stop them later.

Idea Hub: Feasibility

Now that you have identified a potential suite of solutions and assessed their feasibility, discuss the following questions with your team.

» Will these solutions, if implemented with fidelity, reduce the problem's chances of occurring again?

» What, if any, solutions are risky to implement?

Drafting Goal Statements

You have completed the analysis. You have explored possible solutions. Now, you are ready to write your improvement goals. We recommend using the SMART+IE format (specific, measurable, attainable, relevant, time bound, inclusive, and equitable; Waters & Farwell, 2022). Figure 3.8 will help your team craft effective improvement goals.

Instructions: Use this worksheet to develop and refine collective and individual goals. Guide your team members as they discuss their responses to the questions for each section. Use the outputs of the discussion to refine the team's collective big rock and individual big rocks.	
Specific	1. What, in specific terms, do we want to accomplish? 2. Why is it important?
Measurable	1. What criteria will we use to track and measure progress and determine when the goal is achieved? 2. What metrics will we use? 3. How will we capture those metrics?

FIGURE 3.8: Success tool—SMART+IE goal worksheet.

continued ▶

Success Tool Notes:

Attainable	1. Is the goal realistic and achievable given the available time, resources, and other constraints?
	2. What can we do to increase the probability of it being achievable?
Relevant	1. Is the goal aligned with the school's mission?
	2. Is it seen as a priority?
	3. Is there support for the overall improvement plan?
Time Bound	1. What is the specific period or deadline for achieving the goal?
	2. Are there milestones we can use to show and celebrate progress?

Inclusive	1. Are the students who will be impacted included in the work of accomplishing the goal? 2. Have we engaged those who can contribute to achieving the goal?
Equitable	1. Will students who are impacted feel supported, valued, and included in the work of this goal? 2. What can we do to purposefully support and value students and stakeholders?

Visit go.SolutionTree.com/schoolimprovement for a free reproducible version of this figure.

Reviewing Examples of Standard 3

To help you use what you have learned in chapter 3, we have included an example of an effective practice and an example of a less effective practice. Comparing these examples will help you determine what to do and what to avoid when applying the work of standard 3.

An Effective Example

Principal Tijuan Johnson and assistant principal Hassana Scott were in their third year of leading Sydney Park Elementary. In the past, they had studied the school's data and developed the school's improvement plan. This year, Johnson and Scott wanted to involve everyone more deeply in the process. Their first analysis showed the school's needs matched the district's strategic plan. They needed to improve reading, mathematics, attendance, discipline, student engagement, and teacher performance. They knew there were no quick fixes, so they had to involve everyone who could make a difference.

Success Tool Notes:

_____
_____
_____
_____
_____
_____
_____
_____
_____
_____
_____
_____
_____
_____
_____
_____
_____
_____
_____
_____
_____
_____
_____
_____
_____
_____
_____
_____
_____
_____
_____

Johnson and Scott led groups in using the fishbone diagram (see figure 3.1, page 61) to find causes of the problems. They used the five whys protocol (see figure 3.2, page 62) to dig deeper. They guided the groups through the performance-factors solutions consideration list (see figure 3.6, page 68). After they chose solutions, they used the feasibility analysis worksheet (see figure 3.7, page 70) to determine the possibilities of implementing them.

Everyone agreed on causes to address and their solutions. They made sure their goals were specific, measurable, attainable, relevant, time bound, inclusive, and equitable. They added the goals to the school-improvement plan. They were ready to plan their improvement projects. Looking back, Johnson and Scott saw that involving everyone led to better understanding and commitment.

A Less Effective Example

Asana Bowers was a mathematics coach at an elementary school. Her principal asked her to help the mathematics teachers and their assistants better understand why some students were struggling with mathematics and had trouble with reading. The school leaders had looked at some data and found that mathematics teachers needed to collaboratively come up with ways to help students who were struggling to read.

Bowers shared the leaders' request with the mathematics teachers and asked them to look at the data and discuss what might be causing mathematics problems related to reading skills. The teachers agreed that reading skills affected mathematics, but they were more interested in new teaching methods that they had learned about at a summer mathematics conference. They decided that the main reason for the mathematics problems was that they needed better teaching tools. They set a goal to use some online training from the conference to improve their mathematics teaching. Bowers then sent this goal to the school leaders to include in the school-improvement plan.

Idea Hub: Reflection

Reflect individually on what you learned in this chapter, and record your thoughts. Then use your individual reflections to collaboratively answer the following questions with your team.

» What did Johnson and Scott do that aligns with the guidance in this chapter?

» What did Bowers do that misaligns with the guidance in this chapter?

» What are your and your team's biggest takeaways?

» How will you embrace the work of chapter 3?

» Who will you engage in the work of chapter 3?

Conclusion

This chapter introduced you to the differences among root causes, causal factors, and symptoms. We presented several tools to help you determine these things: The fishbone diagram helps you identify causes; the five whys protocol helps you dig deeper to uncover the root causes or causal factors; the environment and worker analysis helps you determine why a performance gap might exist; and the causes priority protocol helps you set priorities before brainstorming possible solutions.

The chapter discussed that for every performance challenge, there can be at least three causes and four solutions. The performance-factors solutions consideration list helps you organize your chosen solutions by considering performance factors. Using it could help those who did not take part in the factors analysis understand the factors impacting performance. The feasibility analysis worksheet helps you decide what is possible. Finally, you can use the SMART+IE goal worksheet to record your improvement goals.

Next, it is time to move to standard 4, plan and record. Chapter 4 will introduce tools and processes designed to help you develop efficient and effective plans for achieving and sustaining your improvement goals.

Before moving on to chapter 4, complete the "Standard 3: Do and Avoid Chart" and "Standard 3: Plan-Ahead Chart" reproducibles (pages 78 and 79) with your team to reflect on and process the work you accomplished for standard 3 and plan ahead for next steps.

Standard 3: Do and Avoid Chart

As you move through the standards for improvement, you will find things to do and things to avoid. After reading the effective and less effective practice examples and reflecting on them and the work of standard 3, complete the following do and avoid chart to help you record your thoughts about the work of this standard.

Instructions: Record what you plan to do and avoid. Consider the following questions.

1. How will you introduce your team to the processes introduced in this chapter?
2. How will you help your team use the processes and tools in this chapter?
3. How will you help your team investigate the causes of gaps in performance?
4. How will you help your team identify who can impact causal factors and root causes?
5. How will you help your team identify what the priorities are?
6. How will you facilitate identifying suites of solutions that can address the gaps in performance?
7. How will you help your team agree on and set SMART+IE goals?

Do	Avoid

Standard 3: Plan-Ahead Chart

To get a clearer perspective on the next steps, consider your do and avoid chart as you complete the following plan-ahead chart. The work of standard 3 prepares you to analyze root causes and causal factors of gaps in performance, determine who and what can impact the causes and factors, identify a suite of solutions that can address the gaps, and agree on their goals.

Instructions: Use the information from chapter 3 to identify your and your team's next steps to complete each action.		
Actions	**Person or People Responsible**	**Due Date**
Use the fishbone diagram (see figure 3.1, page 61) to identify and explore causes of issues and their effects.		
Use the five whys protocol (see figure 3.2, page 62) to dig deeper into the causes you identified in the fishbone diagram.		
Complete the environment and worker analysis (see figure 3.4, page 65) to conduct a deeper systemic analysis of workers and factors beyond the workers.		
Use the causes priority protocol (see figure 3.5, page 66) to decide what causes will add the most value to solving the problem at hand and achieving the desired results.		
Use the performance-factors solutions consideration list (see figure 3.6, page 68) to gain insight from and tap the expertise of people who did not take part in performance-factors analysis, and determine the best solutions.		
Use the feasibility analysis worksheet (see figure 3.7, page 70) to determine whether the solutions you selected are practical, realistic, and achievable within your current context.		
Use the SMART+IE goal worksheet (see figure 3.8, page 73) to develop and refine collective and individual goals.		

Chapter 4

Standard 4: Plan and Record

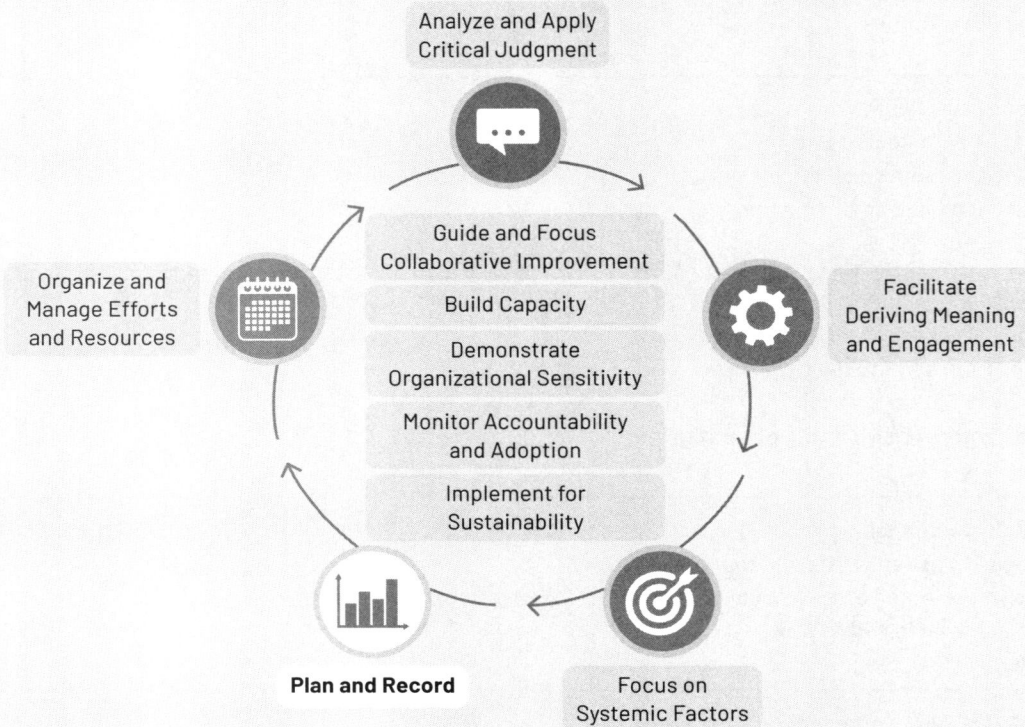

Analyze and Apply
Critical Judgment

Guide and Focus
Collaborative Improvement

Build Capacity

Demonstrate
Organizational Sensitivity

Monitor Accountability
and Adoption

Implement for
Sustainability

Facilitate
Deriving Meaning
and Engagement

Focus on
Systemic Factors

Plan and Record

Organize and
Manage Efforts
and Resources

$\mathcal{S}$tandard 4 is about planning the methods, resources, and high-impact practices that will take your school-improvement goals from vision to reality. It is about recording those practices for future replication or revision. Planning and recording serve as the backbone for achieving continuous improvement, fostering innovation, and ensuring successful implementation. It takes commitment to get the work done. Then, the work must be continually communicated to all stakeholders. School-improvement planning is either a compliance requirement or a strategic choice of a school or school system. This chapter helps educators make a shift from compliance to strategic choices.

In this chapter, you will learn how to move from your school-improvement goals to more meaningful and actionable project plans. The school-improvement team might have one large project plan or split the school-improvement plan into smaller project plans. You will learn how to develop the project plans needed for each school-improvement plan goal, including documenting the plans, assigning accountability, gaining commitment, and communicating with all stakeholders.

Ensuring Alignment and Focus in School-Improvement Plans

At the beginning of this book, we asked you to identify a big rock—an area for which your leadership team or lead school-improvement team recognized the need for improvement. This need may be addressed at various levels: schoolwide; by departments, grade levels, or content areas; or through cross-functional collaboration. As you analyzed data in chapters 1–3, you identified performance factors, potential causes, and priorities. Through that process, you may have refined your original big rock focus, uncovered a high-priority need that was not part of your initial description, or even discovered a new big rock or reframed the issue as a more specific "priority pebble." These shifts are expected and appropriate when working with complex challenges that have multiple contributing causes.

As your understanding of the problem evolves, so too must your focus, clarifying exactly where to concentrate people's energy and resources. At the same time, maintaining alignment ensures that the priorities you have selected stay connected to your school's broader vision, goals, and improvement strategy. Together, alignment and focus create the conditions for coherent, coordinated action moving forward.

Alignment

Alignment means ensuring identified priorities, strategies, and actions are connected to broader school or district goals so that all improvement efforts are working in the same direction. Alignment ensures the work you are guiding is connected to and supported by the broader goals, strategies, and improvement efforts of the school or district. You are aligning your team's identified big rock, its causal factors and root causes, and proposed solutions with the school's mission, vision, improvement plan, and available resources. Ideally, your school's improvement plan, which your big rock is aligned to, is well developed with clear priorities. However, you may not have access to a solid school-improvement plan, or you may not have participated in its development.

It is also possible that during analysis with your team, you uncovered a high-priority challenge that is not currently reflected in the school-improvement plan. In that case, this is the time to share your findings with those responsible for developing and updating the plan. Informing them allows you to maintain alignment with school priorities while also elevating additional gaps, needs, and potential solutions that may require attention. In all these cases, once you have permission to move ahead, the next step is to develop a solid project plan—or a set of plans—that clearly outlines how your team will address the aligned priorities.

Focus

Focus refers to narrowing attention and resources to the highest-priority need, ensuring the team directs its efforts toward what will make the greatest impact. School-improvement plans are beneficial because they provide clarity and focus. When developed collaboratively by those who implement the plans, they can build ownership and commitment. Likely, the school or school system has adopted or adapted a school-improvement plan format required by the state, the province, or some other governing entity. We encourage you to find the template and requirements specific to your state or province. Some states, provinces, or districts may have more prescriptive requirements than others.

The work completed in the first three chapters of this book can support schools in completing their needed analysis and help you determine where you should focus your attention, funds, and time to improve student achievement and growth. Focus shifts from needs analysis informed by opinions to rigorous analysis. The analysis in chapters 1–3 and the planning processes in this chapter are best practices for all schools, regardless of their level of academic performance. Every school has areas they can improve or enhance.

At the end of chapter 3, you and your team identified needs and prioritized them before developing at least one SMART+IE goal for your big rock. That big rock could be part of the school-improvement plan. You also explored possible solutions for your big rock and checked the feasibility of those solutions. For your school-improvement plan, we recommend revisiting the data and crafting additional SMART+IE goals for all prioritized areas. A school might have goals related to achievement or growth; culture, climate, and community; and organizational operations. Setting priorities and crafting goals requires a strategic mindset with an emphasis on focus.

School-improvement plans that include extensive lists of priority areas weaken the momentum of the school. We recommend that your school targets three to five priorities or big rocks within your school-improvement plan. Having too many areas of focus can be overwhelming and weaken staff capacity to effectively address them all. Focusing on the most important three to five areas ensures stakeholders maintain hope and enthusiasm for achieving their goals. This does not mean other needs will never be addressed. They might be an action step under a priority. To keep this process streamlined without redundancies, we recommend that the school-improvement plan function as an overarching master plan. It will include your prioritized goals. For each goal you identify, list one or two interventions or initiatives that the team believes will address the goal. This ensures alignment and keeps the team focused on specific projects and actions to drive improvement.

Developing Project Plans

Project plans clearly explain and document how the interventions or initiatives will be implemented to accomplish the school-improvement plan's goals. You may need several project plans for all the goals in your school-improvement plan. These project plans will document the work needed to achieve your big rock goal.

Figure 4.1 (page 84) shows an example of how goals in the school-improvement plan may require more than one project plan and several teams to facilitate achievement. You can use the project plan summary chart to list the goals in your school-improvement plan and the needed interventions or initiatives.

After identifying the specific project plans, determine who will lead or manage these projects. This may be school leaders, members of the lead or core school-improvement team, or other individuals who have the ability and authority to guide others to do the work of the plans. Distributing this leadership and having multiple teams involved gives educators opportunities to own part of the school-improvement plan. When recruiting and determining the role each person will play, you must ensure a diverse range of expertise, roles, and perspectives. You may include faculty; staff; and district, regional, and state or provincial resource personnel or students, families, and community stakeholders who commit to collaborating to reach the goals. You must also select project team leaders who are committed to leading the work. Once a team is formed, the team leader can plan a kickoff to get everyone on the same page and begin moving forward with the plan.

Success
Tool Notes:

Instructions: List your school-improvement plan goals in the left column. Think about the project plans needed to accomplish each goal, and list them in the right column. Project plan statements in the right column should reflect the goals of each project required to achieve the school-improvement plan goal in the left column.

School-Improvement Plan Goal	Project Plans Needed
1. Improve reading comprehension of all student subgroups in grades 6–8 by at least 6 percent by the end of next school year, as measured by the reading comprehension scores on the state reading test.	a. Improve reading comprehension instructional strategies that ensure equitable access. b. Provide family university courses about family engagement with reading at home.
2. Decrease discipline problems in grades 6–8 by 5 percent for all subgroups by the end of next school year, as indicated by a decrease in the number of discipline referrals recorded in the student management system.	a. Create a positive and equitable school environment that addresses the diverse needs of students.
3. Ninety percent of students in grades 6–8 will be present in class at least 85 percent of the time each month, as measured by the monthly attendance report.	a. Increase student engagement by addressing the affective, behavioral, and cognitive domains. b. Increase wraparound services through school and community partnerships.

FIGURE 4.1: Success tool—Project plan summary chart example.

Visit go.SolutionTree.com/schoolimprovement for a free blank reproducible version of this figure.

Phase 1: Kick Off the Project Plan

Kickoffs are critical to building core teams of people who must collaborate to reach their goals. These sessions communicate the goal that their project supports. They also promote excitement among team members about the work to be planned. Perhaps more importantly, they build the momentum needed to launch the planning. Kickoffs begin by onboarding the team to the planning and implementation of the work ahead. If team members were not engaged in the analysis that led to the development of the goals and objectives, the kickoff is an opportunity to help them understand why their participation is needed. It also helps them understand what led to the goals.

A kickoff is a time to orient new team members and map out the variety of factors that will lead to successful implementation. You may need a half- to full-day retreat or workshop to dedicate the time and effort to building a cohesive plan. Begin with facilitating understanding of the project and the school-improvement goal it addresses. Complete the following steps collaboratively.

1. Share the school-improvement plan goal that this project aligns with and a quick overview of the data that led to the goal.
2. Identify team members, team leaders, and other stakeholders.

3. Define the project's goal and the outcomes. If this project goes well, what will be the result, and what evidence will you show to demonstrate the improvements? Include measures of student outcomes.

4. Brainstorm or provide a project title.

5. Define the duration, or how long this project should last.

6. Identify the tasks that must be accomplished to meet the project goal.

    + **Tip:** Refer to the set of solutions you identified in chapter 3 (see figure 3.6, page 68). You checked their feasibility and determined the support needed to implement them. This information will assist you in determining the tasks to include in your project plan. For example, a task for improving reading comprehension instructional strategies might be "Provide equitable access to core instruction."

7. Define and list the activities to accomplish each task.

8. Determine who is responsible for each action step and what stakeholder groups will be involved.

9. List the specific, observable changes in adult behaviors, practices, or routines that need to occur to accomplish the goal. These may include actions such as implementing new instructional strategies, collaborating regularly in planning meetings, using data to inform decisions, or consistently following agreed-on protocols.

    + **Tip:** Identify the qualitative or quantitative evidence you will collect to document implementation and clarify who is responsible for collecting it. This evidence might include informal assessment data, meeting minutes, observation notes, walkthrough checklists, survey results, coaching logs, or program usage reports.

10. Determine the evidence to be collected, who will collect it, and when it will be collected. The formative process of monitoring or assessing a plan throughout the year can allow a team to check progress and adjust as needed.

11. List the resources you will need to complete each task in the project plan. For example, what materials, professional learning, structures, equipment, support, permissions, and budget are needed to complete each task?

    + **Tip:** You must work within a realistic budget and identify the funds available so that you do not encounter unnecessary roadblocks along the way. Share the budget that the principal or the funding source has given you for this project with your team.

12. Determine the start and end dates for each task. These will be specific dates, not "ongoing" or "yearlong."

13. Plan the communication process to ensure who you will communicate with, when, how, and by whom.

Discussing and collaboratively addressing these steps with your team builds shared ownership of the project. The project plan will also be stronger by involving more than just one or two people. The variety of perspectives helps encourage thinking that is only possible when a diverse group works together.

Now think about who on the team has decision-making authority and to what degree they have it. How will this person keep the principal or district office, if necessary, informed of progress? Do any of the action steps require external approval, or can they be accomplished with resources within the school? Taking the time to consider these additional pieces ensures a project team does not face preventable adversity.

Phase 2: Document the Project Plan

The research that led to the development and validation of the ten CSIS standards found an interesting and concerning gap in the work of those who guide improvement. These people noted that they did not plan their own work in writing. The team or school leaders kept their plans in their heads. If plans are not in writing, the work would not endure should the person guiding the work suddenly be unable to continue to lead it. A new person would be starting over, so the work to date may not be sustained, and valuable time would be wasted. In addition, plans that are not in writing could not be replicated or reflected on for initiatives or interventions that need to continue, be revised, or be deleted.

Participants in the LAUNCH!™ school-improvement development program at The Institute for Performance Improvement have consistently shared that detailed planning and documentation has helped them achieve clarity, focus, and continuity. This helps new leaders move in and pick up where prior administration left off. To establish a strong plan, each project team must take time to consider a variety of factors. The improvement project planning template in figure 4.2 provides a series of questions that teams can ask to consider those factors and outline their project plan.

Instructions: Use this tool to capture what must be done to achieve your project goals. To complete your project plan, answer the following questions.

- **Tasks:** What are the key tasks needed to accomplish the project?
- **Actions:** What actions or activities for each task will lead to the desired outcomes?
- **Who is responsible:** Who is responsible for each action step? What stakeholder groups are involved in each action?
- **Evidence:** What products, artifacts, or outputs will be collected as evidence?
- **Outcomes:** What are the ultimate desired results or value added that you want? (Clarify the *value added* by defining the ultimate outcomes your team is working toward.) What positive impact do you want for students, educators, or the school community as a result of this work? (These are your *measures of success*—such as improved student achievement, increased engagement, stronger instructional practices, or greater collaboration—and they should directly connect to the goal.) Clearly identifying these outcomes helps ensure your efforts lead to meaningful and measurable improvements.
- **Resources:** What resources, professional learning, structures, equipment, permissions, and budget will you need to do the work?
- **Start and end dates:** What are the specific start and end dates for each task or action? *Remember not to use "ongoing" or "yearlong."*

Name of Project:	Duration:

Related School-Improvement Plan Goal:

This Project's Goal:

This Project's Outcomes:

The Evidence to Collect:

Team Members:	Team Leads:
	Other Stakeholders:

Tasks	Actions	Who Is Responsible	Evidence	Outcomes	Resources	Start and End Dates

Success Tool Notes:

FIGURE 4.2: Success tool—Improvement project planning template.

*Visit **go.SolutionTree.com/schoolimprovement** for a free reproducible version of this figure.*

The results of these conversations and the completed template can be presented to the school's administration, if necessary, for approval before action. We encourage taking that step to make sure everyone agrees with your intended actions. Great plans can go awry when a lack of resources or action steps leads to frustration and false starts. Plans for communication are addressed in more detail later in this chapter.

Participants in the LAUNCH! program often ask their instructors, "When is it necessary to develop a project plan?" The instructor's response is "Only when you want to get the work done successfully and achieve its goals" (A. Gray, personal communication, October 1, 2017). Participants from schools, school districts, and other education agencies have reported developing, following, and updating their project plans as being key to achieving the needed engagement and results. The project-planning process has also helped participants successfully document their efforts. It has enabled others who joined the work in progress, or needed to take over guidance due to changes in personnel or assignments, to clearly see what had been planned.

Idea Hub: Project Planning

Ask yourself the following questions, and then discuss them with your team.

» How can you use the improvement project planning template (see figure 4.2, page 86) to plan the work of your project goal in detail?

» How will this plan help you achieve the work of your big rock?

» Are there other project plans related to your big rock? If so, how will you ensure collaboration and communication between these project teams?

Once the improvement project plan is complete, your team should take proactive steps to get organized and determine a clear location for all materials. This location might be a shared drive or folder. Furthermore, we recommend that teams create a visual of their project plan. A Gantt chart, such as the one featured in figure 4.3, is a useful tool for visualizing timelines for tasks and activities in the project plan (Ramachandran & Karthick, 2019). Five key features comprise a Gantt chart.

1. **Timeline:** The horizontal axis represents the timeline, which can be in days, weeks, or months, depending on the project's duration.

2. **Tasks:** The vertical axis lists the tasks and activities that need to be completed.

3. **Bars:** Horizontal bars represent each task, with the length of the bar showing the duration of the task. The position of the bar on the timeline indicates the start and end dates.

4. **Dependencies:** Gantt charts can include lines or arrows to show dependencies between tasks, indicating which tasks must be completed before others can start. The critical path, which is the longest stretch of dependent activities, and the time required to complete them, can be easily identified.

5. **Milestones:** Key events or deadlines can be marked with milestones, often represented as diamonds or special symbols on the chart.

Task 1	Month 1				Month 2				Month 3			
	Week 1	Week 2	Week 3	Week 4	Week 1	Week 2	Week 3	Week 4	Week 1	Week 2	Week 3	Week 4
Activity 1					*							
Activity 2												
Activity 3									*			
Activity 4												

Task 2	Month 1				Month 2				Month 3			
	Week 1	Week 2	Week 3	Week 4	Week 1	Week 2	Week 3	Week 4	Week 1	Week 2	Week 3	Week 4
Activity 1							*					
Activity 2											*	
Activity 3												

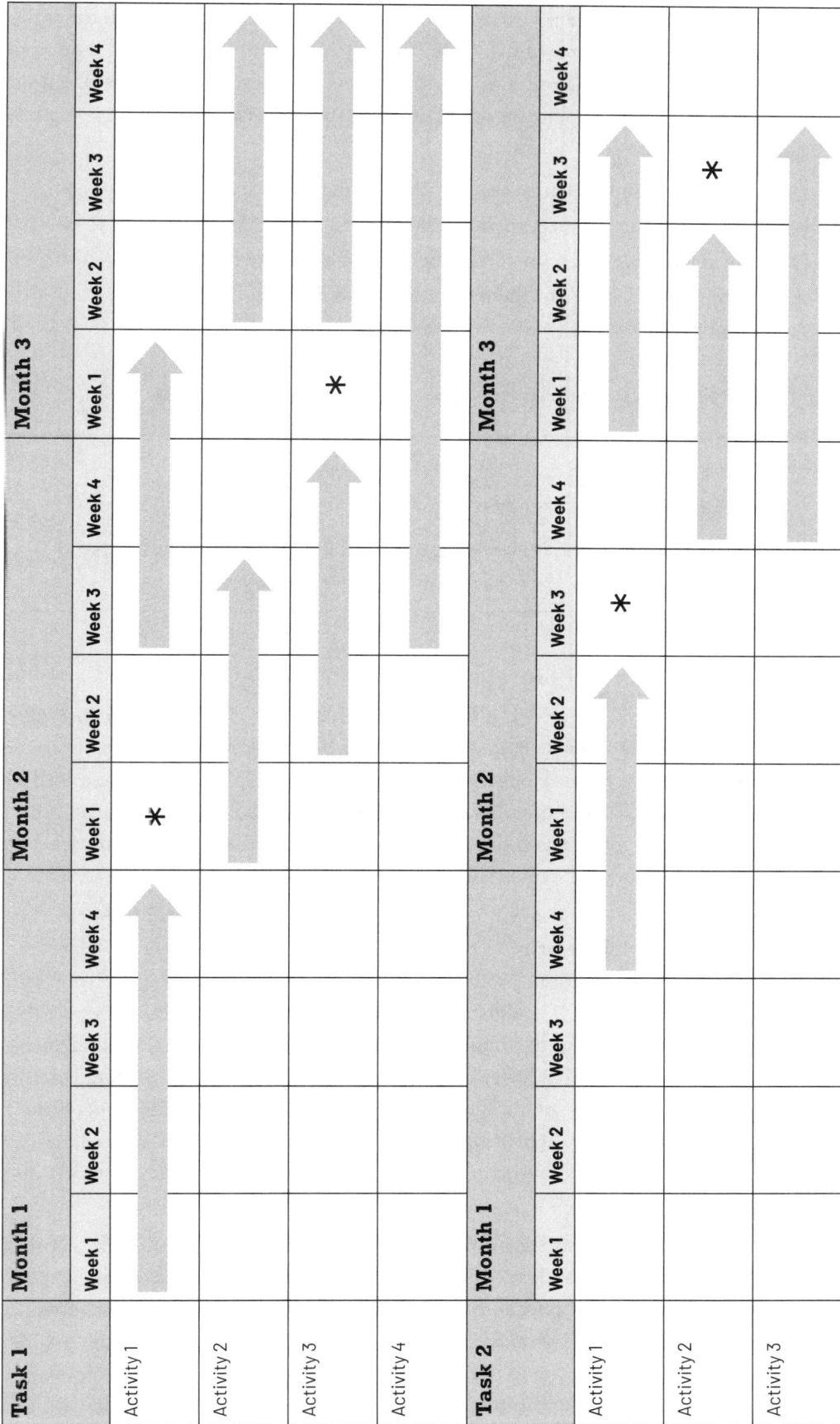

Source: Adapted from Ramachandran & Karthick, 2019.

FIGURE 4.3: Gantt chart example.

*Visit **go.SolutionTree.com/schoolimprovement** for a free blank reproducible version of this figure.*

Gantt charts can help your team visualize action steps and stay accountable to timelines and goals. They also serve to intentionally plan time for your team to meet and reflect on what you are learning and observing during this process. Reflections should be based on evidence and allow for independent thought before group conversation. Consider the following questions to guide your reflections.

- How did your individual actions contribute to the project?
- Did the team members meet their deadlines?
- Does our data show we are making progress and are ready for the next step?
- If the project stalls, how can the team adjust its actions to move the project forward?

Idea Hub: Planning Time

Ask yourself the following question and discuss it with your team.

» How does your team currently plan time to reflect?

Take time to consider your individual actions and the status of the project and determine what the next steps will be to continue moving forward.

Phase 3: Commit to the Plan

This type of planning takes time, but it is time well spent at the beginning to ensure more efficient and productive implementation later. One important thing to keep in mind is that those doing projects are not locked into every detail of the planning, as described in the plan. As the work progresses, the plan may need to be updated or revised. This kind of planning produces a clear, written record of decisions, actions, and intended outcomes—documents that can be updated, revised, and refined as needed.

What's essential is that teams commit to the shared goals, direction, and priorities outlined in the plan, even while remaining flexible about how to achieve them. This shared commitment provides a foundation for coordinated action, adaptive problem solving, and progress monitoring over time. If leadership changes, the project plans serve as a valuable reference, helping new leaders understand the rationale behind past decisions and maintain momentum. This continuity lowers the risk of work being stalled or derailed and helps preserve the commitment of those who have been investing time and energy into improvement and innovation. Remember the adage "If it is not documented, it did not happen." Taking time to document the plan supports transparency, continuity, and long-term success.

Formally committing to the work outlined in the improvement project plan or other written plans increases accountability—it gives autonomy to the workers who are responsible for completing the work, and autonomy fuels motivation to engage in the work, support the work, and ensure the work is successful. Committing to the work can look like a team signing a formal contract with details of the project and what they are responsible for completing. It can also be as simple as having the team members sign their initials on a draft of the project plan or shared goals. For example, a school leadership team may want to revamp its mission and create shared ownership. After engaging stakeholders in the development of the new mission, the team can post it on chart or poster paper where teachers, leaders, and parents and community members on the local school council can all sign their initials around the mission to illustrate their commitment.

Phase 4: Communicate the Plan

Once you develop the project plan, you can share it with a broader range of stakeholders. As always, those who receive the plan are expected to support it. They must have the opportunity to understand what led to the plan's development and why they should care and be engaged. It may be necessary to hold another kickoff for the completed improvement project plan. This promotes understanding of the plan for stakeholders outside the planning team. It also builds enthusiasm for the work they will be asked to do.

You can use figure 4.4 to record who is responsible for crafting and approving key decisions and actions. This worksheet also designates to whom and how often these decisions and actions will be communicated. It is necessary to consider stakeholder accessibility to technology in communication efforts. For example, if families do not have access to the internet or social media, other forms of communication must be used to communicate improvement efforts.

Success Tool Notes:

Instructions: Answer the following questions with your team about communication needed for the project plan.

Who must be informed?	Through which media are they informed?	Who crafts the message?	Who approves it?	Who sends the message?	How often do you communicate?

FIGURE 4.4: Success tool—Communication worksheet.

*Visit **go.SolutionTree.com/schoolimprovement** for a free reproducible version of this figure.*

Reviewing Examples of Standard 4

To help you use what you have learned in chapter 4, we have included an example of an effective practice and an example of a less effective practice. Comparing these examples will help you determine what to do and what to avoid when applying the work of standard 4.

An Effective Example

Jounida Ekard was the principal of a high school with instructional coaches across the curriculum. With the support of the school system curriculum directors, she had chosen to focus the coaches on guiding teachers to use strategies that would promote deeper learning. Data supported the need to engage students in complex tasks and projects that would require them to apply knowledge in meaningful contexts.

During preplanning at the start of the school year, Ekard guided the instructional coaches in conducting a gap analysis to define the desired state of instructional strategies. They also identified the current state of the school. She led the research analysis, which helped determine the impact of deeper learning instructional strategies on student success. The factors analysis and causal analysis helped identify barriers and opportunities to support teachers in understanding why changes in their practices could produce better student learning outcomes.

They crafted a SMART+IE goal that 100 percent of teachers would collaboratively develop a project-based lesson aligned to their curriculum, which would increase student engagement and learning, and Ekard guided the coaches to develop a project plan for the year. They called it their "deeper learning project plan" and named it Project Horizon.

As Ekard guided the coaches in using the improvement project planning template, they achieved clarity in defining the work ahead. This included the support that teachers would need. The coaches determined how they would assess the project milestones and learn from the process. They decided to focus on this project and iterate it until the end of the school year, getting ready to take it to the next level in the next school year. Each coach committed to support the professional learning teams and their assigned teachers to collaboratively plan to reach the goal in their classrooms.

The school had attempted to introduce deeper learning as a concept five years before. The teachers challenged themselves to learn about it and try it. However, most expressed they were too busy to do it and were unable to figure it out by trial and error, so they did not pursue it.

This time, teachers across the curriculum areas engaged in developing an interdisciplinary project-based learning unit focused on solving a simulated crime. Early in the school year, instructional coaches guided teachers to analyze standards, learn new strategies, and collaboratively plan lessons that would allow students to investigate and solve the staged crime using skills from various subjects. As the process unfolded, teacher collaboration and enthusiasm grew steadily.

Teachers who had previously mastered project-based learning strategies began informally coaching their peers, sharing ideas, and helping others design lessons that connected to the overarching crime-solving theme. This collaboration led to integrated planning across subjects—science teachers developed forensic labs, English teachers guided students in writing case reports, and social studies teachers explored the legal and ethical aspects of crime solving.

Inspired by this momentum, a group of teachers challenged the rest of the faculty to cocreate an immersive experience: a simulated crime scene and investigation that would be woven into students' coursework. The entire initiative culminated in April with a student-led showcase where learners presented their findings and demonstrated how they applied academic content to solve real-world problems.

Students adapted to new roles, collaborated across disciplines, and produced impressive work products. Their efforts drew attention from the local television station, which highlighted the project and praised both students and teachers. Many students also created YouTube videos documenting their experiences, further showcasing their learning and engagement.

Surveys of student engagement at the beginning of the school year and in April showed a spike of 42 percent, while teacher efficacy, learning design, and delivery also increased. Interim assessments aligned to the curriculum that was covered through the project-based approach showed gains for most student subgroups.

Teachers shared and celebrated their individual designs. They used their final collaborative team time to choose another data-identified schoolwide challenge for the coming year.

A Less Effective Example

Mikale Boone was a strong instructional leader and a high-performing mathematics teacher at a middle school before he became its assistant principal. In May of his last year as an assistant principal, he was offered the position of principal. After he accepted the role, he developed three goals for the coming year: (1) Conduct an assessment of teachers' instructional proficiency, (2) provide academic coaching for teachers in courses with standardized testing, and (3) create collaborative teams focused on deeper learning across the curriculum.

Over the summer, Boone and the assistant principals developed action plans for these three goals. At the preplanning meeting, he presented the plans to the faculty and staff. He let them know that these plans were going to be implemented, and they would be participating in professional learning on project-based learning. During the school year, the teachers received a half day of professional learning on project-based lessons. A few teachers focused on developing these types of lessons in their classrooms. Most did not.

There was no consistent focus and support for implementing the plans that Boone presented. There was no understanding of how the goals had been developed. Therefore, the teachers were not invested in making this shift in instruction.

Idea Hub: Reflection

Reflect individually on what you learned in this chapter, and record your thoughts. Then use your individual reflections to collaboratively answer the following questions with your team.

» What did Ekard and the teacher team do that aligns with the guidance in this chapter?

» What did Boone do that misaligns with the guidance in this chapter?

» How will you use what you have learned to develop plans that engage others and gain their commitment?

» What are your and your team's biggest takeaways?

» How will you embrace the work of chapter 4?

» Who will you engage in the work of chapter 4?

Conclusion

School-improvement efforts require buy-in and engagement. Written plans that record the work ahead facilitate clarity and keep stakeholders focused on the identified tasks. After the school-improvement plan is developed, the tools and processes in this chapter help you gain the stakeholder input necessary to successfully design project plans that can achieve the selected goals.

Now that the project plans are developed, people are committed to the work, and the plans are communicated, you are ready to organize and manage resources required for success. Chapter 5 discusses how to facilitate the processes that enable teams to successfully implement the plans they have developed. It specifically focuses on how to break down tasks into feasible steps and actions and how to organize the required resources.

Before moving on to chapter 5, complete the "Standard 4: Do and Avoid Chart" and "Standard 4: Plan-Ahead Chart" reproducibles (pages 95 and 96) with your team to reflect on and process the work you accomplished for standard 4 and plan ahead for next steps.

Standard 4: Do and Avoid Chart

As you move through the standards for improvement, you will find things to do and things to avoid. After reading the effective and less effective practice examples and reflecting on them and the work of standard 4, complete the following do and avoid chart to help you record your thoughts about the work of this standard.

Instructions: Record what you plan to do and avoid. Consider the following questions.

1. How will you introduce your team to the processes introduced in this chapter?
2. How will you determine the project plans needed to meet school-improvement plan goals?
3. How will you select the project-planning team and leader?
4. How will you help those you guide use the project-planning guidance and template?
5. How will you guide the team to develop a project commitment statement and gain the commitment needed for successful implementation?
6. How will you facilitate communication efforts that share the work ahead with all stakeholders?

Do	Avoid

Standard 4: Plan-Ahead Chart

To get a clearer perspective on the next steps, consider your do and avoid chart as you complete the following plan-ahead chart. The work of standard 4 prepares you to plan and support the right work for students and adults after the school-improvement plan is in place. Gaining the commitment of the workers and communicating the plan are included.

Instructions: Use the information from chapter 4 to identify your and your team's next steps to complete each action.

Actions	Person or People Responsible	Due Date
Complete the project plan summary chart (see figure 4.1, page 84) to determine what project plans are needed to accomplish each school-improvement plan goal.		
Use the improvement project planning template (see figure 4.2, page 86) to plan the specific work of your project goal.		
Develop a Gantt chart (see figure 4.3, page 89) to help your team visualize action steps and stay accountable to timelines and goals.		
Complete the communication worksheet (see figure 4.4, page 91) to plan details for communication, promote understanding of the plan for stakeholders outside the planning team, and gain enthusiasm for the work the stakeholders will be asked to do.		

Chapter 5

Standard 5: Organize and Manage Efforts and Resources

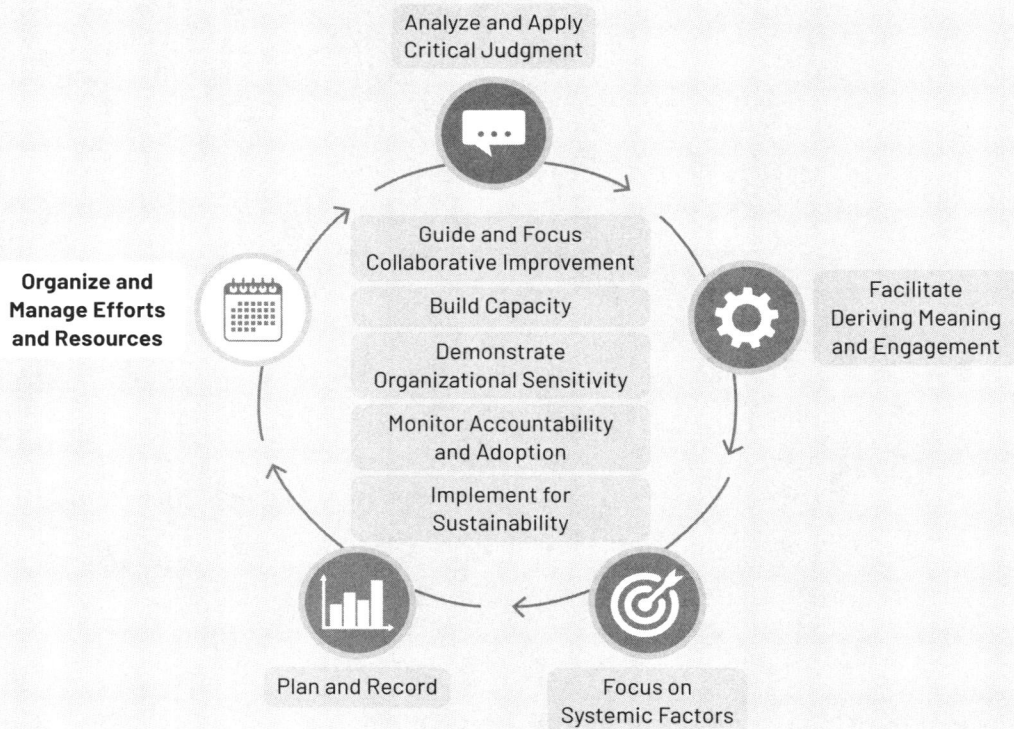

Analyze and Apply
Critical Judgment

Guide and Focus
Collaborative Improvement

Build Capacity

Demonstrate
Organizational Sensitivity

Monitor Accountability
and Adoption

Implement for
Sustainability

Organize and
Manage Efforts
and Resources

Facilitate
Deriving Meaning
and Engagement

Plan and Record

Focus on
Systemic Factors

$\mathcal{S}$ tandard 5 is about organizing the tasks to be done by breaking them down into steps and actions. It is about coordinating the efforts, schedules, and human and financial resources in ways that will lead to expected outcomes and effectively managing resources such as time. Organizing and managing efforts and resources effectively facilitates improvement and implementation and also supports innovation. The work of this standard ensures that education systems remain adaptive, equitable, and impactful, which, in turn, respects educators' time and workloads.

In this chapter, you will explore how to think ahead in decision making. Proactive decisions will save you time when something that happens has the potential to derail the work once it is in progress. You will learn how to break down tasks in the project plan into specific steps and actions to facilitate success. You will also learn how job aids assist staff in conducting tasks that are important but infrequent—those that they need support to perform before they have reached mastery and those for which the consequences of errors are high and self-correction is appropriate.

This chapter reviews how you can promote commitment rather than compliance. Empower educators by distributing work, responsibility, authority, and leadership. When they are engaged in decision making and planning, educators feel ownership for the shared work.

Breaking Down Tasks

You have identified and explained the work tasks listed in your project plan. Now the focus shifts to delegating those tasks to assist team members in accomplishing and distributing the work so that those guiding the work do not fall into the trap of trying to do it all. Coordinating and organizing efforts ensures tasks and people are aligned and the necessary support and resources are available. This section introduces tools for breaking down the tasks in the project plan into collaborative steps and actions.

We employ *task analysis*, a process from the field of adult instructional design, to break down tasks into steps and related actions. Task analysis prompts consideration of the consequences of doing the tasks well or not and helps teams prepare themselves to respond effectively to challenges. This also supports thinking about what people need to know to perform the tasks, which helps avoid a major enemy of implementation, learning, and growth: making assumptions.

Idea Hub: Task Breakdown

Think about the current tasks needed to achieve your school-improvement plan or project plan.
» How has the school clearly defined expectations for these tasks in the past?
» How has the school defined the steps necessary to complete a task?
» Are these steps easy to access and reference as needed?

It is important to respect educators' knowledge and experience. It is equally important not to assume what they know and can do. This analysis helps prevent the trap of making assumptions as individuals or as groups that lead to negative outcomes or missed opportunities. When a person or group knows what to do and how to do it, a common error is to assume others know as well. This is an easy mistake to make when those guiding the work know how to do the task fluently without having to think about what they are doing and why. Breaking down tasks into steps seems unnecessary to those who know the procedure. However, it is important to get what to do and how to do it out of the minds of experts by making the knowledge explicit so others can do the work well. Quality work requires clarity in the tasks to be accomplished that support goal achievement.

An Example of Making Assumptions

Consider what happened to a team that was planning a summer professional learning event at a school. The team, consisting of the professional learning director from the school system and the school's academic coaches, decided to host the event in the school library. The team members worked hard on their agenda and content. They arranged catering and made copies of materials. They ensured extra power cords and outlets were ready for use of technology. Meanwhile, the principal was attending a summer conference in another town on the day of the event, and she assumed the team planning it was taking care of everything they needed.

The event kicked off at 9:00 a.m. By 10:00 a.m., the participants were fanning themselves. The library's temperature had become uncomfortably hot. They asked if the air-conditioning could be turned lower. As the team worked to adjust the thermostat, they found that the library air-conditioning was deactivated during the months that school was not in session. The principal knew this and had assumed those planning the event knew it, but the team had overlooked this important detail. They moved the session to a cooler space, but the interruption impacted their carefully planned day.

This is a low-consequence example of making an assumption or overlooking a needed action, but the ramifications can be much graver. When leading improvement or developing aspiring leaders, you must break priority performances into tasks, steps, and actions. This lowers the risk of overlooking valuable information and decisions that impact performance and results.

Proactive Decision Making

Proactively thinking through what they will do should certain events occur while they are implementing a task will save teams time before, during, and after the work. Teams can proactively consider *if-then* decisions and list them at the end of a task breakdown. For example, a team of professional learning facilitators might complete a task breakdown for a safety training session that is being scheduled for all the employees in a school system.

Proactive thinking is needed to determine what will be done if certain employees cannot attend the training at their school. The decision can be stated as follows: "*If* faculty and staff are unable to attend the safety training in their own school, *then* the professional learning coordinators and the principals will coordinate their attendance in another school." Making this decision in advance allows the facilitators to carefully think through and prepare to communicate a plan. Proactive decision making eliminates reactive, situational decisions that could result in undesirable and unintended consequences.

Task Analysis

Experts involved in task analysis may experience "brain pain" because they are digging deep into their experience and expertise, which have been acquired and refined over time. *Metacognition*—the process of thinking about one's thinking—is important to being able to teach or train others to do the task at hand. It takes effort for experts to bring what they normally do fluently, without even thinking, to a conscious level to help others know what to do. This is normal and to be expected.

Collaborating with a peer or set of peers to break down a task into specific steps and actions may help experts identify questions about the task. It may help them determine what is missing, assumed, or placed out of order. As the facilitator of improvement, you can allow those assigned the responsibility of completing a task analysis to draft it using the task breakdown chart. Then you can build the workers' capacity by having a coaching conversation with them about that task breakdown. After that, the workers can sustain use of the task breakdowns to increase their chances of success.

The example in figure 5.1 (page 102) demonstrates how to break down a task using the task breakdown chart. Note that steps and actions begin with verbs.

Success Tool Notes:

Task: Develop writing prompts aligned with content-area unit plans to be used weekly by content-area teachers, career and technical education (career tech) teachers, and special education content-area teachers.

Step	Actions
1. Check with the principal to determine the summer calendar dates available for professional learning with teachers.	a. Meet with the principal to review open dates on the school and system calendar.
2. Collect possible dates for the regional literacy coordinator, school-improvement specialist, and instructional coaches to be available to conduct training.	a. Meet with experts to clarify what staff will need to know and do, the desired results, and goals of the training. b. Review available dates for experts.
3. Schedule training dates for teachers.	a. Select professional learning dates, and verify them with the principal, regional coordinator, school-improvement specialist, and instructional coaches. b. Determine the training site and room availability. c. Check logistics: air-conditioning or heat, parking, facility access, food, and snack access. d. List and collect the materials and resources needed.
4. Research content-area and career tech writing prompts for ideas to share in collaborating with teachers.	a. Access all available state or provincial and national resources to collect samples of writing prompts.
5. Design the course plan for professional learning to develop writing prompts.	a. Review reading and writing scores. b. Share research about the relationship between writing and reading achievement. c. Review writing standards. d. Share a collection of resources for content-area and career tech writing prompts. e. Review curriculum maps to brainstorm writing prompts that could be used weekly aligned to specific content and career tech instruction. f. Write prompts aligned to unit plans. g. Collect a bank of prompts. h. Add writing prompts to curriculum maps. i. Develop a scoring rubric for content-area writing.
6. Convene the individual academic, career tech, and special education departments on scheduled professional learning dates.	a. Conduct the designed professional learning.
7. Communicate expectations for weekly use of prompts to all staff.	a. Distribute written expectations and review them in collaborative planning meetings and professional learning teams. b. Provide time for questions.

8. Model and monitor weekly use of writing prompts in content-area, career tech, and special education classrooms.	a. Model writing instruction as needed in content-area and other classrooms. b. Conduct observations to check for transfer of learning. c. Provide specific feedback. d. Use the established monitoring and feedback form to provide feedback and support to all teachers.
9. Monitor the quality of teacher feedback to students for writing prompts.	a. Discuss and share meaningful and specific formative feedback at collaborative planning meetings about the important work teachers do every day for students. b. Provide additional professional learning as needed. c. Provide additional coaching as needed.
10. Select exemplars of student writing.	a. Develop a process for collecting student writing samples. b. Share anonymous student writing at collaborative planning meetings and have all teachers score it. c. Discuss similarities and differences in scoring and reach a consensus to select exemplars. d. Use exemplars for models in instruction.

Decisions

- If there are no current state or provincial scores available to review, then use formative assessments.
- If a teacher cannot attend a meeting, then provide scheduled makeup sessions.
- If a teacher needs additional help, then arrange for additional coaching support.

FIGURE 5.1: Success tool—Task breakdown chart example.

*Visit **go.SolutionTree.com/schoolimprovement** for a free reproducible version of this figure.*

Developing and Using Job Aids

Task analysis also helps leaders, academic coaches, and improvement teams unleash the potential of job aids. Job aids help someone perform a task or set of tasks, what instructional designers refer to as *performance*. Job aids can take the form of checklists, flowcharts, infographics, numbered lists, or hybrids, and are designed for the following.

- Providing information and support
- Influencing perspective and decision making
- Giving educators guidance (not specific instruction) before, during, and after the task performance
- Providing immediate assistance to get the work done
- Supporting useful tasks that are performed infrequently *or* are not part of a person's regular job
- Reducing the length of time for recall
- Signaling when to act
- Giving general directions

Success Tool Notes:

Analyzing and breaking down tasks provides a chance to scan the work and consider which of the steps may need resources. This scan might lead to further breakdown of the task so it can be taught to, or scaffolded for, those who have not yet attained mastery in performing it. With protocols or job aids, those who are less experienced in the task can get the support they need.

Job aids are most useful when they support infrequently performed tasks, the consequences of errors are high, and self-correction is appropriate. If there is a large or changing knowledge base, job aids are useful for informing people and keeping them up to date. If training resources are limited, job aids can be just enough and just in time to support consistent task performance. Avoid job aids if those using them cannot perform the task and their use will not support effective performance. Do not use a job aid when having it in hand might hurt your credibility, such as when in a conference with students and family members. Job aids are inappropriate with work that must be performed quickly or requires rapid responses.

The job aid example in figure 5.2 demonstrates the last step in the preceding task breakdown: Select exemplars of student writing. It will guide educators in each content area and grade level to effectively collect student writing samples and select exemplars for instructional purposes, assessment, or the sharing of best practices.

Step 1: Organize Collection of Student Writing

1. *Decide on format.*
   + *Determine whether you will collect physical submissions (notebooks or papers), digital submissions (via Google Classroom, a learning management system, or email), or hybrid submissions (a combination of both physical and digital formats).*
2. *Set clear expectations.*
   + *Communicate deadlines and formatting guidelines to students. (Include instructions for word count, font size, file type, and more.)*
   + *Select the writing prompt that all students will use in a particular content area.*
   + *Provide the scoring rubric developed for students to self-assess before submission.*
3. *Create a submission system.*
   + *For digital work, use a learning management system to organize and track submissions.*
   + *For physical work, designate a specific location (such as an inbox tray) or time for submission.*
   + *Label work with student name, class or period, and assignment title to avoid confusion.*

Step 2: Review and Assess Writing (All Teachers in a Content Area)

1. *Review all submissions.*
   + *Skim each piece to gain a general sense of performance.*
   + *Look for key elements of writing such as structure, creativity, grammar, and alignment with the assignment prompt.*
2. *Evaluate against the rubric.*
   + *Use the rubric or scoring guide provided to students to fairly assess each submission.*
   + *Look for consistency in scoring by focusing on the criteria (content, organization, voice, mechanics, and more).*
3. *Annotate or provide feedback.*
   + *Offer constructive feedback that is clear and encourages improvement.*
   + *Highlight strengths and areas for development.*

Step 3: Select Exemplars

1. Define what makes an exemplar.
    + Identify characteristics of strong writing.
        1. Clarity of ideas—Does the writing express a clear argument or narrative?
        2. Creativity or originality—Does it stand out with unique ideas or perspectives?
        3. Technical proficiency—Are the grammar, syntax, and structure strong?
        4. Engagement—Does the piece engage the reader and achieve the assignment's purpose?
2. Ensure diverse representation.
    + Choose a variety of exemplars that showcase different strengths (such as a strong voice, a creative approach, and a solid structure).
    + Select exemplars of a range of performance levels (such as high-performing, midlevel, and improved) to show growth and development.
3. Gain permission.
    + Obtain permission from the students whose work will be used as exemplars.
    + Ensure students' anonymity, or offer to use their initials if students prefer that.

Step 4: Share Exemplars With the Class

1. Explain the purpose.
    + Share the reason for showing exemplars (such as to illustrate expectations or to celebrate creativity).
2. Discuss the strengths.
    + Walk students through the exemplars, highlighting specific features that meet or exceed expectations.
    + Encourage students to ask questions and learn from the work of their peers.
3. Use the exemplars for reflection or peer review.
    + Allow students to reflect on the exemplars and compare them with their own work.
    + Consider organizing peer review sessions where students can offer feedback inspired by the exemplars.

Step 5: Continue to Improve

1. Reflect on the process.
    + Evaluate how well the submission-collection and exemplar-selection process worked. Were there challenges in organizing submissions, or was the rubric effective?
2. Refine the rubric or process.
    + Adjust the rubric or submission guidelines to improve clarity and consistency in future assessments.
3. Incorporate exemplars into future instruction.
    + Use the selected exemplars in future lessons as models for students to emulate or learn from.

FIGURE 5.2: Job aid example.

Visit **go.SolutionTree.com/schoolimprovement** *for a free blank reproducible version of this figure.*

> **Idea Hub:** Job Aids

Think of a task that is relevant for your role (teacher, coach, administrator, and so on) but not necessary to have memorized. For example, a teacher might need to know how to differentiate instruction but does not need to have every detail memorized. An administrator might need to know testing guidelines and procedures but not have to commit them to memory.

» Is there a job aid or resource that provides the necessary details to accomplish this task?

+ If not, how might a job aid help someone in your role do this task?

+ If so, how would this job aid help someone during the induction phase of your role?

» How might you use job aids without overwhelming educators?

Distributing the Work

Distributing the work you have planned is necessary to get the work done and achieve the needed results, and it is also a way to build shared, or distributed, leadership. Distributed leadership is more than just task delegation—it is a leadership approach that intentionally shares decision-making authority and responsibility among multiple individuals across an organization. As defined by researcher and educator Darlene García Torres (2019), distributed leadership influences school culture by fostering professional collaboration and enhancing educators' sense of self-efficacy. Unlike the act of simply assigning duties, distributed leadership empowers team members to own aspects of planning, implementation, and improvement, leading to greater job satisfaction and stronger student outcomes—especially in high-need schools.

To distribute work effectively, leaders must make deliberate choices about what to delegate. A helpful starting point is to consider the following factors.

- Tasks that others can do 80 percent as well as or better than the leader
- Responsibilities that will help others grow, such as coordinating a meeting, analyzing data, or leading a collaborative group
- Routine operational tasks that free up the leader to focus on strategic work

Conversely, leaders should be cautious about distributing the following.

- High-stakes decisions that require broad perspective or authority that only the leader has
- Tasks requiring confidential information or sensitive personnel issues
- Critical systems-level design work without scaffolding or coaching

A common trap that leaders may fall into is doing the work themselves, believing, "It is faster if I just do it myself." While this may seem efficient in the short term, it is what we call *fake time management*. It delays others' development, keeps the leader overextended, and weakens the team's long-term capacity. Sustainable improvement depends on developing others, not being the only expert.

When a leader or coach hears, "Just tell me what to do," it signals that person is not yet invested or confident. While assigning tasks may provide quick direction, it misses the opportunity to build ownership. Leaders should shift from telling to coaching, helping team members clarify goals, understand expectations, and build their capacity to contribute. This is the difference between compliance and commitment, which is critical to the success of collaborative school-improvement efforts and the sustainability of implementation.

To implement distributed leadership, it is essential to coordinate shared work effectively. Leaders and teams must align schedules, budgets, and roles. Once a team has developed a project plan with clear deliverables and milestones, the team must assign responsibility and monitor progress. Teams working on the planned projects may use digital supports like Google Workspace or Microsoft Teams for collaboration and document sharing, including job aids to guide and support tasks. By conducting regular check-ins, they can assess progress and adjust course when needed.

Once the project plans are complete, school leaders and school-improvement teams can review the plans, looking for opportunities to distribute leadership while ensuring clarity of the following.

- What tasks need to be done
- Who has the skills or wants the opportunity to do them
- What support they will need
- When the work happens and will be reviewed

By using these strategies, leaders don't just get the work done—they build the leadership capacity of others, foster collaboration, and create more sustainable and scalable school improvement.

Idea Hub: Work Distribution

Ask yourself the following questions, and then discuss them with your team.

» How does the school currently distribute leadership?

» Is work distribution a new practice that is not yet in place, or is it established as an expectation?

+ If it is not in place, what shifts might need to occur with administrators, teachers, and staff members to make this happen?

+ If it is already in place, how does the school ensure ownership and accountability to those with responsibilities?

» How is the distribution equitable and supported to achieve school goals?

» Who should be responsible for different tasks in your project plans?

Reviewing Examples of Standard 5

To help you use what you have learned in chapter 5, we have included an example of an effective practice and an example of a less effective practice. Comparing these examples will help you determine what to do and what to avoid when applying the work of standard 5.

An Effective Example

Elementary school principal Daundria Habash was pleased with the improvement project plans that the academic coaches had developed to support literacy growth across the school. The plans identified specific instructional strategies each teacher would work to master, with the expectation that teachers would later coach their peers supported by the academic coaches. To ensure the work was implemented effectively and equitably, Habash met with the six coaches to intentionally distribute leadership and clarify responsibilities.

After reviewing and approving their project plans, Habash collaborated with the coaches to identify the key implementation tasks they would complete in partnership with their assigned teachers. To model shared leadership and encourage peer collaboration, she paired coaches and assigned each pair responsibility for one key task across their project plans—completing a task breakdown chart with their teachers. This chart required coaches and teachers to define the steps and actions needed to implement each literacy strategy effectively. The charts were later developed into job aids for teachers and coaches.

Each coach was then responsible for guiding their assigned teachers through that breakdown process and providing targeted coaching as teachers worked to implement the strategies in classrooms. They embedded this coaching into existing professional learning teams, reinforcing collaboration and ensuring planning and implementation were integrated into regular instructional improvement efforts.

Habash distributed leadership as she shifted ownership of key elements of the work to coaches and teachers, aligning tasks with their strengths and encouraging peer-led growth. Rather than directing every action herself, she built the team's capacity to lead the work, fostering a culture of ownership, collaboration, and sustainable improvement.

A Less Effective Example

Nick Foah was the leader of Malone High's school-improvement team. He guided the team to develop improvement project plans for the school-improvement initiative. Then they met to decide the next steps for completion. The team used the plans to identify who would be engaged in each project. They also conducted kickoffs for each of the teacher teams.

During the kickoffs, the plans were reviewed with the teacher teams, who were instructed to start implementation. There were questions as the teams began discussing what they needed to do. Foah and the improvement team assured the teacher teams that they would be available to help them complete the work. Afterward, the school-improvement team shared concerns that the teacher teams did not know how to do the work. They decided they would tell them what to do and how to do it.

Idea Hub: Reflection

Reflect individually on what you learned in this chapter, and record your thoughts. Then use your individual reflections to collaboratively answer the following questions with your team.

» What did Habash do that aligns with the guidance in this chapter?

» What did Foah do that misaligns with the guidance in this chapter?

» What are your and your team's biggest takeaways?

» How will you embrace the work of chapter 5?

» Who will you engage in the work of chapter 5?

Conclusion

This chapter demonstrated how to use the task breakdown chart to break tasks into steps and actions, which makes the tasks in the improvement project plan more manageable and easier to monitor. It also examined how job aids can promote successful performance and how distributing leadership empowers people and makes them feel valued. Distributing leadership also increases ownership of the work and makes the work more efficient. By facilitating the organization of human, material, time, and financial resources, you enable teams to implement the plans you have helped them develop.

Chapter 6 is about guiding and focusing collaborative improvement. You will be successful if you can influence others to take the right actions and make the right decisions. You may be used to influencing people to let you do what you know how to do rather than getting others to contribute. It is important to do both. You want others to trust your judgment and recognize the expertise of the core team, but they must follow through on doing the work. Chapter 6 will guide you through tools and processes to focus stakeholders on the importance of collaboration in accomplishing the improvement goals they have set and planned to achieve.

Before moving on to chapter 6, complete the "Standard 5: Do and Avoid Chart" and "Standard 5: Plan-Ahead Chart" reproducibles (pages 110 and 111) with your team to reflect on and process the work you accomplished for standard 5 and plan ahead for next steps.

Standard 5: Do and Avoid Chart

As you move through the standards for improvement, you will find things to do and things to avoid. After reading the effective and less effective practice examples and reflecting on them and the work of standard 5, complete the following do and avoid chart to help you record your thoughts about the work of this standard.

Instructions: Record what you plan to do and avoid. Consider the following questions.

1. How will you introduce your team to the processes introduced in this chapter?
2. How will you facilitate teams to break the tasks in the project plans into steps and actions?
3. How will you help those you guide decide when job aids are needed and help them guide implementation?
4. How will you distribute the work and coordinate efforts?

Do	Avoid

Standard 5: Plan-Ahead Chart

To get a clearer perspective on the next steps, consider your do and avoid chart as you complete the following plan-ahead chart. The work of standard 5 prepares you to break tasks into steps and actions and develop job aids, as needed, to facilitate success. By distributing the work, responsibility, authority, and leadership, you empower educators and promote commitment instead of compliance.

Actions	Person or People Responsible	Due Date
Instructions: Use the information from chapter 5 to identify your and your team's next steps to complete each action.		
Use the task breakdown chart (see figure 5.1, page 102) to break down tasks in the project plans into steps and actions.		
Identify job aids needed to support people in completing tasks.		
Distribute the work to empower team members to own aspects of planning, implementation, and improvement and assist in task efficiency.		

Part 2

Systemic Perspectives

*Y*ou have now completed part 1, "Systematic Processes." Now, you will move into part 2, "Systemic Perspectives." Chapters 6–10 take a deeper dive into the systemic best practices necessary for doing the work of standards 1–5. The performance of educators and students is impacted by a broad range of factors. This makes education a complex system. Those factors include school infrastructure, the skills of teachers and leaders, and a culture that fosters learning and accountability. There is no place for blame or shifting the blame. Another important factor is a willingness to recognize and celebrate all contributions to progress.

The chapters in part 2 explain how to promote collaboration, build the skills and knowledge of your team to do the work, and demonstrate the organizational sensitivity necessary to make collaborative improvement possible. They also explain how to monitor progress in a way that encourages accountability and long-term sustainability. In addition, they include the processes that facilitate successful implementation of the school-improvement plan. All these practices are continuously applied throughout the school-improvement process.

Chapter 6

Standard 6: Guide and Focus Collaborative Improvement

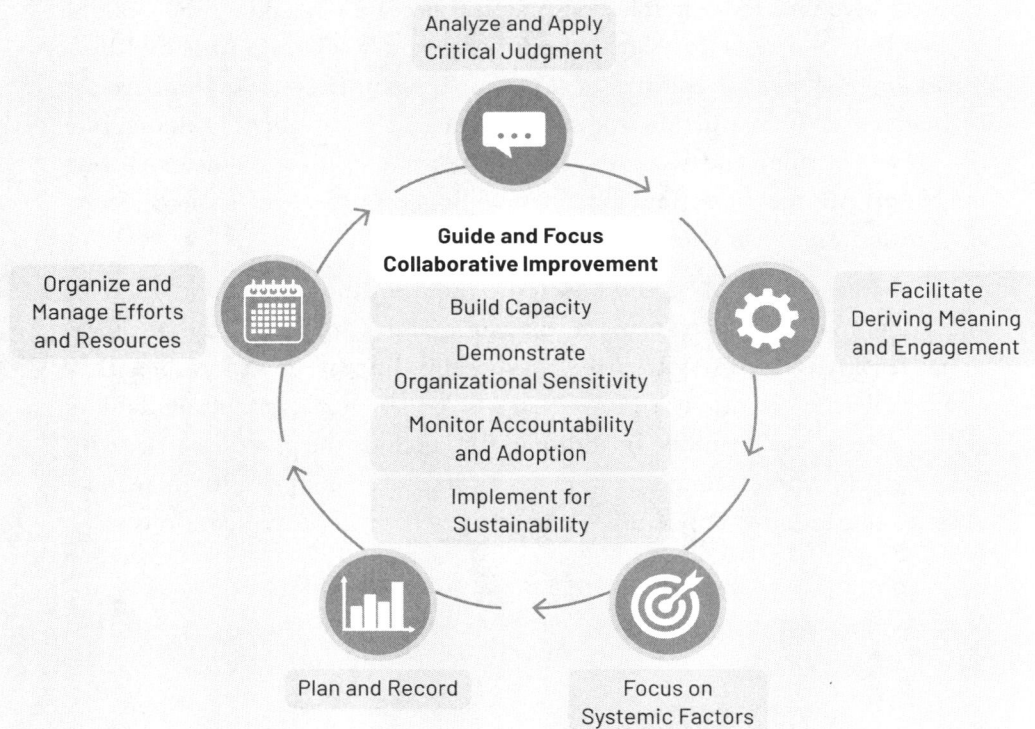

Analyze and Apply
Critical Judgment

**Guide and Focus
Collaborative Improvement**

Build Capacity

Demonstrate
Organizational Sensitivity

Monitor Accountability
and Adoption

Implement for
Sustainability

Organize and
Manage Efforts
and Resources

Facilitate
Deriving Meaning
and Engagement

Plan and Record

Focus on
Systemic Factors

*T*he goal of standard 6 is to guide educators to be influencers of positive change. Guiding and focusing collaborative improvement creates fertile ground for innovation by harnessing diverse perspectives, fostering trust, and encouraging risk taking. It ensures that the implementation of innovative practices is systematic, inclusive, and sustainable in schools. This chapter's standard is about influencing people to implement the work, change their behavior, or develop new or more helpful opinions. It is also about advocating for or making people aware of school-improvement needs and the work required to achieve success. Your team's influence can facilitate stakeholder engagement and commitment, the latter of which is important for team members to develop throughout the improvement process, as discussed in chapters 2 and 4. This results in a shared vision of outcomes and commitment to the work.

The strategies in this chapter are provided as a deeper dive into the work presented in chapter 2, where you help your team derive meaning and engage through collaborative analysis. These strategies help you influence others in improvement efforts so there is clarity and shared understanding of the behaviors needed to achieve your goals. Even when you do not have the positional authority to guide others, you can influence them. School-improvement teams that command engagement can result in compliance and fail to achieve the outcomes that committed teams can achieve. You and your team must do what you know how to do and influence others to do what they need to do. In this chapter, you will determine which people are in your inner circle of influence and how best to engage them. Then you will think about the people in a wider circle of influence who are important to consider for successful work. You will learn how to gain the support of those people by using tools designed specifically for thinking about who can influence the work.

This chapter also reviews the importance of aligning actions and foundational commitments to ensure the school's vision and mission align with its goals. You will learn a protocol to engage stakeholders in ongoing collaborative conversations to encourage their commitment and creativity and facilitate achievement of the goals they have set.

Identifying Your Circles of Influence

As noted in chapter 2, in guiding collaborative work, you need to identify the critical mass needed for engagement, commitment, and implementation. Hale (2012) defines *critical mass* as "51 percent of the right people"—those individuals who have the credibility, influence, and positional leverage to move the work forward. When this group is aligned and actively engaged, it can propel the effort to what author Malcolm Gladwell (2000) describes as the *tipping point*—the moment when an idea, behavior, or change crosses a threshold and gains unstoppable momentum.

In the context of school improvement, the tipping point occurs when enough people within the school adopt the needed collaborative mindsets and engage in the analysis, goal setting, selection of sets of solutions, planning, and implementation of the plans with true commitment to their shared goals. Once you reach the tipping point, change often accelerates. Collaborative improvement, innovation, and implementation become more widespread and integrated into the school's culture and operations. The people who you believe have the greatest potential to positively influence others are the first group of people you must reach to champion the planned work to all who can impact results.

Crafting Inner and Outer Circles of Influence

In thinking about how to influence the behavior of stakeholders and guide them in collaborative work, consider two groups of individuals. The first group is those within your personal circle of influence. Your personal circle of influence is often the starting point for achieving a critical mass. If you can persuade those in your immediate circle to adopt a behavior or idea, they can, in turn, influence others in their own circles. This creates a ripple effect that can expand far beyond your direct influence. The concept of critical mass amplifies the impact of what begins within a personal circle of influence. As your ideas or actions spread, they may reach a tipping point where larger groups adopt them.

Your personal circle of influence includes everything you have the power to affect or control. Think of it as the space where your actions, decisions, efforts, reputation, and relationships can have influence with others inside that zone. In this circle, you can guide, encourage, convince, inspire, and engage. Consider these nine guidelines for working with people who are in your personal circle of influence.

1. Engage them in a conversation about the improvement you wish to advance by asking questions and listening more than talking.
2. Identify the similarities you have with the person or people you directly engage. Make sure that, through the conversation, you cover points of agreement that strengthen rapport. Conversely, identify the points of difference that make collaboration so important.

3. Relate stories or use metaphors to create mental images that are persuasive.

4. Avoid using the phrase *have to*, the verb *must*, or other terms that communicate that someone *should* do something or *should not* do something. Things will rarely turn out exactly as you want or expect. If you avoid the "you have to do it this way" approach to persuasion and instead facilitate those you are influencing to come to their own conclusion, they will be more likely to own and have accountability for the results.

5. Focus the conversation on a better outcome that others can support, and when asked, share your ideas for specific things your audience can do to contribute to that outcome. Present these as possibilities, not stringent *to-do*s. Invite your audience to join you in inquiry to define better ways of reaching goals. One way to frame *change* is that it is only one letter away from the *chance* to make better outcomes happen.

6. Connect to the sense of identity of each person you talk with so that what you need them to do reflects their unique identity in this context—for example, let them know, "You are a technologist who other technologists respect," or "You are a person who connects others to resources." (Note: This approach lets you focus on what you observe the person say or do, as opposed to trying to guess what is going on between their ears that could drive their future actions or decisions.)

7. Provide a few vivid details or credible data points, and communicate that information to help people make up their own minds.

8. Determine what the other person or group wants or needs that you may be able to provide or support while working to meet the performance targets and goals.

9. Encourage those who you need to participate in or support needed changes. Then they will feel good about you, themselves, and the possibilities.

Idea Hub: Leadership Style

Ask yourself the following questions, and then discuss them with your team.

» What is your team's current approach to sharing the school's goals?

+ **Authoritarian:** A top-down approach with mandates

+ **Authoritative:** A clear direction and shared commitment toward common goals

+ **Permissive:** A focus on keeping people happy rather than sharing accountability

+ **Neglectful:** A failure to communicate with staff

» What is one step your team might take to get closer to an authoritative style? If you are already there, what is one step to take to ensure you do not veer into other styles?

Using Roles and Responsibilities to Determine Individual Circle Placement

For high-priority actions and decisions, you might use the RASGO roles and responsibilities chart shown in figure 6.1 (Stolovitch & Keeps, 1999). *RASGO* is an acronym that outlines five distinct roles for people: (1) those who are *responsible*, (2) those who are *accountable*, (3) those who provide *support*, (4) those who can *guide* the efforts, and (5) *observers* who might influence outcomes.

Instructions: Use the chart to determine roles and responsibilities for a planned improvement project. Refer to the definitions of each role as you think about the people to involve. You may list job titles or names.

Task	Responsible People	Accountable People	Supporters	Guides	Observers

Source: Adapted from Stolovitch & Keeps, 1999.

Success Tool Notes:

FIGURE 6.1: Success tool—RASGO roles and responsibilities chart.

*Visit **go.SolutionTree.com/schoolimprovement** for a free reproducible version of this figure.*

Roles similar to those in the chart were originally developed by Harold D. Stolovitch and Erica J. Keeps (1999) as a tool to clarify responsibilities in collaborative work and ensure accountability in decision-making processes. For this book's purposes, we've adapted them to support your work of collaborative school improvement with guidelines for communicating with people in each role.

- *Responsible people* are people or teams who will do the planned work. Clarify expectations for them, provide updates, remove obstacles, and give and receive feedback. This requires frequent two-way communication to ensure real-time problem solving, adaptation, and shared ownership.

- *Accountable people* have the authority to approve the actions and decisions of responsible people. There is only one person in this category for each task. This person must ensure alignment, monitor progress, and make or approve key decisions. This person also needs regular updates and timely, decision-focused communication to avoid delays or misalignment.

- *Supporters* or sponsors are those who need to be in favor of the work as planned and openly support your actions while providing resources, tools, or assistance to those doing the work. Provide them with two-way communication, as needed.

- *Guides* have special expertise or knowledge about how to do the work. These individuals are typically subject-matter experts, and they can provide guidance and even help evaluate the work. Leverage their expertise, engage them in design decisions and adaptations, and co-reflect on results. Create opportunities to solicit their advice, ask questions about how to act on their advice, and confirm that what you are doing is in the spirit of their advice. Ongoing two-way communication with them is essential.

- *Observers* are interested parties who may not actively participate in the work but who watch progress and may be impacted by it or can influence outcomes. Keep observers informed, build their understanding and trust, and invite their feedback when appropriate. Provide them with periodic one-way progress updates, usually at key milestones and at the end of the work, with optional feedback. Providing transparent communication, even if less interactive, builds observers' broader understanding, trust, and support.

The chart supports the necessary consideration of those who must be influenced or engaged as well as their roles and responsibilities on the project. By considering who falls into each of the categories, you can then determine which of them are within your direct circle of influence and which are outside it.

To help clarify your engagement strategies with the people in these categories who are either inside or outside your personal circle of influence, you might code each person: Mark their name with an *I* if they are inside your personal circle of influence or an *O* if they are outside of it. This simple coding helps you quickly assess where you have the most direct influence and where you may need to build new relationships or rely on others to help engage key individuals. It allows you to focus your time and efforts strategically, leveraging strong connections where you can directly influence actions and plan intentional outreach where influence is less direct.

Your role is to facilitate collective investment in the plan of action and purposeful engagement or support. Gaining engagement and moving educators and stakeholders to act take time and effort. Every person wants to know the personal benefits of investing in something like your project. They consider the personal and professional risks and benefits of any new initiative. By facilitating shared understanding and collaborative action, you can encourage them to take risks to improve outcomes for themselves and students.

Infrastructures, routines, and protocols that support opportunities for collaboration are important, but infrastructures alone will not ensure collaboration. The research reveals a collaborative culture as the intervening mechanism that translates servant leadership to project team performance (Nauman, Bhatti, Imam, & Khan, 2021). Leaders must articulate a vision for a collaborative school culture that values increased teacher voice and leadership. School-improvement teams contribute to that collaborative culture. In addition, collaboration among teachers for improved instruction will thrive (Nauman et al., 2021).

Widening Your Circles of Influence

After using the adapted RASGO roles and responsibilities chart to identify key people and the roles they will play in achieving the work, you now know which people are internal and external to your personal circle of influence. You may know the people in your personal circle of influence; however, it is impossible for you to fully understand what would motivate them to make changes, persevere, and do the work needed to reach their shared goals. Thinking you understand people's motivations, even if you know the people well, is not enough. You are not a mind reader! Conducting empathy interviews (see figure 2.4, page 46) and other approaches to better understand what people are thinking and feeling can prevent you from guessing or assuming. Also, facilitating conversations and analyzing together helps with examining the differences among what they know, what they think they know, and what the facts are.

Now, consider your outer circle of influence. In organizational change, your outer circle of influence consists of people or groups who are not directly under your control but whose support is critical to the success of the change. These are people who have the influence to engage others and whose cooperation is needed. They might include district, regional, state, provincial, or other senior leaders who set direction and approve resources for improvement. Their buy-in is essential for justifying and driving change. External stakeholders such as families, community organizations, project partners, employers, government agencies, and others can impact the success of efforts that cannot be accomplished without external collaboration. Engaging them early can help you align expectations and gain their commitment.

You must expand your range of influence into your outer circle of influence in a purposeful way. Effectively engaging your outer circle means finding ways to clearly communicate your goals and facilitate shared understandings so people will see the benefits. Show them that by building alliances, you are creating opportunities for shared success. When you have a wider circle of influence, you can impact more people or variables. And the more people you can influence, the quicker you can build momentum toward achieving the tipping point and reaching a critical mass. In a scientific or nuclear physics context, *critical mass* refers to the amount of material needed to maintain a chain reaction. In school improvement, a wider circle of influence helps create a chain reaction. Increasing influence might enhance the effects of the chain reaction once that threshold of critical mass is reached.

Since your results and your reputation can be impacted by the reputations of those who advocate for you, carefully consider the following.

- How will the association of your work with people from your outer circle impact your credibility and reputation? Is this desirable?
- How well do the people from your outer circle understand what you are doing and why? Do you need to support them with key points in writing so that they accurately tell your story? What are the pros and cons of supporting those in your outer circle when they approach others to gain support for the work?
- How does becoming advocates benefit those in your outer circle? How does becoming advocates reinforce or shape their self-images (such as seeing themselves as experts in obtaining funding)?

In general, if you are seeking to build collaborative or coordinated arrangements, have the people who are collaborating perform the following steps.

1. Discuss and clarify why they are doing this together.
2. Define the arrangement. (Is it a partnership? A sponsorship? A shared or distributed work of leadership? Are there other deliberate ways of working together to reach the desired results or benefits?)
3. Indicate in writing their agreement with the purpose and structure of the arrangement and what each person will or will not do.

More importantly, be clear in your purpose: Are you trying to build collaboration or get people to work together? Collaborating requires sharing the vision and purpose that working together does not. If you observe that the adults you are guiding do not share ways of thinking about their work or its results, you may need to revisit the foundational commitments (the stated mission, vision, values, or beliefs).

Leveraging the Outer Circle

Community members and the media influence public perceptions. They also shape the narrative around needed changes and improvements. Positive engagement with these groups can build public support and minimize resistance. Even vendors and suppliers who provide essential products or services can have an influence. Their cooperation might be needed to adjust to new processes or requirements as part of the change.

Effectively engaging your outer circle of influence involves clear communication. You must build relationships and understand the outer circle's interests to align them with the change objectives. You may not have influence over those who must do the work or make key decisions. You may not have a way to effectively communicate with people whose support is needed. You will have to identify others who can influence and inform them on your behalf. This type of indirect influence is also needed when you have been unable to influence someone directly. That may be because the person or group of people is resistant, is highly assertive, or appears disinterested. It may also be because influencing them directly would be inappropriate.

For example, a project-planning team was working on the task of reducing the number of discipline infractions in a middle school. Decreasing discipline infractions was a goal in the school's improvement plan. One task in the improvement project plan was to provide incentives for students who had no infractions every nine weeks. There were several activities for this task. Some activities involved incentives that the school could provide students at no cost, including homework passes and extra time with mentor teachers during school club periods. Other activities required funding. Funds were limited, so the team members knew they had to reach out to a wider circle of influence to find help. One member personally knew the chamber of commerce president, who could arrange for members of the project-planning team to be on the chamber meeting agenda. The team wanted to inform business owners and community businesspeople about the need for incentives.

The team member contacted the chamber president, who attended one of the project-planning team meetings. During the meeting, the team shared the discipline data and the project plan to address discipline and explained the need to reduce discipline infractions and focus on student achievement. The incentives would be a huge help in motivating students to follow the discipline management plan. The chamber president put three team members on the next chamber meeting agenda. As a result, the team was able to get free incentives and funding for incentives from chamber members to motivate appropriate student behavior. The businesses that donated funds received credit in newsletters to parents and were listed as sponsors on the school website. The businesses that donated giveaways got free advertising. The project-planning team member was able to use her influence with the chamber president to impact the work. The president was in the team's wider circle of influence, and his help and influence impacted the achievement of one of the school goals.

Idea Hub: Stakeholder Collaboration

Ask yourself the following questions, and then discuss them with your team.

- » How does your team currently collaborate with leadership and external stakeholders?
- » Are leadership and external stakeholders involved in the planning or implementation process?
- » How might you create shared understanding and support with your wider circle of influence?

Identifying Which Individuals Have Influence and Where

Identify and engage those who have the credibility to introduce you to someone with whom you cannot directly engage. In this way, you can temporarily borrow these individuals' influence until you can prove your own value, integrity, and credibility. If you are working with a group that is already committed to the change, figure 6.2 may help you work together to influence a wider circle than the improvement team.

Instructions: Work with your team to identify whom outside your group you want to influence or whose influence you can use. Utilize the planner to help you think about who those people are, what their position may be on the initiatives you are working on, and how best to work with them.

Who outside our team can influence or impact our success?	What is their position? (Circle one.)	Who in our group can best communicate with them?	Who outside our group can influence them? Which of us can gain that support?
	• Resister • Supporter • Neutral party • Other		
	• Resister • Supporter • Neutral party • Other		
	• Resister • Supporter • Neutral party • Other		

FIGURE 6.2: Success tool—Influence planner.

Visit go.SolutionTree.com/schoolimprovement for a free reproducible version of this figure.

Success Tool Notes:

Consider the following questions when determining your ability to influence a wider circle. Use figure 6.2 to help determine your answers.

- Can you get access to key stakeholders beyond your own group?
- If you need the support of other stakeholders, can you get to the people who can help make this happen?
- When asked to facilitate an improvement project, can you access others who can help you find out how it fits into the larger picture of the school, district, and community?
- When you see an opportunity to make significant improvements, but it requires changing the behaviors of people in other parts of the school, district, or community, can you get to the people who are able to champion your idea?
- When you need advice from someone outside your circle of influence, do you know where to get it?

- When you need to understand the underlying issues, informal dynamics, or political landscape affecting a situation, do you know who has that insight and can be trusted to share it accurately?
- Can you effectively identify the official and unofficial flows of power, such as teachers who are highly credible to other teachers, and leverage them?

Review the lists of people in your RASGO roles and responsibilities chart and your influence planner. List the people by the degree to which you believe they will support the work and they are deemed influential, as shown in figure 6.3.

	People Who Are More Likely to Support the Work	People Who Are More Likely to Resist or Not Actively Support the Work
People Who Have Influence or Are Seen as Credible by the Larger Group	Focus on this group first to get their public endorsement and involvement and their commitment to coach or influence others to support the work.	Focus on this group second to hear their concerns and identify ways to address them. Also identify peers they admire who may be supporters and who might help by either engaging in this group or minimizing any potential negative effect the group might have.
People Who Are Deemed to Have Little or No Influence Over the Larger Group	Focus on this group third and identify ways to increase their level of influence.	Focus on this group last, even if they are the most vocal resisters. Eventually work to get others to help minimize their resistance or change their position.

FIGURE 6.3: Influencers and best approaches for interacting.

Aligning Actions and Foundational Commitments

Identifying circles of influence and widening them are critical for successful collaboration in meeting project and school-improvement goals. Also, collaborative improvement efforts must align with the school and school district's foundational commitments to ensure coherence and sustainability. During the research that led to the development of the ten standards that form the framework for this book, interviewees consistently emphasized the importance of ensuring alignment between collaborative improvement work and the school or district's *foundational commitments*—the established and communicated mission, vision, values, and beliefs. This alignment is critical because it ensures the planned collaborative work has legitimacy, relevance, and organizational support. When collaborative efforts are clearly connected to the institution's core identity and strategic direction, they are more likely to gain stakeholder buy-in, attract necessary resources, and achieve a lasting impact.

Without this alignment, collaborative work can be perceived as disconnected, optional, or even disruptive, leading to confusion, resistance, or duplication of efforts. Misalignment can cause friction among teams, leadership, and broader stakeholders, undermining trust and slowing influence, ownership, support, and progress.

When misalignment is identified, it must be addressed directly and constructively. This may involve revisiting the purpose and scope of the improvement effort, seeking clarification from your leadership, or adjusting the focus of the work to ensure coherence with organizational priorities. In some cases, it may also require engaging in courageous conversations to surface hidden assumptions or revisit outdated or conflicting beliefs. Alignment is not a one-time check; it must be revisited regularly to ensure collaborative work continues to support the shared vision and moves the school community forward together.

For example, an improvement team was working to implement its English language arts curriculum. One team member observed, "Our school district's vision statement is 'Every graduate will attain a technical certification, military training, or a two-year or four-year degree.' How can we find out what our English language arts department's current thinking is regarding how curriculum implementation is aligned with and supports our vision statement?" As leaders guide and support the work of collaborative school improvement, you may see the necessity to update those foundational commitments to meet new or changing needs. School-improvement teams may also be part of recognizing this necessity.

Idea Hub: Foundational Commitments

Ask yourself the following questions, and then discuss them with your team.

» What are the current mission, vision, values, and beliefs of your school?

» How is the school collectively working toward these foundations?

» When was the last time these were updated? Do you need to update them to better align with the goals of the school?

A key to sustainable and meaningful school improvement is guiding collaborative dialogue among stakeholders to inform actions and foundational commitments. Guiding collaborative dialogue allows educators to explore and agree on what matters most, clarifying expectations, priorities, and intended outcomes. To align actions, everyone needs a common understanding of foundational commitments.

Aligned performance requires ongoing monitoring and adaptation to build capacity and accountability. Collaborative discussions create a space for accountability, reflection, and feedback. Teams can check whether their actions are leading to the desired outcomes and make course corrections. Sustaining alignment requires consistent communication across time, teams, and stakeholders. For example, regular, guided dialogue reinforces focus and coherence across departments or grade levels, preventing a drift away from foundational goals.

Aligning actions and foundational commitments gives school-improvement efforts a direction and purpose. Guiding collaborative dialogue is the engine that ensures everyone moves in the same direction—through shared meaning, co-constructed strategies, and mutual accountability.

Guiding Collaborative Dialogue

Facilitation of, and participation in, different types of dialogue can support stakeholder engagement and creativity. This dialogue may be between stakeholders within the school, between school- and system-level stakeholders, between the school and external stakeholders, or between educators and their school board. For example, connecting and dialoguing with external stakeholders who can partner on providing real-world projects and problems can support both educators and students. Conversations may lead to teacher externships and employers' support for content-area and career and technical education teachers to create engaging and effective instruction that supports curriculum mastery. This collaboration can develop the types of high-demand skills that employers are seeking while relationships are built and feedback is sought and given.

Use the following eight protocols to guide your dialogue with stakeholder groups, and encourage this communication and engagement.

1. **Visionary dialogue:** This type of conversation is about discussing the long-term goals and dreams for the school or specific efforts, like the school's vision for innovation and improvement. It helps everyone get on the same page with a shared purpose and direction.

    a. *"What kind of future do we imagine for students in terms of both their academic success and their personal development?"* The intent is to encourage stakeholders to think beyond the present, focusing on long-term outcomes and the broader impact they can have on students' lives.

    b. *"If there were one significant change to the education system that would better prepare students for the future, what would it be and why?"* The intent is to invite stakeholders to reflect on innovative solutions and think critically about the larger educational landscape, pushing them to envision transformative possibilities.

2. **Problem-solving dialogue:** The focus of this dialogue is on identifying challenges and obstacles in the way of improvement. It is about brainstorming solutions, creating action plans to overcome these challenges, and encouraging critical thinking and new ideas.

    a. *"What are the biggest obstacles that students face when it comes to developing strong critical thinking skills? What can we do to help them overcome those obstacles?"* The intent is to identify specific challenges or barriers and encourage stakeholders to propose actions.

    b. *"In what ways do current curriculum or instructional strategies help or hinder students' ability to think critically, and how might we address those limitations?"* The intent is to encourage educators to challenge their practices and suggest changes or innovations.

3. **Reflective dialogue:** This dialogue involves looking back at past efforts, evaluating how well they worked, and learning from both successes and failures. The goal is to refine strategies for future improvements and decide what practices should be continued or abandoned.

a.   *"Looking back, what approaches or strategies have been most successful in achieving our learning goals, and why did those practices work?"* The intent is to get your team to reflect on its successes, identify key factors behind those successes, and consider what practices should be continued.

b.   *"What challenges or setbacks have we encountered, and what adjustments or changes might make our efforts more effective?"* The intent is for the group members to think about their failures or challenges in a way that encourages them to develop new strategies and be willing to abandon or adjust their past practices.

4.   **Inclusive dialogue:** This ensures all stakeholders—teachers, students, families, administrators, and community members—have a chance to learn from one another and have a say in the improvement process. It values diverse opinions while preventing uninformed assumptions, biases, and misunderstandings from harming collaborative efforts.

a.   *"What can we do to ensure all stakeholders—teachers, students, families, administrators, and community members—feel heard and valued in the process of developing improvement strategies?"* The intent is to encourage teams to think about inclusivity and how to genuinely solicit and consider diverse perspectives from all stakeholders.

b.   *"What steps can we take to prevent assumptions or biases from influencing how we interpret feedback from stakeholders? How can we make sure that decisions are based on accurate and well-rounded information?"* The intent is to stress the importance of objectivity and to think critically about how to gather, interpret, and act on stakeholder input without allowing preconceived notions to interfere with effective collaboration.

5.   **Data-driven dialogue:** This type of dialogue focuses on analyzing relevant data, such as academic performance, student feedback, and demographic information, to make informed decisions and measure progress toward improvement goals.

a.   *What types of data—such as academic performance, student feedback, and demographic information—are most relevant for measuring progress toward improvement goals, and why?"* The intent is for teams to reflect on the types of data that will be most useful in making informed decisions and tracking progress, while encouraging a conversation about prioritizing key metrics.

b.   *"How can teams use the collected data to identify areas for improvement and ensure strategies are directly aligned with the needs of students and the school community?"* The intent is for teams to think about how to translate data into actionable insights, ensuring decisions are rooted in evidence and geared toward measurable outcomes.

6.   **Collaborative dialogue:** Emphasizing teamwork, this dialogue fosters a culture where all stakeholders share responsibility and work together to achieve school improvement and innovation.

a. *"What steps can we take to build stronger partnerships among teachers, students, families, administrators, and community members so that everyone feels responsible and invested in school success?"* The intent is to encourage teams to think about concrete actions that can strengthen collaboration and shared ownership of improvement efforts.

b. *"How can we create opportunities for regular communication and collaboration among all stakeholders to ensure everyone's ideas and perspectives are contributing to meaningful innovation?"* The intent is to stress the importance of open communication and collaboration and to invite teams to consider how to structure ongoing dialogue and joint efforts for improvement.

7. **Creative dialogue:** This dialogue encourages thinking outside the box, exploring new ideas, and trying innovative approaches to teaching, learning, and school improvement.

a. *"If there were no limitations—such as time, resources, or traditional expectations—what bold new ideas could we try to enhance student learning?"* The intent is to invite stakeholders to think freely without constraints so that you spark imaginative thinking and encourage them to propose innovative solutions or approaches.

b. *"What are some successful or cutting-edge practices from other schools, industries, or fields that we might adapt or experiment with to improve our school's outcomes?"* The intent is to look beyond traditional education models and draw inspiration from a variety of sources to foster cross-disciplinary thinking and open the door to creative experimentation.

8. **Empathetic dialogue:** This focuses on understanding and addressing the needs, concerns, and perspectives of everyone involved. It builds trust, empathy, and mutual respect among all stakeholders.

a. *"How can stakeholders actively listen to and understand the unique needs and concerns of students, families, teachers, and community members to ensure everyone's voice is heard and respected?"* The intent is to prompt stakeholders to think about how to create spaces for meaningful dialogue and engagement, emphasizing the importance of active listening and empathy.

b. *"What can we do to foster a culture of mutual respect and trust where all stakeholders feel comfortable sharing their perspectives, even when they differ from the majority or challenge existing practices?"* The intent is to reflect on how to create an environment of psychological safety where diverse perspectives are valued, promoting collaboration and deeper understanding.

Each of these dialogue types offers a structured way to foster meaningful conversations that go beyond surface-level agreement and into authentic collaboration. By intentionally selecting and using the appropriate type of dialogue, leaders can create space for trust, critical thinking, creative problem solving, and shared accountability. These protocols support the core leadership work of guiding collaboration by engaging stakeholders in ways that build buy-in, deepen understanding, and cultivate shared ownership of both the challenges and the solutions. They support strategic accomplishment of the school's and district's foundational commitments and may inform revisions of those commitments when needed. Thoughtful facilitation of these conversations helps influence not just actions but attitudes and relationships and lays the groundwork for sustained commitment and collective success.

Reviewing Examples of Standard 6

To help you use what you have learned in chapter 6, we have included an example of an effective practice and an example of a less effective practice. Comparing these examples will help you determine what to do and what to avoid when applying the work of standard 6.

An Effective Example

At Stanley High School, a cross-functional school-improvement team led by principal Miki Berenguer identified chronic absenteeism and low postsecondary readiness as persistent barriers to student success. Instead of launching disconnected initiatives, the team developed strategies to build influence and guide collaborative improvement from within the school and beyond its walls.

The team began by engaging educators in reflective dialogue about the data to guide their understanding of the situation, draw on past experiences, and collaboratively decide on new, targeted strategies. Teachers, counselors, and administrators codeveloped early warning systems to flag attendance issues and created grade-level teams to follow up with students and families. To strengthen internal trust and buy-in, they held inclusive conversations that honored diverse perspectives and aligned efforts with the school's mission to prepare students for lifelong success.

Simultaneously, the school-improvement team expanded its circle of influence by partnering with community organizations, local employers, and a nearby technical college. These partners codesigned career-exposure days, mentorship programs, and dual enrollment opportunities that gave students a clearer pathway to postsecondary success. The team also provided wraparound supports for students facing chronic challenges that impacted attendance and engagement.

Through consistent, intentional communication and use of stakeholder engagement protocols, the team fostered a culture of shared ownership. Teachers reported stronger collaboration across departments, while families and students felt more connected and supported. Over two years, Stanley High saw a 15 percent reduction in chronic absenteeism, a notable increase in course completion rates, and a 20 percent jump in students earning industry credentials or college credits before graduation.

At a school board meeting, the Economic Development Authority honored the school with its RISE (Resilient, Inspired, Skilled, and Empowered) Award for both modeling and developing the skills students need in order to succeed. The chair of the school board said, "The entire team at Stanley High and its families and community partners demonstrated the power of influencing commitment, not just compliance, and aligning internal actions with external partnerships to produce systemic, sustainable change. The school-improvement team did not rely solely on authority but used strategic collaboration and communication to lead the school forward."

A Less Effective Example

Principal Bronson Britt met with the members of his school's improvement team to focus on the need to complete their state-required analysis. They developed a draft of the school-improvement plan for the year. The team had been working for several weeks on a comprehensive needs assessment.

Britt stressed, "We need to have our plan in place and an aligned budget right away. You have brought your experience and points of view to the analysis and know what needs to be done this coming year. Just a reminder—we need to let the central office know our funding needs so they can allocate them for us by the deadline. Since it is the middle of April, we need that plan completed as soon as possible."

When members of the improvement team reminded Britt that they wanted to involve more people in the school and community in collaborative analysis to inform the plan, he responded that he was hopeful they could do that. But he added that since annual testing was in progress, and school ended in late May, there would be limited time to engage others in planning. He charged them to complete the plan and engage others in implementing it in the fall.

Idea Hub: Reflection

Reflect individually on what you learned in this chapter, and record your thoughts. Then use your individual reflections to collaboratively answer the following questions with your team.

» What did the school-improvement team at Stanley High School do that aligns with the guidance in this chapter?

» What did Britt do that misaligns with the guidance in this chapter?

» What are your and your team's biggest takeaways?

» How will you embrace the work of chapter 6?

» Who will you engage in the work of chapter 6?

Conclusion

Sustainable school improvement depends not only on sound planning but also on your ability to build trust, foster collaboration, and influence others to act with a shared purpose. As explored in this chapter, true collaboration goes beyond simply working together; it requires a unified vision, mutual commitment, and the willingness to shape behavior and decisions in support of collective goals.

To guide effective improvement, leaders must think strategically about their circles of influence, identifying who needs to be engaged, who can champion the work, and how to build the relationships that make successful collaboration and shared success possible. This includes aligning collaborative actions with the school's foundational commitments—its mission, vision, values, and goals—so every effort moves in the same direction.

This chapter presented protocols for collaborative dialogue as practical tools to spark meaningful engagement, invite diverse perspectives, and generate creative, evidence-based solutions. These conversations encourage participation, foster ownership, fuel innovation, and lay the groundwork for a culture of sustained improvement. By guiding these conversations with intention, leaders can activate the power of collaboration to overcome barriers, build support, and drive real, lasting change.

Chapter 7 focuses on what successful school-improvement teams point to as one of the most important aspects of their efforts—building their own capacity and that of others to ensure the work is successful and sustainable.

Before moving on to chapter 7, complete the "Standard 6: Do and Avoid Chart" and "Standard 6: Plan-Ahead Chart" reproducibles (pages 132 and 133) with your team to reflect on and process the work you accomplished for standard 6 and plan ahead for next steps.

Standard 6: Do and Avoid Chart

As you move through the standards for improvement, you will find things to do and things to avoid. After reading the effective and less effective practice examples and reflecting on them and the work of standard 6, complete the following do and avoid chart to help you record your thoughts about the work of this standard.

Instructions: Record what you plan to do and avoid. Consider the following questions.

1. How will you introduce your team to the processes introduced in this chapter?
2. How will you facilitate discussions about how to promote stakeholder collaboration?
3. How will you identify your personal circle of influence and assign roles and responsibilities?
4. How will you identify people outside your personal circle of influence whom you need to support the work?
5. How will you use the influence planner (see figure 6.2, page 123) and the influencers and best approaches for interacting chart (see figure 6.3, page 124) to guide your work?
6. How will you ensure you align actions and foundational commitments?
7. How can you use different types of dialogue to sustain alignment of actions and foundational commitments while supporting communication and engagement?

Do	Avoid

Standard 6: Plan-Ahead Chart

To get a clearer perspective on the next steps, consider your do and avoid chart as you complete the following plan-ahead chart. The work of standard 6 prepares you to facilitate and focus collaboration to achieve improvement goals.

Instructions: Use the information from chapter 6 to identify your and your team's next steps to complete each action.

Actions	Person or People Responsible	Due Date
Complete the RASGO roles and responsibilities chart (see figure 6.1, page 118) to determine roles and responsibilities for a planned improvement project and consider which people to involve.		
Use the influence planner (see figure 6.2, page 123) and the influencers and best approaches for interacting chart (see figure 6.3, page 124) to identify which people outside your team you want to influence or whose influence you might bring into your initiatives and how best to work with them.		
Align actions and foundational commitments to give school-improvement efforts direction and purpose.		
Use the eight dialogue protocols (see pages 126–128) to ensure stakeholders move in the same direction through shared meaning, co-constructed strategies, and mutual accountability.		

Chapter 7

Standard 7: Build Capacity

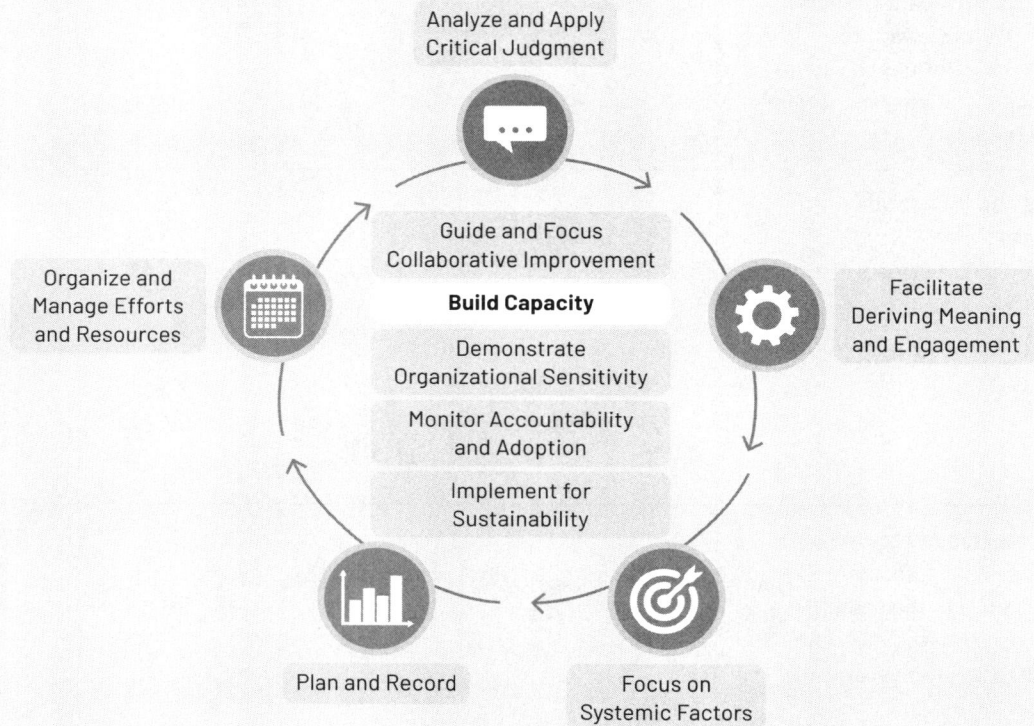

Analyze and Apply
Critical Judgment

Organize and
Manage Efforts
and Resources

Guide and Focus
Collaborative Improvement

Build Capacity

Demonstrate
Organizational Sensitivity

Monitor Accountability
and Adoption

Implement for
Sustainability

Facilitate
Deriving Meaning
and Engagement

Plan and Record

Focus on
Systemic Factors

*S*tandard 7 is about advocating for developing educators' abilities to improve their performance. Building capacity serves as the foundation for innovation by ensuring educators and stakeholders are prepared, confident, and equipped to embrace, implement, and sustain change. In our work, we have explored the practices of those who successfully guide school improvement. That research taught us that building capacity is one of the most critical aspects in the work of school-improvement practitioners and school-improvement teams.

This chapter will help your school-improvement team understand how important it is to ensure teachers and other school staff are continuously learning, which leads to ongoing improvement. While your team may not be directly responsible for providing professional learning, you play a key role. This role is to recommend and request effective development and support for educators. Even though you are not responsible for delivering professional learning, the performance of educators directly impacts student success. Your school-improvement team should advocate for effective processes and tools that can help build educators' skills and abilities. This chapter will help your team:

- Recommend practices for professional learning based on adult learning science
- Support efforts to evaluate the impact of professional learning on teaching and practice
- Identify areas where educators need development
- Evaluate existing professional learning and advocate for improvements

By advocating for quality professional learning that results in practical improvements, you contribute to an environment where educators can better support students. Being able to support your school with more effective development for educators requires first understanding the foundation of how adult learners learn. You must understand how adults transfer their knowledge to effective practice.

Understanding How Adults Learn

In education, time is both limited and vital. Schools must ensure their approaches to improvement match their data and identified goals. When professional learning is necessary, it must be "sustained (not stand-alone, one-day, or short-term workshops), intensive, collaborative, job-embedded, data-driven, and classroom-focused" (Learning Forward, n.d.). Development for educators that does not lead to better practices wastes time, effort, and money. It can also cause frustration and stress among educators. By ensuring professional learning is effective, you are making your school a better place for both educators and students.

A key part of advocating for effective development for educators is understanding how adults learn. Traditional K–12 professional learning often relies on teaching methods designed for students, not adults. Follow these guidelines to ensure adults learn and effectively apply their learning (Shank, 2017).

- **Readability and usability:** Ensure professional learning materials are clear and easy to use. The goal is to make information easily understood and applied in the classroom.
- **Prior knowledge:** Professional learning should be built on what educators already know. Avoid the pitfalls of assuming too much and offering one-size-fits-all training.
- **Mental effort and memory:** Adult learners need professional learning that is designed to be memorable and not overwhelming. Using strategies that align with how adults process and retain information will help ensure that learning sticks and can be applied in real situations.
- **Appropriate difficulty:** Adults learn best when they are challenged in ways that enhance long-term retention but do not overwhelm their abilities. Professional learning should include the right levels of challenge to deepen learning. As Patti Shank (2025) emphasizes through her evidence-based approach, instructional methods should be adapted to match learner expertise—novices benefit more from studying worked examples, while more skilled learners benefit more from solving problems.
- **Social learning:** Adults also learn from interacting with others. They can learn through discussions, group activities, mentoring, or peer coaching. Professional learning should include opportunities for social learning to enhance collaboration and problem solving.
- **Relevance:** This is one of the most important issues for adult learners. Adults should see the importance of professional learning, and it should serve a specific purpose related to their job. Relevant experiences help establish the foundation for professional learning to transfer to practice.

Educators need to understand why their training is important. Too often, professional learning is provided without a clear explanation of its purpose. When educators understand the rationale behind training and how it will improve their teaching, they are more motivated to engage in and apply what they learn. Training programs should clearly state what teachers will achieve by the end. An example is "In order to achieve student engagement, teachers will practice strategies for active learning in the classroom." Educators are more likely to commit to effectively implementing new strategies when they know why a specific professional learning program or initiative is necessary and how it will impact their performance.

Research shows that high-quality professional development that engages educators in well-designed, discipline-specific professional learning, along with active learning, expert coaching, and sustained duration of practice, results in meaningful improvements in their practice and confidence (Lau & Yuen, 2019; Van Driel, Borko, & Osborne, 2023; Wilson, 2013). It also reveals that enhanced educator self-efficacy and instructional skills can produce better classroom experiences and stronger student outcomes, reflected in higher achievement. These findings provide compelling evidence that districts should prioritize ongoing, relevant professional learning as a strategic lever to improve both teacher capacity and student achievement.

Applying Learning on the Job

For professional learning to be truly effective, it must transfer to the real world of teaching and learning. Your team can advocate for professional learning that includes modeling, practice, and feedback so educators can apply what they have learned.

The SEDA (Situation → Evaluation → Decision → Action) model is a reflective decision-making framework that helps clarify the distinction between decision making and task performance by describing how people move through realworld situations—as they perceive and evaluate a situation, make a decision, and then act (Thalheimer, 2018).

You can advocate for this model as part of educator development, particularly in coaching, mentoring, and school-improvement processes. It supports both individual and team-based learning by reinforcing a continuous cycle of evaluation, decision making, and intentional action.

1. **Situation:** An educator learns about or is experiencing a situation and then gathers information about it—such as student data, classroom dynamics, or instructional challenges. For example, a teacher might observe that students are disengaged during mathematics lessons and begin to gather data on participation, student feedback, and assessment results to define the core problem.

2. **Experience:** The educator reflects on past experiences—both personal and shared with peers—related to similar challenges. They might consider what instructional strategies they have tried before, which students responded well, and what the outcomes were. A team might share insights during a collaborative meeting to identify patterns or missed opportunities.

3. **Decision:** With input from reflection and dialogue, the educator or team collaborates to identify potential solutions. In this example, they might decide to implement differentiated mathematics stations and use formative assessments to monitor understanding. They weigh the potential benefits and challenges of this approach based on their situation and past experiences.

4. **Act:** The team puts the plan into action. The educator organizes the new learning stations, sets a timeline, and commits to regular student check-ins. After implementation, the educator reflects on the impact—monitoring engagement levels and student growth. Based on the results, the team may refine the strategy or introduce additional supports.

By guiding educators through this process, the SEDA model builds capacity for reflective practice and adaptive decision making. It encourages intentional responses to complex classroom and school-level challenges. This structured yet flexible approach also supports leadership development and improves instructional decision making, so it is especially useful in professional learning, coaching, and improvement-planning contexts. It also reinforces a continuous cycle of evaluation, decision making, and action. This helps educators reflect and be more intentional in their practice.

Idea Hub: Quality Check

Think of a recent professional learning session you attended. Considering the list of guidelines from the Understanding How Adults Learn section (see pages 136–137 and the SEDA model (see pages 137–138), rate the quality of the session on a scale of 1–4 (*1* means "strongly disagree" and *4* means "strongly agree"). After you have had a chance to rate the professional learning session individually, discuss your ratings as a team.

>   » The session provided meaningful opportunities to collaborate and learn from others (for example, discussions, peer sharing, and group activities).

>   » The learning was personally relevant and connected to your day-to-day work as an educator.

>   » The session appropriately challenged your thinking without being overwhelming. The mental effort required was productive and purposeful.

>   » The learning honored what you already know and provided space for reflection and experience sharing.

>   » The materials and delivery were clear, easy to follow, and applicable to your instructional context.

>   » The strategies and key ideas were presented in a way that helped you remember them.

>   » The learning matched your level of expertise, stretching your thinking with just the right level of challenge.

>   » After training, you were able to apply your learning and achieve the expected results.

Consider how you might provide this feedback to the person who delivered the professional learning or use this list to help evaluate the quality of professional learning before it is delivered.

Recommending Professional Learning for Educators

As a school-improvement team, you can advocate for professional learning that aligns with the goals of your school-improvement plan. You do not need to provide the training yourself. You can identify when professional learning is necessary and make informed recommendations for its implementation or improvement.

Through your team's gap analysis (see chapters 1 and 3), factors analysis (see chapters 1 and 2), causal analysis (see chapter 3), and environment and worker analysis (see chapter 3), you may find your team needs professional learning. To confirm whether professional learning for educators is the right solution, ask, "Could our staff do what is needed and expected if they absolutely had to do it?" Consider what each of the following answers means for your next steps.

- If the answer is *no*, it means training is needed or barriers preventing success must be removed.
- If the answer is *yes*, the issue is likely one of willingness, and the focus should be on motivating or requiring the staff to perform the task.
- In rare cases, you might realize the task itself is unachievable, which calls for further analysis and leader involvement to reassess the situation.

It is important to note that sometimes professional learning is not the right solution. Reflect on the work you did in chapter 3 using the environment and worker analysis (see figure 3.4, page 65). Professional learning or development interventions are needed only for the individual Knowledge and Skills cell. Before recommending professional learning, also check for other key issues to ensure training is the best approach. It is *not* a capacity-building need in the following cases.

- **Expectations are unclear:** If poor performance is due to a lack of communication or clarity of expectations, the issue is not skill, will, or readiness.
- **External barriers exist:** If there are obstacles in the marketplace, workplace, or processes that prevent educators from doing their work well, and they already have the necessary skills, training will not solve the issue.

If either of these conditions is true, professional learning will not address the problem, and you should consider other interventions. If your team has conducted the analysis explained in chapter 3, you have identified both the causes and the needed solutions. Your team may have determined other interventions that are more appropriate than professional learning, or perhaps other solutions are needed. Use the following guidance to develop recommendations to meet the identified teacher needs.

- **Curriculum alignment:** Recommend interventions in curriculum alignment when assessments show gaps between the taught curriculum and the written curriculum (Eaker & Marzano, 2020).

- **Instructional practices:** Recommend professional learning in instructional practices when student data or classroom observations show ineffective or inconsistent teaching methods.
- **Classroom management:** Recommend classroom management support when discipline data or teacher feedback highlights disruptions that negatively impact the learning environment.
- **Collaborative planning:** Suggest collaborative planning support when teachers work in isolation, leading to inconsistencies across classrooms.
- **Coaching:** Develop and use a rubric for educator growth and impact after professional learning, and consider coaching interventions for more personalized, ongoing support when teachers are not progressing.
- **Data-driven decision making:** Recommend data-driven decision-making strategies when there's limited use of data in instructional planning. In addition, student outcomes might suggest a need for better analysis of student needs.
- **Technology integration:** Advocate for technology integration support when teachers struggle to use digital tools effectively. It may also be that students are not using technology to enhance learning.
- **Family and community engagement:** Promote family and community engagement initiatives when external factors like low family involvement or weak community partnerships hinder student success.

After analyzing the situation, your school-improvement team can prioritize professional learning when the following factors are true.

- Educators express a lack of confidence in their subject knowledge or instructional strategies.
- Student outcomes indicate the need for skill enhancement. Targeted professional learning with coaching can address these gaps against clear performance criteria.

This approach ensures professional learning efforts are aligned with actual needs. It also ensures other supportive interventions are considered where necessary.

Idea Hub: Professional Learning for Educators

Return to chapter 3, or provide the group requesting professional learning with a copy of the environment and worker analysis tool you completed (see figure 3.4, page 65).

» What professional learning is currently required for your school?

» Does this professional learning align with the identified needs in the environment and worker analysis tool? If yes, great! If not, share this tool with the group requesting professional learning.

» What recommendations for alternative solutions or supports will you provide based on this analysis?

Effective professional learning goes beyond workshops and training sessions. It requires intentional support structures that ensure learning translates into practice. As noted earlier, coaching is a critical component of sustained professional growth. Coaching provides personalized, job-embedded guidance that reinforces learning and fosters continuous improvement. Induction supports new educators with structured onboarding and mentorship, helping them navigate expectations and build confidence. Evaluation ensures accountability and informs improvement by assessing both the quality and the impact of professional learning on educator practice and student outcomes. Together, these strategies build a coherent system that supports educators at every stage of their growth journey.

Coaching to Develop Educators

Coaching is one of the most effective interventions to support educators' development and practice improvement (Turner, 2023). Like any performance intervention, coaching's quality directly impacts its success. To ensure high-quality teacher coaching, consider the following essential elements.

- **Clear goals and expectations:** Set specific, measurable objectives for teacher growth and improvement.
- **Trusting relationships:** Establish relationships based on mutual respect and trust between coach and teacher.
- **Frequent, focused feedback:** Provide timely, actionable feedback that aligns with the teachers' goals for development.
- **Collaborative reflection:** Encourage teachers to reflect on their practices and work with the coach to solve problems.
- **Modeling of best practices:** Demonstrate effective, high-impact instructional strategies for teachers to observe and implement.
- **Job-embedded support:** Integrate coaching into daily teaching routines for real-time, practical support.
- **Data-driven conversations:** Use student performance data to guide coaching discussions and track progress.
- **Sustained follow-up:** Ensure continuous support by regularly revisiting goals and assessing progress.

Idea Hub: Coaching and Capacity Building

Ask yourself the following questions, and then discuss them with your team.

» How can the school-improvement team support effective educator coaching in your school?

» What capacity-building supports or solutions are needed based on your school-improvement goals and project plans?

» How might you communicate your ideas to the project teams if they are not part of the school-improvement team?

Focusing on Induction

A critical process in supporting professional learning is the induction or transition of educators to new roles, teams, or jobs. Effective induction ensures educators have the support and clarity they need to succeed in their new positions. The tool in figure 7.1 can help you assess whether effective induction practices are in place for educators at all levels.

Instructions: Read each item and determine whether the practice is in place. Circle *Yes* or *No*.	
Yes No	Providing handbooks and job aids
Yes No	Ensuring completion of structured practice assignments aligned with day-to-day work with clear preset criteria
Yes No	Providing feedback on practices corresponding with clear preset criteria
Yes No	Providing peer groups or networks of other inductees
Yes No	Implementing a group or network of support by more expert performers who model expected behaviors and practices
Yes No	Offering regular reflection on practice and setting achievable goals for growth, improvement, and results with coaching
Yes No	Identifying and addressing performance barriers outside the inductee's control
Yes No	Offering training and development
Yes No	Providing structured mentoring and support, including check-ins with a compatible peer mentor or induction coach
Yes No	Offering support for navigating operational processes
Yes No	Providing structured orientations
Yes No	Ensuring access to a coach, professional developer, or other supporting individual
Yes No	Offering social-emotional support
Yes No	Providing access to resources for development
Yes No	Giving celebrations of achievements, whether big or small
Yes No	Establishing learning communities
Yes No	Offering cultural competence training
Yes No	Developing mindsets that support learning
Yes No	Providing learning management systems

FIGURE 7.1: Success tool—Induction worksheet.

*Visit **go.SolutionTree.com/schoolimprovement** for a free reproducible version of this figure.*

Evaluating Development and Support of Educators

Evaluating teacher training is crucial to ensure it actually improves both teaching practices and student learning outcomes. The following three categories of questions can support the evaluation of teacher training.

1. **Focus on results:** When considering professional learning options, first determine what results the development aims to achieve. This is especially important when external vendors provide development. Instead of focusing on whether educators enjoy the training, the key is understanding what they learn and how they will apply it on the job. This means asking questions about what educators intend to do differently in their teaching practices. It also means asking how likely they are to make those changes. For example, after practicing developing a project-based lesson plan as a team, you might ask, "How and why will you use individual and group reflection in the project-based lessons you design? How likely are you to develop project-based lessons aligned to the curriculum? Why?"

2. **Review participant feedback:** Feedback forms are often provided after professional learning sessions for educators. However, many times, the forms do not measure what is important. Look for evaluation questions that go beyond "Did you enjoy the session?" or "Did you learn something?" Instead, focus on questions like the following.

   a. "What did you learn that you can apply in your teaching?"

   b. "How confident are you in applying what you learned?"

   c. "What changes will you make in your classroom because of this training?"

   These questions provide more meaningful insights into whether the development for educators will lead to improved performance in the classroom.

3. **Evaluate performance, not just experience:** The goal of professional learning is to improve what educators do in their day-to-day work. When evaluating or selecting professional learning, focus on how it will help teachers make better decisions and improve their teaching practices. Focus on how it will meet specific goals (such as improving student outcomes). This means asking the following.

   a. "What are the specific goals of this development?"

   b. "What observable changes will we see in teachers' practices?"

   c. "What will educators practice during the session, and what will they do differently on the job?"

Achieving effective development, like achieving other school-improvement goals, takes planning and collaboration. As performance-improvement expert Robert Brinkerhoff (2017) points out, most training does not work because people often go back to their old ways of doing things. To avoid this, it is important to create the right conditions for learning to transfer to performance. These include the following.

- **Focus and direction:** Make sure there are clear links between the training, what educators need to do, and their goals. Educators should know what is expected of them and be held accountable.
- **Learning engagement:** Ensure learning activities are relevant and allow for enough practice with feedback. Educators should have control over their learning. Tools like job aids can support them in practice.
- **Performance and application:** Support educators in applying what they have learned by providing ongoing coaching and feedback.

Reflecting on Professional Learning and Practices

To improve development for educators, it is helpful to reflect on what is working and what needs improvement. Use these ten questions to guide your team in evaluating professional learning efforts.

1. What were you trying to achieve with this development?
2. Was professional learning successful? How can you tell?
3. What materials or strategies were used, and how effective were they?
4. What techniques did you use, and how did they work?
5. What happened, or what do you expect will happen, after the development?
6. Did you have to adjust your approach? If so, why and how?
7. What problems did you face during the process?
8. What were you thinking and feeling while working on this?
9. What did you accomplish, and what would you change next time?
10. What did you learn about your professional learning practices?

Using these reflective questions can help your team continually improve professional learning efforts and support educators in meaningful ways.

Reviewing Examples of Standard 7

To help you use what you have learned in chapter 7, we have included an example of an effective practice and an example of a less effective practice. Comparing these examples will help you determine what to do and what to avoid when applying the work of standard 7.

An Effective Example

A new principal, Declan Fields, was assigned to Bennett High School. The school-improvement team met with him during the summer to discuss plans for professional learning. Fields had reviewed the school-improvement plan and the professional learning scheduled for the school. He had questions about how some of the professional learning connected to the goals in the improvement plan.

Fields knew from his twenty years of experience that professional learning must align with the school goals and transfer to classroom practice if it is going to be truly effective. He told the team members that he needed their help to review the connection between the planned professional learning and the goals in the school plan. He also wanted to ensure that the planned professional learning was truly based on capacity-building needs, not unclear expectations or other barriers causing the underperformance.

The school-improvement team members expressed that they wanted professional learning that included modeling, practice, and feedback so teachers could apply what they learned. They thought that some of the planned professional learning did not align with the improvement plan goals. They also said that some professional learning in the past really had not connected to current goals, and there had been no follow-through in the classroom. Many teachers felt a lot of time was wasted. They shared that the training done was ineffective because it was mostly sit-and-get training with no modeling, opportunities for practice, or feedback to ensure transfer of learning to their classrooms.

Fields suggested that the team first review the planned professional learning to determine whether it was directly tied to school goals and resulted from a capacity-building need. He explained that some underperformance is a result of will, not skill, and some is a result of poor communication or unclear expectations.

In addition, team members needed to establish whether obstacles in the marketplace, workplace, or processes were preventing teachers from using necessary skills they already had to do their work well. If any of these other reasons for underperformance were the case, no amount of training would solve the problem. Fields did not want to waste teachers' or other staff's valuable time on unneeded training. The team agreed and set a time to review the school goals and professional learning planned. Fields would provide guidance.

Fields then explained that, after determining whether the professional learning in the plan was truly a capacity-building need, the next step would be knowing how to select quality development opportunities. Professional learning must result in the transfer to practice of what was learned. Fields discussed the SEDA model and told the team that it could use this framework to review professional learning needs and opportunities. He explained that the process combines decision making and reflection with feedback, as well as opportunities to learn and practice in different situations. One must consider different classroom circumstances as well as situational awareness to accurately assess and respond to different contexts before acting. Fields also expressed the need for a continuous cycle of evaluation, decision making, and action. This process would help the team reflect and be more intentional in its practice. The team agreed that the SEDA model would be very helpful.

Fields charged the team with advocating for quality professional learning. He assured team members that they would work together to ensure all professional learning going forward was tied to school goals, truly needed, effective, and evaluated for a positive impact on teaching and learning in the classroom. He said they would discuss the characteristics of quality professional learning at their next meeting. Fields stressed that planning and implementing quality educator development would be a collaborative process. As a result, the team left the meeting excited about the upcoming school year.

A Less Effective Example

Katrina Montoya was frustrated. She was a member of her school's improvement team and saw what she believed to be signs that something was lacking in teachers' professional learning for improving literacy instruction. The state had chosen a mandatory thirty-hour online program for teachers and also developed a two-day professional learning program for academic coaches in regional education agencies.

Six months into the initiative, the academic coaches in the school were complaining that the professional learning was ineffective. They did not see teachers consistently and effectively using the practices that they had been taught online and assessed to verify their learning. They requested additional professional learning to support the teachers. The leadership team asked the school-improvement team to review the request and recommend what should be done next. The team members could see what they thought were necessary changes. However, they were not sure how to determine the best approaches.

Idea Hub: Reflection

Reflect individually on what you learned in this chapter, and record your thoughts. Then use your individual reflections to collaboratively answer the following questions with your team.

» What did Fields do that aligns with the guidance in this chapter?

» How did the process in Montoya's state misalign with the guidance in this chapter?

» What are your and your team's biggest takeaways?

» How will you embrace the work of chapter 7?

» Who will you engage in the work of chapter 7?

Conclusion

This chapter discussed the importance of ensuring improvement and transformation continue during ongoing school change. It focused on developing the people who do the work and helping them be continuous learners. School-improvement teams must be able to assess professional learning to ensure educators' valuable time is not wasted. Time is wasted if professional learning does not result in successful application of learning. It is up to your team to advocate for the best professional learning and support that can improve staff's capacity to achieve at their highest level.

Chapter 8 focuses on developing organizational sensitivity, which includes monitoring people and processes. Those trained and certified as school-improvement facilitators often point to this concept as most important to support success. Organizational sensitivity is critical when you are supporting others to collaboratively set and meet shared goals for improvement and innovation.

Before moving on to chapter 8, complete the "Standard 7: Do and Avoid Chart" and "Standard 7: Plan-Ahead Chart" reproducibles (pages 148 and 149) with your team to reflect on and process the work you accomplished for standard 7 and plan ahead for next steps.

Standard 7: Do and Avoid Chart

As you move through the standards for improvement, you will find things to do and things to avoid. After reading the effective and less effective practice examples and reflecting on them and the work of standard 7, complete the following do and avoid chart to help you record your thoughts about the work of this standard.

Instructions: Record what you plan to do and avoid. Consider the following questions.

1. How will you introduce your team to the processes introduced in this chapter?
2. How will you facilitate your team to use the SEDA model (see pages 137–138)?
3. How will your team determine whether professional learning or other ways of building capacity are needed?
4. How will your team assess the quality of coaching for capacity building?
5. How will your team evaluate professional learning and the facilitation of transfer to practice?
6. How will your team provide opportunities for reflection?

Do	Avoid

Standard 7: Plan-Ahead Chart

To get a clearer perspective on the next steps, consider your do and avoid chart as you complete the following plan-ahead chart. The work of standard 7 prepares you to be the ambassador for developing and supporting educators. This requires you to be knowledgeable and engaged in assessing current efforts and results and in recommending effective practices, processes, tools, and models for building educator capacity.

Instructions: Use the information from chapter 7 to identify your and your team's next steps to complete each action.

Actions	Person or People Responsible	Due Date
Use the guidelines for adult learning and transfer (see pages 136–137) to ensure adults learn and effectively apply their learning.		
Use the SEDA model (see pages 137–138) to build capacity for reflective practice and adaptive decision making.		
Review the essential elements of good coaching (see page 141) to ensure high-quality coaching of teachers.		
Complete the induction worksheet (see figure 7.1, page 142) to ensure educators have the support and clarity they need to succeed in their new positions.		
Evaluate educator development and support to ensure it actually improves both teaching practices and student learning outcomes. Use the three categories of questions on page 143 to guide your evaluation.		
Use the ten reflective questions on page 144 to reflect on professional learning and practices to improve educator development.		

Chapter 8

Standard 8: Demonstrate Organizational Sensitivity

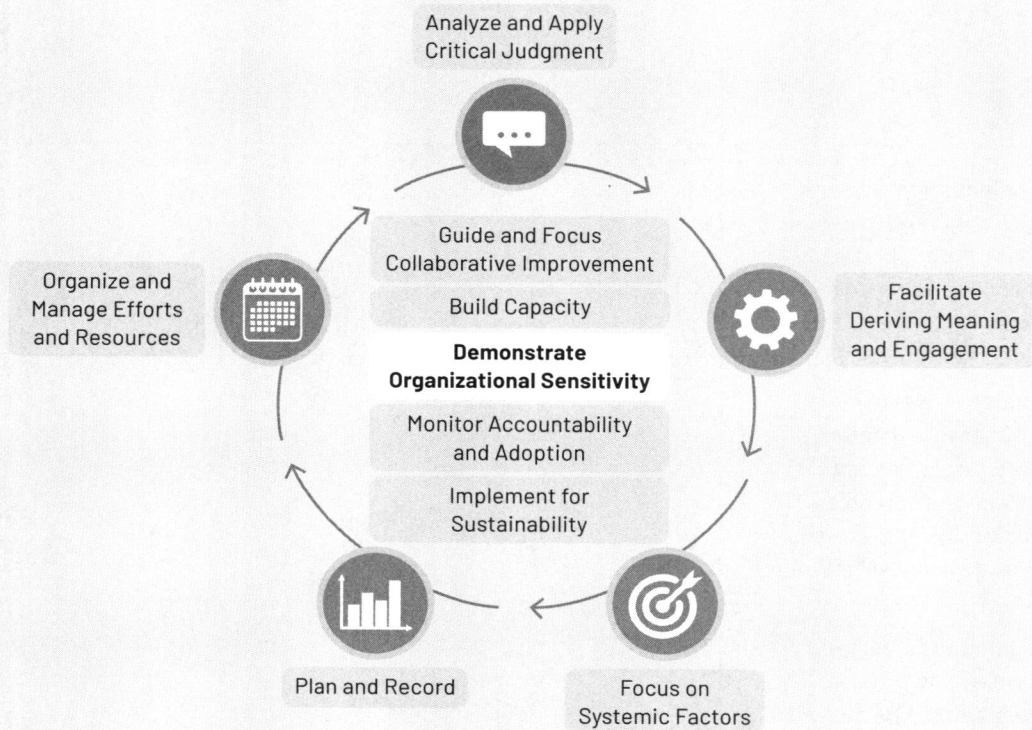

Analyze and Apply
Critical Judgment

Guide and Focus
Collaborative Improvement

Build Capacity

**Demonstrate
Organizational Sensitivity**

Monitor Accountability
and Adoption

Implement for
Sustainability

Organize and
Manage Efforts
and Resources

Facilitate
Deriving Meaning
and Engagement

Plan and Record

Focus on
Systemic Factors

*S*tandard 8 is about paying attention to *people* while you execute the performance-improvement *processes*. It emphasizes being aware of people's needs and valuing their points of view by recognizing, respecting, and leveraging each person's unique background, perspective, and skill. This enhances collaboration, creativity, and overall team performance. It also increases the likelihood that people will stay engaged and honor their commitments.

By now, if you have been applying the processes and tools in this book, you and your team are well on your way to collaboratively addressing your big rocks. You may have whittled down the original challenge or opportunity to a smaller focus or morphed or changed it as you have worked together. The required work of standard 8 focuses on your processes as well as the people collaborating to achieve your shared goals. If things have gone as they normally do, not everything has been easy or without conflicts or challenges. This focus on demonstrating organizational sensitivity will help you navigate those challenges while developing shared understandings with respect for the diverse perspectives and experiences of those you are guiding and influencing to support your efforts.

The work of standard 8 must be demonstrated every day; it is crucial to all improvement work. If you want to achieve success, you must monitor the people as well as the processes. By fostering a culture of sensitivity to people and processes, organizations can drive continuous improvement, sustain innovation, and achieve effective implementation. This creates long-term value for all stakeholders.

This chapter describes how school-improvement teams can model and cultivate others' abilities to thrive even amid challenges and change. It establishes a clear definition of culture and shares practical ways to maintain, build, or advocate for a positive culture. It also discusses how to create the conditions for successful collaboration and the role that communication plays in successful improvement efforts. Finally, this chapter concludes with ways to promote a healthy work-life balance and how to conduct a culture audit to ensure your school culture is positive and supportive of improvement efforts.

Facilitating Organizational Sensitivity

School improvement, innovation, and effective implementation of change depend on the people who do the work. People are more likely to embrace change when their concerns are acknowledged and addressed. Being attentive to people and nurturing the school's culture throughout the collaborative improvement process are critical. A positive culture is also a key factor in attracting and maintaining quality workers. Sensitivity to people's physical, emotional, and professional needs reduces burnout and improves productivity. It also allows the people who do the work to focus on improving the processes required for successful school improvement. When people feel valued and heard, they are more likely to share innovative ideas (Ghani, Hyder, Yoo, & Han, 2023).

School-improvement teams' ability to be sensitive to the needs of those affected by proposed changes impacts their ability to gain and maintain support. Attention to people is key. Facilitators cannot turn a blind eye toward the feelings and opinions of the people whose commitment to the work is essential. A pervasive mindset of "collaboration is the way we get things done around here" enables continuous improvement and supports the implementation of innovative solutions.

Organizational sensitivity follows two parallel processes, and school-improvement teams have more success when they use both. One is "keeping an eye on processes," such as performance analysis, causal analysis, and intervention selection, implementation, and evaluation. The other is "keeping an eye on people" by developing, nurturing, and supporting those who do the work of the school. This organizational sensitivity requires a culture that includes exercising hope and resilience, creating the conditions for successful collaboration, and focusing on communication-informed decision making and a healthy work-life balance.

Focusing on School Culture

The culture of a school is the glue that holds it together and the compass that provides direction. *Culture* refers to the collective beliefs, values, customs, traditions, languages, and norms that characterize a school or group (Cordeiro, 2021). It is the way individuals within the school interact and communicate. It is broad, long term, and deeply rooted and offers uniqueness to the organization. Organizational culture is the personality of a school that guides how employees think and act on the job (Azorín & Fullan, 2022). It is the way they learn and make meaning of their experiences within the school or system. Culture is an essential element that influences the performance of a school, including its stability, cohesion, unity, and adoption of reforms (Kythreotis, Pashiardis, & Kyriakides, 2010). When you conducted a factors analysis, you likely identified the school culture as a significant workplace factor.

A culture of support facilitates teacher confidence and motivation. Recognizing and appreciating diverse backgrounds, perspectives, and identities among students, teachers, administrators, and other stakeholders facilitates collaborative practices and strategies, and these strategies help establish a positive culture that enables collaboration and a growth mindset. School-improvement teams have a role in facilitating and promoting a positive culture because the school culture impacts performance.

A school's culture is not built overnight—it is shaped through intentional actions and collaborative efforts. Schools can cultivate cultures where student and staff performance thrives. Practicing hope and resilience and having a growth mindset are intentional actions that contribute to a positive school culture.

Hope

Michael Duncan, who wrote this book's foreword, points to hope and resilience as critical behaviors in building a positive school culture that facilitates success. Psychologist C. R. Snyder (2002) defines *hope* as "the perceived capability to derive pathways to desired goals, and motivate oneself via agency thinking" (p. 249). In *The Oxford Handbook of Hope*, Matthew W. Gallagher (2018) defines *hope* as goals, pathways, and agency. Hope often involves thinking flexibly to envision solutions to problems and remaining open to continuous learning. It aligns with maintaining a positive mindset even when facing difficulties.

Global analytics and advisory firm Gallup has done extensive research on hope and its impact on student success. Gallup has found that by creating a school culture driven by student engagement and hope, schools can provide a positive atmosphere that encourages involvement in and enthusiasm for school, while promoting students' ideas and energy for the future. As a result of increasing student engagement and hope, schools can decrease negative student behavior outcomes such as chronic absenteeism and suspensions (Gallup, 2019a). You can learn more about engagement and hope and their impact on student success via the Gallup (2019b) Student Poll analysis.

Resilience

Resilience is the ability to bounce back from setbacks, adapt, and keep going in the face of adversity (American Psychological Association, n.d.). Habits of mind, such as persistence, thoughtful listening, and impulse management, directly contribute to resilience (Costa & Kallick, 2008).

School leaders and school-improvement teams can embrace habits of mind by modeling and cultivating positive dispositions during collaborative planning and decision making. By approaching challenges with curiosity, flexibility, and a commitment to continuous learning, you can create a culture in which inquiry and reflection drive improvement. Practicing these habits in interactions with others fosters psychological safety, strengthens relationships, and encourages deeper, more respectful engagement across the school community.

Growth Mindset

Developing a growth mindset is a cornerstone for building resilience and fostering hope. *Growth mindset* is the belief that people can enhance their abilities and intelligence through effort, effective strategies, and input from others. This concept, developed by psychologist Carol S. Dweck (2006), emphasizes learning and persistence over innate talent. School leaders and school-improvement teams can embrace and model growth mindsets by creating a culture where effort, reflection, and continuous improvement are valued over perfection. This involves celebrating progress, encouraging people to take risks and learn from failure, and providing constructive feedback that focuses on strategies and processes rather than fixed traits.

By embedding growth mindset language into coaching, goal setting, and professional learning, leaders reinforce the belief that all educators and students can grow through deliberate practice and support. This mindset lays a strong foundation for resilience—helping teams of educators and stakeholders adapt in the face of challenges—and fosters hope by reinforcing that future success is achievable with sustained effort and collaboration. Helping collaborators focus on the things over which they have influence is also part of a growth mindset. This can propel people to work together in a cycle of continuous improvement. Then they continuously imagine and seek innovative solutions to any challenge they encounter.

Given the many changes, challenges, and complexities of education, the behaviors associated with hope and resilience are foundational for the success of educators, students, and communities. The tool in figure 8.1 can help you set a baseline for your behaviors, determine how you could be more aware of the positive behaviors, and decide how you will guide others to adopt and demonstrate these behaviors for mutual benefit as you focus on your big rock.

Instructions: Rate each behavior on a scale of 1–4 according to its current level of performance.

1 = Not yet
2 = Developing
3 = Performing
4 = Modeling effectiveness

Use your ratings to celebrate your behaviors and identify how to adopt better ones.

Rating	Behaviors
	Setting aspirational goals: Consistently setting and communicating ambitious, clear, and achievable goals for students and staff
	Focusing on long-term outcomes: Committing to the larger vision of student success and deeper learning even during setbacks
	Celebrating progress: Acknowledging small wins and milestones to motivate staff and students and build momentum
	Highlighting strengths: Emphasizing what is working well as a foundation for further growth

	Collaborating and teaming: Encouraging strong partnerships among educators, students, families, and the wider community
	Building trust and empathy: Creating a culture where students and staff understand one another and can rely on each other
	Demonstrating calm and constructive behavior: Managing stress visibly and showing how to manage challenges without giving up
	Promoting self-care: Fostering practices that help maintain physical and mental health
	Proactively identifying challenges: Addressing obstacles early and focusing on solutions rather than dwelling on setbacks
	Using data-informed decision making: Using data as a tool for growth and continuous improvement rather than as a measure of failure
	Sustaining effort over time: Maintaining dedication to school-improvement goals despite difficulties or slow progress
	Encouraging a "learn and try again" mentality: Cultivating an environment where mistakes are seen as learning opportunities rather than failures
	Believing in potential: Trusting in the ability of students, staff, and the school community to grow and achieve deep learning
	Inspiring hope: Nurturing a hopeful perspective by communicating confidence in the school's path and the capacities of all involved
	Reflecting regularly on practices: Evaluating what works and what needs to change to foster an adaptive and evolving school culture
	Encouraging lifelong learning: Supporting ongoing professional learning for all to promote resilience and adaptability

Success Tool Notes:

FIGURE 8.1: Success tool—Hope and resilience assessment.

Visit **go.SolutionTree.com/schoolimprovement** *for a free reproducible version of this figure.*

Idea Hub: Hope and Resilience

Reflect on your ratings in the hope and resilience assessment in figure 8.1 to determine how well your behaviors are reinforcing a culture of hope and resilience and creating an environment where adults and students can flourish. What do you need to do or change?

In addition to fostering hope and resilience through embracing habits of mind and establishing a growth mindset, collaboration is the engine that drives a positive school culture. Without collaboration, efforts to improve the climate, relationships, and performance will be fragmented and unsustainable.

Creating the Conditions for Successful Collaboration

Collaboration is a source of fresh ideas that lead to innovation and improvement. Effective collaboration leverages diverse perspectives and skills to tackle complex problems. When teams understand the conditions that allow people to feel safe sharing creative ideas, they can focus on collective problem solving rather than individual conflicts or confusion.

Your work in chapter 2 to establish team norms focused on creating shared norms to build trust, promote accountability, and form a collaborative culture focused on achieving common goals. The research that led to the development of standard 8 revealed the need to pay attention to broader social norms when guiding school improvement. *Social norms* are shared standards of acceptable group behavior. They support respectful, inclusive collaboration with all stakeholders by honoring community values and unspoken expectations. Social norms are powerful drivers of human behavior. Sensitivity to interpersonal dynamics enhances teamwork, creating a fertile ground for innovative solutions. Norms "prescribe how to make decisions in social situations," and they "play a crucial role in sustaining cooperative relationships and coordinating collective action" (Gross & Vostroknutov, 2022, p. 1). Social norms can be informal understandings that govern the behaviors of a group as well as formal rules or policies.

Having awareness of social norms may be difficult for a school-improvement team member who is asked to work on an improvement initiative with a different department or grade level. They may lack familiarity with the assigned grade level or department's norms. If you are assigned to facilitate a new group, take time to observe the established social norms. Have conversations with people who know the social norms of the group before beginning work. This can reduce the chances you will accidentally create barriers that could be difficult to overcome. The beginning of collaborative and productive work will be delayed if barriers are created.

💡 **Idea Hub:** Successful Collaboration

Ask yourself the following questions, and then discuss them with your team.

- » What conditions currently support successful collaboration in your team?
- » How can you nurture these conditions?
- » How do you currently cocreate with stakeholders?
- » What development and support do you and other stakeholders need to do this well?

Improvement facilitators must recognize the diversity of backgrounds and perspectives among students, teachers, administrators, and other stakeholders, and they should consider that diversity in collaborative practices and strategies to promote a positive culture and achieve improvement goals. Demonstrating sensitivity in building, maintaining, and working through social norms also requires navigating bias and cultivating empathy.

Navigating Bias and Cultivating Empathy

Demonstrating empathy and cultural competence requires understanding and valuing diverse perspectives. Actively listen to the unique experiences of teachers, students, and families, and acknowledge their voices. It is more difficult to reflect on your own behavior, as it can surface your implicit biases. *Implicit biases* refers to "the attitudes or stereotypes that unconsciously affect our understanding, actions, and decisions" (Travers, 2024). These biases often operate without our awareness, shaping how we perceive and interact with people based on factors like race, gender, age, or other characteristics. Unlike *explicit biases*, which are deliberate and conscious, implicit biases can influence behavior even when individuals believe they are impartial. Everyone has their own mental model about how things work. It is easy to forget that not everyone has the same understanding or mental model.

Encourage team members to examine their mental models to foster an environment of mutual respect. They may view the big rock from varying perspectives based on their mental models, and these points of view provide an opportunity to focus systemically. In *Beyond Implicit and Explicit Bias*, ClauDean ChiNaka Kizart (2025) examines how specific unconscious biases—such as anchoring, herd mentality, intergroup biases, decision fatigue, scarcity mindset, and the Dunning–Kruger effect—shape decisions and behaviors in educational settings. For example, the Dunning–Kruger effect is a cognitive bias in which people with low ability or knowledge in a particular area overestimate their competence, while those with high ability may underestimate their relative expertise. Using Kizart's self-assessment tools, real-world school scenarios, reflective questions, and reproducible resources can help staff recognize and manage their own biases and implement improvement strategies to avoid them. As you practice fostering inclusive dialogue, you can engage stakeholders, teachers, students, parents, and other relevant parties in key decisions, ensuring their input is both heard and incorporated.

Just as you assess the effectiveness of teacher development to improve instructional practices and student outcomes, you must also evaluate your own empathy and cultural competence. Professional growth requires honest self-reflection about how our perspectives and biases influence our interactions with all stakeholders. When educators examine both their explicit *and* implicit biases, they can implement meaningful improvements in practice.

Ensuring Psychological Safety

Psychological safety is the invisible foundation of a school where people feel connected, motivated, and ready to grow. Without it, even the best strategies and programs cannot thrive. As a guide and practitioner of collaborative improvement, you must consider how you ensure psychological safety. In *The Culture Code: The Secrets of Highly Successful Groups*, Daniel Coyle (2018) speaks about safety, vulnerability, and purpose as three vital ingredients of organizational culture. To ensure a sense of psychological safety, you can advocate for and support shared work and create consistent routines and structures like collaborative planning sessions, peer observations, and inquiry cycles. You can also use platforms and processes that support teamwork, such as shared workspaces and cocreation software.

Ensuring psychological safety allows educators and students to take calculated risks without fear of retribution, and to turn failures into learning opportunities. When you share and encourage others to safely share challenges and learning experiences, you can foster an environment where others feel comfortable doing the same. Sharing without fear of criticism or judgment builds relationships and trust. It can even lead to innovative solutions. Consider starting meetings or projects with relationship-strengthening exercises that deepen connections, such as one-word check-ins (each member shares a word that reflects how they're feeling), strength spotlights (team members highlight a peer's recent contribution), or purpose postcards (members write and share a short note on why their work matters). These simple yet intentional practices help build trust, recognize and appreciate each team member's unique strengths and efforts, and reinforce the team's shared purpose.

Michael Duncan recommends using a predictive behavioral analytics instrument called a *culture index* to "determine the hardwired traits members bring to the team. This helps to align their traits to their collaborative work and helps leaders reinforce positive traits" (M. Duncan, personal communication, November 23, 2024). School-improvement teams interested in leveraging a culture index can access it directly through Culture Index (www.cultureindex.com), the firm that developed and supports the instrument.

Fostering psychological safety, the belief that it is safe to speak up, take risks, and express ideas without fear of ridicule or retribution, is essential for effective collaboration. Rather than expecting collaboration to evolve organically, provide training in collaborative practices and tools that build trust and mutual respect—key foundations of a strong culture. When there is trust and respect, individuals are more willing to share ideas and support each other. In times of difficulty or change—such as policy shifts or budget constraints—trust between stakeholders ensures the school community can come together and navigate challenges more effectively.

Observing how group members interact allows facilitators to plan ways to engage everyone. You may use the tool in figure 8.2 for gathering data about group interactions, which can provide insights into the level of trust between group members.

Instructions: Follow these steps to understand whom the group considers trustworthy.

1. Plan.
   + Decide what you want to learn. For example, do you want to identify potential leaders and experts or understand how group members relate to each other?
   + Develop two or three questions asking group members whom they can depend on—for example, "Who do you go to when you feel you are out of your depth?" and "Who can you count on to know what is really going on?"
2. Ask each group member the questions. Let people know that their responses will be confidential.
3. Compile the responses on a chart. For each question, place the names of the group members you questioned in column 1 and the names of the people they chose in column 2.
4. Tally the number of times each person's name appears in column 2, and put the total in column 3.
5. Review the chart and note the following.
   + Those who were chosen most often
   + Those who were never chosen
   + Pairs who chose each other
   + Those in pairs or small groups who were not chosen by anyone outside their pair or small group (they appear separate from the larger group)

6. Note the number of individuals who exchange information (they chose each other) and the number of individuals who just give or receive information (the choosing was not reciprocal).

7. Formulate hypotheses as to why the pattern is as it seems.

8. Consider other data or pursue other data-collection methods to confirm or disprove your hypotheses.

Question 1:

Group Members	Who They Chose	Times Chosen	Comments

Question 2:

Group Members	Who They Chose	Times Chosen	Comments

FIGURE 8.2: Success tool—Trust meter chart.

*Visit **go.SolutionTree.com/schoolimprovement** for a free reproducible version of this figure.*

The ability to communicate effectively is foundational to the previous notions of creating the conditions for successful collaboration and cultivating a positive, psychologically safe environment where empathy is regularly exercised and biases are gently challenged and changed.

Focusing on Communication

Communication is essential in building a positive school culture because it shapes how people connect, collaborate, and make meaning together. In schools, strong communication is the glue that binds relationships and aligns actions that facilitate school improvement. Open and transparent communication is necessary to engage others and grow together. To encourage authentic dialogue, you must create spaces for honest conversations where all team members feel safe to express ideas, concerns, and feedback. This requires clarifying your purpose and goals and regularly communicating your vision and objectives so they align with the shared values of the school community. Consider whether those who impact the big rock, or a portion of it, can relay the purpose and goals of their participation and why it makes a positive difference.

Listening more than speaking demonstrates respect for others' ideas. Asking guiding questions can engage groups in deeper thinking about how to develop and implement solutions. Be aware that there may be an unexpressed intent behind a message being shared. It is important to listen and interpret what messages might lie beyond the spoken words. People may withhold information because they feel it will not be taken seriously. They watch how you and your team react to what they and others say. They are looking for consistency in behavior. They hope the message beyond their words will be heard, understood, and valued.

Encourage others to use the tools featured throughout this book to foster active listening, facilitation, and consensus building. As noted in chapter 7, create opportunities for your team members to pause, reflect, and talk openly about the quality of their collaborative efforts and how they might improve. Gather continuous feedback using surveys, focus groups, interviews, and informal check-ins to understand the team's dynamics and ensure everyone feels heard and valued. Be flexible in revising plans based on new insights and changing circumstances within the school and community. This reinforces that you are responsive, inclusive, and committed to creating a psychologically safe environment where everyone can contribute.

You can solicit the opinions of group members through techniques such as empathy interviews or the nominal group technique described in chapter 2 (see figure 2.10, page 53). These techniques allow people who are uncomfortable sharing in front of a group to express their thoughts. In addition, they allow you to confirm your understanding of the information being shared. Being sensitive to both differences and consensus facilitates success. Adopt protocols for communicating with team members and for setting norms for meetings.

Seamless communication between stakeholders promotes transparency and more transparent processes for schools to enhance teachers' job performance (Elegbeleye, 2005). Effective and efficient communication requires knowing how to pass relevant information on to all contacts who have a stake in the work. It also requires knowing how to receive and act on that input. This does not mean agreeing with all input or always acting on it. It means acknowledging that input has been received and valuing it as an important part of the decision-making process.

Finally, change is a process, and your team's knowledge of the change process is important to facilitate open and honest communication. Sensitivity to the impact of change ensures employees remain motivated throughout the improvement and implementation process of your current big rock and others in the future. Team members must continuously model and communicate the work of improvement and engage people in the decisions that lead to change. They must communicate the message of cohesiveness and support for all stake-holders as they guide the work of improvement and move through the change process. This means being sensitive to people's implicit and explicit biases and their ability to accept change. To help implementation go smoothly, model open, empathetic communication regarding staff emotions during the change process to build collaborative relationships. This also helps foster a risk-free environment where innovation can thrive.

Idea Hub: Communication Improvement

Ask yourself the following questions, and then discuss them with your team.

» What are your current modes of communication with different stakeholder groups?

» In what ways do these modes encourage two-way communication and feedback?

» How might your team improve communication within the team, across the school, and with external stakeholders?

» How does your current communication approach foster trust, inclusiveness, and shared understanding?

» How would you describe the current level of trust between those facilitating school improvement and those implementing it?

» What actions could you take to strengthen that trust?

Communication is key to decisions and actions in the work of school improvement because it forms the bridge between planning and implementation. Without clear, transparent, and inclusive communication, even the best decisions and actions can fail to gain traction or lead to sustainable change.

Exploring Decisions and Actions

Decisions and actions influence an organization's culture (Tharp, 2009). Decisions can have positive or negative consequences. Those consequences can advance the work or contribute to its failure, and they can result in positive or negative morale. A simple *if-then* consequences chart, shown in figure 8.3 (page 162), can help your team operate more proactively by considering and being sensitive to the consequences of a decision. This is

**Success
Tool Notes:**

_____

_____

_____

_____

_____

_____

_____

_____

_____

_____

_____

_____

_____

_____

_____

_____

_____

_____

_____

_____

_____

_____

similar to the decision tree process, which outlines a decision's potential pros and cons. With either of these tools, your team or facilitator can explore the positive, negative, and possible unintended consequences that may occur. Exploring positive and negative consequences before implementing a change can reduce the chances of failure and prevent unintended consequences. You can use the consequences as a resource for making future decisions or for rethinking past decisions. Try this out for your big rock.

Instructions:

1. State the decision you are considering in the first column.

2. State the intended results of the decision in the second column.

3. List the possible consequences of the decision in the third column, thinking about the whole organization and its interdependent working parts.

4. Label each consequence as *positive* (+), *negative* (–), or *possible unintended* (U).

Decision	Intended Results If the decision is made, then . . .	Possible Consequences

FIGURE 8.3: Success tool—*If-then* consequences chart.

*Visit **go.SolutionTree.com/schoolimprovement** for a free reproducible version of this figure.*

After completing this chart, reflect on the results by answering these questions.

- Are there more positive than negative consequences?

- How could the possible unintended consequences that we have identified impact the performance of various parts of the organization?

- Are we confident that the decision will contribute to performance success and goal achievement while benefiting the whole school?

Your team can regularly conduct "premortems" by holding meetings or discussions before taking actions to identify risks and potential problems. You can conduct postmortems, or what the U.S. military terms *after-action reviews*, by holding meetings to determine which projects or collaborative efforts went well, which did not, and where there are areas for improvement in the future (U.S. Department of the Army, 1993). These practices also help you keep consequences in mind, support better outcomes, and celebrate what is working.

Promoting a Work-Life Balance

The decisions leaders make directly shape the conditions in which educators work—and ultimately, how sustainable and healthy those conditions are. Decisions that support a work-life balance are not just about wellness; these strategic choices strengthen school culture, staff performance, and long-term school improvement.

School-improvement teams should promote a workplace that is sensitive to staff needs. This type of workplace makes gaining and sustaining commitment and engagement more likely. The retention rate of employees increases when employees are happy at work and feel involved in goal setting and planning (Toropova, Myrberg, & Johansson, 2021).

The concept of work-life balance has existed for quite a while, but the women's liberation movement of the 1980s is credited with bringing it back to prominence in American culture (Raja & Stein, 2014). After the COVID-19 pandemic, the parameters and definition of work-life balance have continued to shift. For example, many educators now expect greater flexibility in when and where they work, such as opportunities for hybrid professional learning or designated planning time from home, recognizing that balance is not just about hours worked but about autonomy, well-being, and sustainability. People value their careers but also treasure time with family and friends outside the workplace.

Making mental health and wellness a priority in the workplace is becoming even more critical (Peart, 2020). Employees are juggling complicated home lives. They may face challenges with children, aging parents, mental or physical abuse, drug addiction, divorce, illnesses, disabilities, and other life stressors. The pressure of juggling a fragmented life while being asked to do more at work can be a significant source of stress. School-improvement teams can help facilitate balancing work and personal time. Psychologist and career consultant Natalia Peart (2020) suggests five ways to improve work-life balance to ease employee stress.

1. **Build a culture of care:** Building a culture of care means promoting a culture where employees feel supported and respected. A high degree of empathy, trust, respect, fairness, compassion, and objectivity in how people are treated results in better performance. Peart (2020) calls it a "psychological contract." Again, consistency in facilitator and team behavior is powerful in demonstrating fairness and objectivity. Distributing small tokens of appreciation, writing personal notes that express appreciation to peers, and simply asking about family members demonstrate that you care about others.

2. **Build a culture of flexibility:** Building a culture of flexibility can be difficult in education when school hours are established. Formal teaching and learning must occur within those set hours. However, there are things for which a school-improvement team can advocate that allow teachers flexibility. For example, teams can advocate to let teachers select the times for before- and

after-school student supervision. Teachers who cannot be at school early for personal reasons can select after-school student supervision assignments. Adjusting after-work meeting times to accommodate the life needs of team members is another way to demonstrate understanding of personal life needs.

3. **Build a culture of trust:** Gaining trust was discussed earlier in this chapter. Keep in mind that ambiguity causes stress. Consistent communication demonstrates transparency and builds a culture of trust. Simply encouraging open and honest communication in a risk-free environment demonstrates an appreciation of all ideas.

4. **Build a culture of health:** A culture of health sets boundaries between work and home hours. It makes mental and physical health a priority. Providing frequent breaks and having healthy snacks in meetings are simple ways to demonstrate sensitivity to people's health needs. Advocating for on-site fitness facilities to be accessible before and after school relieves the need for personal financial investments in health and wellness facilities. Staff incentives for healthy-habit initiatives are fun ways to make health and wellness a priority. Be aware if colleagues and staff are spending excessive hours at work after school and on weekends, and encourage them to honor work and home boundaries.

5. **Build a culture of recognition:** A culture of recognition means that employees are recognized publicly for their contributions and achievements. An improvement team can plan celebrations of success as progress milestones are achieved. Group recognition for quality work or progress toward goals is important. However, individual recognition can also engender more positive feelings. This recognition helps everyone feel valued. It increases connections and a sense of belonging and contributes to the momentum of the work. Building on success enables the organization to look to the future. When people see that their efforts are valued, they are happier and more satisfied in the workplace, and employee retention increases (Toropova et al., 2021).

When employees' contributions and what they receive in return are balanced, performance is more likely to improve. Consider how the work of your big rock is tapping into the power of recognition and celebrations of progress.

Idea Hub: Work-Life Balance

Ask yourself the following questions, and then discuss them with your team.

» What are some ways your school supports a work-life balance?

» How can your team advocate for a work-life balance?

» When the school asks teams to implement a new program or initiative, what do they remove to make time and space for the new idea?

» If this advocacy for work-life balance does not happen, how might this become a common practice moving forward?

Success with school-improvement efforts depends, in part, on the culture of your school. It is important to assess your school culture to get a clear picture of the current reality. A culture audit is one way to identify strengths to celebrate and challenges to address. Data about school culture helps guide decision making and ensures efforts are targeted and relevant rather than based on assumptions. Then, you can create and foster an environment where everyone feels valued and can thrive.

Conducting a Culture Audit

Culture audits can provide valuable information to a school-improvement team. A culture audit comprehensively evaluates an organization's values, beliefs, behaviors, and practices to help people understand the current workplace culture. It identifies things in the culture that facilitators and improvement teams need to be aware of and sensitive to. Assessing culture allows schools to identify disparities in how different groups experience the environment.

You may conduct a culture audit internally or use an outside entity. You can use the culture audit in figure 8.4 to assess the current state of your school's culture, identify strengths and areas for growth, and develop actionable strategies for creating an environment that fosters collaborative improvement, innovation, and implementation for your big rock efforts.

Instructions: Use this tool to gather responses from staff, students, and parents. Review the results collectively, identify common themes, and develop an action plan to strengthen the school's culture.

Section 1: Core Values and Vision

1. **Alignment:** Are the school's stated values and vision clearly articulated, understood, and consistently reflected in daily practices?

2. **Shared understanding:** Do staff, students, and families have a shared understanding of the school's core values and vision?

3. **Focus:** Is shared understanding planned for, modeled, monitored, confronted, and celebrated (DuFour et al., 2024)?

4. **Anti-values:** Are attitudes, behaviors, and practices that undermine a thriving learning environment identified and systemically addressed while positive values are reinforced?

FIGURE 8.4: Success tool—Culture audit.

continued ▶

Success Tool Notes:

Section 2: Communication and Collaboration

1. **Openness:** Is communication among staff open, transparent, and constructive?

2. **Inclusivity:** Are all staff members, including teachers, support staff, and administration, involved in decision-making processes?

3. **Collaborative practices:** Does the school have structures (such as team meetings, collaborative planning, and a guiding coalition) that effectively support collaboration?

Section 3: Trust and Relationships

1. **Trust among staff:** Is there a culture of trust and respect among staff members?

2. **Student-teacher relationships:** Do students feel that teachers are approachable and supportive?

3. **Family and community engagement:** Are families and the community meaningfully engaged in the school's activities and culture?

Section 4: Professional Learning and Growth

1. **Continuous learning:** Are staff provided with opportunities for ongoing professional learning that align with the school's goals and their professional goals?

2. **Reflection practices:** Are reflective practices, such as peer observations and feedback sessions, part of the school's culture?

Section 5: Supportive Environment

1. **Psychological safety:** Do staff and students feel safe expressing ideas and taking risks without fear of judgment or negative consequences?

2. **Support systems:** Are support systems (such as mentorship, coaching, and mental health resources) in place for staff and students?

Section 6: Belonging and Excellence

1. **Representation:** Do the school's leadership and staff reflect the diversity of the student population?

2. **Equitable practices:** Are policies and practices in place to ensure all students have access to the same opportunities for learning and growth?

Section 7: Action Plan Development

1. **Identification of priorities:** What are the key areas identified as strengths?

2. **Areas for improvement:** What are the main areas requiring targeted actions?

3. **Next steps:** What immediate actions will the team take to address identified areas for growth?

Success Tool Notes:

Visit go.SolutionTree.com/schoolimprovement for a free reproducible version of this figure.

After completing the culture audit, school leaders and the school-improvement team should transition from data collection to intentional, collaborative action. First, review the audit responses from staff, students, and families to identify patterns, shared strengths, and pressing areas for growth. Analyze this data collectively in a debrief session with a representative team to ensure transparency and inclusive interpretation of results. Discuss how improvements can be planned for, modeled, monitored, confronted, and celebrated, as Richard DuFour and colleagues (2024) suggest.

Based on your findings, develop a focused culture action plan that outlines two or three priority areas, specific goals, timelines, and responsibilities, aligning them with the school's broader improvement efforts. Communicate a summary of the audit findings and planned actions to the broader school community to reinforce trust and collective ownership. Integrate the plan into existing structures such as collaborative department or grade-level teams, school-improvement plans, and staff development efforts, ensuring regular check-ins to assess progress and adjust strategies as needed. Finally, recognize and celebrate early wins and positive shifts in school culture to build momentum, reinforce shared values, and cultivate a climate where all stakeholders feel safe, valued, and engaged.

Idea Hub: Evaluation of Your Culture

Ask yourself the following questions, and then discuss them with your team.

» How would you describe the culture of your school through the lens of the culture audit (see figure 8.4, page 165)?

» If you had to illustrate your school culture visually, what would that image include and why?

» How might someone outside your team—such as a parent, student, or new staff member—describe your school culture based on their experience?

» Considering both the strengths and areas for growth you identified, how intentionally do you and your team reflect on the perspectives of others, as illustrated in the *if-then* consequences chart (see figure 8.3, page 162)?

Reviewing Examples of Standard 8

To help you use what you have learned in chapter 8, we have included an example of an effective practice and an example of a less effective practice. Comparing these examples will help you determine what to do and what to avoid when applying the work of standard 8.

An Effective Example

The new school-improvement team at Ryder Middle School had a big task ahead for the new school year. The school, which was in a low-income neighborhood in a small rural community, had not met expectations for mathematics achievement based on state achievement test scores. In the past, its state scores always met or exceeded expectations. The school's past achievement levels had resulted from years of hard work and dedication to the students and families in the community. This year's mathematics scores were going to disappoint the staff, who took great pride in their accomplishments over the last five years.

The newly assigned principal, Kenneth Jones, asked a veteran team member, Courtney Kendall, to facilitate the school-improvement team in communicating this new mathematics data to the rest of the school. Kendall knew that the way the lower mathematics achievement was presented would be critical because it could discourage teachers. The members of the school-improvement team had to be sensitive to people's needs as they proceeded with the work. They had always had a positive school culture, but this news could have an impact on that. Kendall and the school-improvement team decided to leverage their established culture of hope and resilience to address the low performance in mathematics.

Kendall guided the team members to consider capitalizing on the school's reading achievement strengths to address mathematics deficiencies as they embarked on analysis and planning. They formed small groups to present the data, begin the analysis, and gather input, involving all staff across departments in completing these processes and in finding the best suite of solutions.

The school-improvement team members knew that changes had to be made, and Kendall knew that they had to work as a team to build awareness of the change process and how some needed changes would impact their fellow teachers. She told them they should be sensitive to the impact of change to ensure the teachers remained motivated and resilient. After approval from the principal, she invited a regional consultant to talk to the team about the change process, how to be more aware of how teachers were navigating it, and ways to recognize their progress and efforts.

During this meeting, one team member pointed out the need to earn trust and respect by being open and honest about the data and areas of weak performance, while maintaining the staff's hope and resilience to face this challenge. Team members decided they had to capitalize on the relationships they had with the guiding coalition in their school to keep lines of communication open. They also had to use the expertise within their school, in the system, and in the region to provide the training needed to build the capacity of their staff.

Another team member suggested that it might be time to focus more on creating the conditions for successful collaboration. Even more collaboration was needed, as the school was facing lower mathematics scores for the first time in many years. They knew people and processes had to be aligned for success. Principal Jones agreed to set up a time for the guiding coalition to explore ways the school could reassess the vertical alignment of mathematics standards. The guiding coalition was an avenue to engage people in decisions that had to be made for the necessary changes. The staff had institutionalized a growth mindset, which was an advantage for the work ahead.

Another team member expressed concerns about the increased meetings and training sessions that might be required. The team discussed the need for all group facilitators to remain aware of the staff's work-life balance. Meeting and training times would occur during the school day as much as possible. Professional learning days were already set in the school calendar, and those days could be used for any training needed. Kendall guided the team members to identify ways they could listen to their peers and support them to relieve as much stress as possible in these areas. They knew that every member of the faculty and staff was impacted by life circumstances. The team could advocate for a work-life balance.

Kendall collected concerns, documented them for the principal, and scheduled a follow-up meeting for the team members to review the presentation about this year's mathematics scores before determining next steps. She reminded them that they were all in this together. The school-improvement team left the meeting knowing that its role was to encourage and support peers while facilitating the work ahead. Team members' attitudes and collaboration would set an example for the work ahead.

A Less Effective Example

The school-improvement team at a low-performing school had a meeting before school started to discuss the upcoming school year. Ryan Brady, the team's facilitator, reminded the team that the school had been on the state's list of schools needing comprehensive support for the last six years. Its achievement scores in all content areas were in the lowest 5 percent for the state. Brady told the team that there was a sense of urgency to immediately implement initiatives to improve test scores and that the plan developed in the spring would not work. He proposed throwing the plan away. The newly assigned principal, however, had charged the team with presenting the school-improvement plan to the staff.

Team members expressed a few concerns, but they also thought they would have to take charge and tell teachers what needed to be done. With the existing plan, they were not getting the school off the improvement list. Brady told the team members they would rewrite the plan and give it to teachers on the first day of preplanning.

The team rewrote the plan. At the teachers' meeting on the first day of preplanning, the team had an outline of all the things that had been done "wrong" over the last few years. The team informed the staff of the new initiatives that would be implemented immediately and announced there would be required grade-level meetings every two weeks at 7:00 a.m. Every staff member was expected to attend—no excuses. Brady told the teachers that the principal would assign the day of the week for each grade level's morning meetings, and that at those meetings, the principal would review informal student assessment data for the last two weeks, and every teacher would present plans to improve instruction in the areas needing improvement. The teachers were not asked for input or allowed questions or concerns.

After the preplanning meeting, the teachers felt disrespected and lost hope of making a difference for students. Morale hit an all-time low. They deemed the members of the school-improvement team the "elitists" who ran the school.

Idea Hub: Reflection

Reflect individually on what you learned in this chapter, and record your thoughts. Then use your individual reflections to collaboratively answer the following questions with your team.

» What did Kendall do that aligns with the guidance in this chapter?

» What did Brady do that misaligns with the guidance in this chapter?

» What are your and your team's biggest takeaways?

» How will you embrace the work of chapter 8?

» Who will you engage in the work of chapter 8?

Conclusion

This chapter explored how to demonstrate organizational sensitivity, which means being attentive to the needs of teachers and staff while keeping an eye on the goal. Organizational sensitivity is a systemic focus that is critical throughout the improvement process. The intentional actions and collaborative efforts described in this chapter enable you to cultivate a positive school culture where student and staff performance thrives. Using a culture audit provides you with valuable information to evaluate your organization's values, beliefs, behaviors, and practices and better understand the workplace culture. Then, you can address identified barriers to a positive school culture.

Chapter 9 discusses standard 9, monitor accountability and adoption. In this chapter, you will learn how to put processes in place that achieve the intended results. These processes include creating the discipline required for monitoring, following through, and ensuring selected interventions are implemented with fidelity.

Before moving on to chapter 9, complete the "Standard 8: Do and Avoid Chart" and "Standard 8: Plan-Ahead Chart" reproducibles (pages 172 and 173) with your team to reflect on and process the work you accomplished for standard 8 and plan ahead for next steps.

Standard 8: Do and Avoid Chart

As you move through the standards for improvement, you will find things to do and things to avoid. After reading the effective and less effective practice examples and reflecting on them and the work of standard 8, complete the following do and avoid chart to help you record your thoughts about the work of this standard.

Instructions: Record what you plan to do and avoid. Consider the following questions.

1. How will you introduce your team to the processes introduced in this chapter?
2. How will your team maintain, build, or advocate for a positive culture?
3. How can your team create the conditions for effective collaboration?
4. How can your team navigate bias and cultivate empathy in your school?
5. In what ways can your team ensure psychological safety so that staff are willing to take risks?
6. How can your team use the trust meter chart to determine the level of trust between team members?
7. How can your team advocate for a work-life balance?
8. How can you use a culture audit to inform your work?

Do	Avoid

Standard 8: Plan-Ahead Chart

To get a clearer perspective on the next steps, consider your do and avoid chart as you complete the following plan-ahead chart. The work of standard 8 prepares you to demonstrate organizational sensitivity.

Instructions: Use the information from chapter 8 to identify your and your team's next steps to complete each action.		
Actions	**Person or People Responsible**	**Due Date**
Use the hope and resilience assessment (see figure 8.1, page 154) to set a baseline for staff behaviors and determine how you can guide others to adopt behaviors that promote the benefits of hope and resilience.		
Create the conditions for successful collaboration (see pages 156–160) to encourage innovation and improvement.		
Use the trust meter chart (see figure 8.2, page 158) to determine the level of trust among team members.		
Use the *if-then* consequences chart (see figure 8.3, page 162) to be proactive in considering the consequences of decisions.		
Promote a work-life balance to make mental health and wellness a priority in the workplace (see pages 163–164).		
Use the culture audit (see figure 8.4, page 165) to evaluate your organization's values, beliefs, behaviors, and practices and better understand the workplace culture. Address any barriers to a positive school culture.		

Chapter 9

Standard 9: Monitor Accountability and Adoption

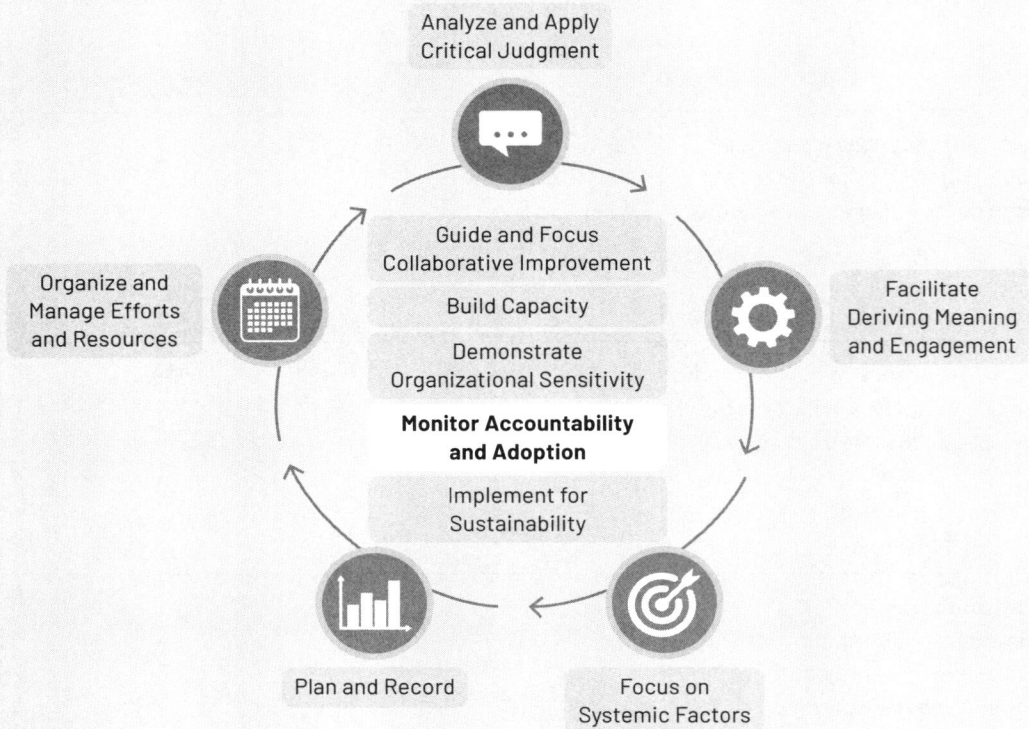

Analyze and Apply
Critical Judgment

Organize and
Manage Efforts
and Resources

Guide and Focus
Collaborative Improvement

Build Capacity

Demonstrate
Organizational Sensitivity

**Monitor Accountability
and Adoption**

Implement for
Sustainability

Facilitate
Deriving Meaning
and Engagement

Plan and Record

Focus on
Systemic Factors

*S*tandard 9 is about empowering your team to create systems that guide and sustain the work of school improvement. By putting processes in place to monitor progress and results, you build a foundation of transparency and trust that supports everyone involved. Monitoring helps you focus on the work, celebrate wins, recognize effort, and ensure all voices stay connected to the mission. School-improvement teams play a vital role by keeping a purposeful eye on performance, conditions, and outcomes. They can use this insight to uplift and energize the work. As you engage others to work toward the goals of your big rock, monitoring will help you check milestones and adjust as needed.

Monitoring accountability and adoption in education serves as a bridge between theory and practice. It ensures improvement initiatives address real needs, innovations deliver measurable benefits, and implementations achieve their intended outcomes. Monitoring pinpoints inefficiencies and areas for growth, driving evidence-based refinements. Accountability supports innovative practices that are sustainable, equitable, and aligned with educational goals. Adoption tracking guarantees that strategies are embraced effectively, reducing the risk of failure.

By embedding monitoring into the educational ecosystem, schools can create a culture of excellence, adaptability, and continuous progress. The ongoing collection of data allows your team to stay on track. It is not a rigid checklist but a dynamic process to inform decision making and inspire growth. Short monitoring cycles create opportunities to learn, adjust, and refine strategies in real time. These cycles ensure your team and supporters remain informed, aligned, and accountable. This accountability is not punitive. It is a collaborative effort to stay true to your commitments and goals. By communicating progress to stakeholders, you build momentum and confidence, reinforcing success even when conditions change.

In this chapter, we introduce tools that make monitoring and accountability approachable and empowering. We show you how to track the adoption of new behaviors and processes through adoption indicators. These indicators offer encouraging signals that the work is progressing. We also offer a checklist of implementation practices to assess best practices. It will help you decide when to adopt strategies, adapt them, or let go of strategies that may no longer serve your school.

We also discuss the importance of aligning monitoring efforts across grade levels, content areas, and the entire school system. Open and consistent communication between groups supports improvement efforts that are collaborative and mutually supportive. Monitoring helps you avoid unintended consequences and amplifies the positive impact of your work. When everyone moves together toward a shared vision, the result is a school culture that thrives on progress, innovation, and collective success.

Finally, we will explore action research, a process that blends inquiry and action to keep your team curious and energized. Through reflection and iteration, action research enables your team to assess your progress and refine practice in real time. Monitoring and measuring are not the end; they are a means to stay connected to the purpose of your work and make thoughtful adjustments along the way.

Monitoring Adoption

Adoption happens when individuals, or the school, fully embrace and consistently use a new practice, program, or initiative, integrating it into their daily routines and systems. *Adoption indicators* are the key behaviors and measurable results that show this integration is underway. These are what you will look for to assess progress, especially changes in behavior. These indicators provide meaningful feedback to guide decisions and actions. Some adoption indicators are straightforward, like how many educators attend a kickoff event. Others require more depth, using tools like surveys, interviews, or focus groups to gather insights.

These indicators are like signposts, helping your team recognize success, adjust course when needed, and build momentum. For example, they might include the percentage of staff participating in professional learning, the number of teachers actively contributing to committees, or the level of collaboration with external partners. By focusing on these measures, you will not only stay on track but also inspire confidence and drive sustainable progress. Use figure 9.1 as a checklist to assess which adoption indicators you may see in your school.

Participation
☐ The percentage of classrooms using prescribed strategies or tools increases.
☐ The number of students participating in activities or interventions associated with the initiative increases.
☐ The number of families and community members participating in initiative activities increases.
☐ Partnerships with local organizations or stakeholders increase.
☐ Student attendance and engagement increase.
☐ The number of teachers participating in professional learning opportunities increases.

School Commitment or Institutionalization

Success Tool Notes:

☐ The inclusion of initiative-related items on meeting agendas increases.

☐ Consistent and continuous improvement in instructional practices is observed and documented.

☐ The school staff consistently demonstrate the ability to effectively allocate and manage resources in implementing initiatives.

☐ Schedules are in place that are conducive to initiative implementation.

☐ Policies, routines, and systems created during the initiative are part of the school's standard operating procedures.

District and School Leadership Support

☐ The time that school and system leaders spend in classrooms or in meetings that support the initiative increases.

☐ Specific feedback given to teachers about initiative implementation increases.

☐ Funding is allocated for initiative-related activities.

☐ Systems are in place to train and prepare staff to sustain efforts.

Use of Initiative Materials and Tools

☐ The number of teachers observed effectively and consistently using the materials and tools increases.

☐ The degree to which the initiative is part of the school's regular practices, routines, and values increases.

☐ School and district leadership's commitment to and support for implementing and sustaining the initiative increase.

Collaboration

☐ The inclusion of initiative-related topics on collaborative planning agendas increases.

☐ Written iterations of plans outline collaborative revisions to original initiative plans.

☐ The number of teachers mentoring one another, and showing a culture of shared learning and collaboration, increases.

☐ The time allotted for teacher and staff collaboration increases.

Capacity Building for Scaling Improvements and Innovations Independently

☐ Improvement in staff's confidence and skills to implement changes without relying on external guidance is observed.

☐ Clear and actionable plans for continuing and scaling initiatives are developed and implemented.

☐ The regular and pervasive use of data and evaluations to make decisions about the effectiveness of initiative efforts increases.

☐ Reports or presentations demonstrate how the school has expanded successful practices to new areas or contexts.

Satisfaction With the Initiative

☐ Surveys and interviews with staff and the community reflect positive changes in attitudes or practices.

☐ Student achievement, attendance, or engagement increases.

☐ The number of teachers who adopt the programs or practices introduced during the initiative increases.

FIGURE 9.1: Success tool—Adoption indicators checklist.

continued ▶

Success Tool Notes:

Student Achievement

- [ ] Scores on formative assessments in all content areas and subgroups improve.
- [ ] Achievement of individual student learning goals (including Lexile scores) increases every nine weeks.
- [ ] Students' skills in verbal self-reflection and self-evaluation about their own achievement improve.
- [ ] Students' demonstration of their application of learned skills improves.

*Visit **go.SolutionTree.com/schoolimprovement** for a free reproducible version of this figure.*

Focus on the adoption indicators that closely align with your goals and that you can realistically measure. Once established, these indicators provide the foundation for systematic monitoring of implementation, allowing you to identify successes, address challenges, and make data-informed adjustments.

Idea Hub: Reflection on Current Efforts to Map Success

Ask yourself the following questions, and then discuss them with your team.

» How does your team monitor progress on school-improvement initiatives or key projects?

» What early signs or adoption indicators (for example, observable shifts in practice, team buy-in, or initial results) might suggest you're moving in the right direction toward your big rock's goals?

» How could you use those indicators to break up the year into meaningful checkpoints for celebrating wins, identifying roadblocks, and making adjustments?

Monitoring Implementation

When implementing solutions and innovations, set up your team for success by identifying the tools and processes that keep the work on track. Start by envisioning what full implementation with fidelity should look like. Think about what success means in practical terms and how you will measure it. By intentionally tracking how closely the program or intervention aligns with its original plan, you empower your team to adapt, improve, and stay focused on the goals that matter.

Figure 9.2 is designed to support you from day one and throughout your journey. It helps your team monitor best practices, making sure every effort is intentional and aligned. Although it is simple, the discipline and work it reflects are critical to success. With the right tools and a clear plan, your team can confidently lead the way to meaningful and sustainable improvement.

Instructions: Use this checklist to ensure best practices are applied to support successful implementation.

- [ ] Establish clear goals and metrics.
- [ ] Conduct regular progress monitoring.
- [ ] Analyze data for trends to determine needed actions and decisions and for reporting.
- [ ] Solicit feedback from stakeholders, and make needed adjustments.
- [ ] Provide expectations, support, and resources, and require accountability.
- [ ] Communicate openly with stakeholders, demonstrating transparency.
- [ ] Acknowledge and celebrate successes and progress.

Success Tool Notes:

Source: Adapted from Fixsen & Blase, 2020.

FIGURE 9.2: Success tool—Implementation practices checklist.

Visit **go.SolutionTree.com/schoolimprovement** *for a free reproducible version of this figure.*

Aligning Efforts

As schools implement multiple initiatives, aligning efforts ensures that their resources and focus remain on the most effective strategies. It is exciting to see schools take on multiple improvement and innovation efforts, but the key to success lies in connecting those efforts. Regular communication across improvement teams, grade-level groups, and content-area coalitions is essential to ensure alignment and prevent overlap or missed opportunities. Schools in the same feeder pattern, for example, can share plans, track progress, and align initiatives to create a seamless experience for students as they move from grade to grade or school to school. While having choices in programs allows schools to meet their unique needs, uncoordinated efforts can lead to challenges like duplicated work or fragmented support.

Align Programs

An urban district with a high level of student transiency discovered that its schools were using fifty-four different literacy programs. This was causing students to struggle due to inconsistent instruction as they moved between schools. These schools collaborated to reduce the number of programs, choose ones aligned to students' needs, and implement them together. This effort improved literacy outcomes as well as created smoother transitions and a more unified learning experience for students. When schools work together, incredible transformations happen.

This example illustrates the power of alignment—not only in selecting the right programs but also in streamlining efforts to reduce fragmentation. Just as too many instructional programs can create inconsistency for students, too many separate initiatives can create confusion and fatigue for staff. When improvement efforts are uncoordinated or competing for time and attention, it becomes difficult to sustain momentum or measure success. That is why alignment must extend beyond programs to include the initiatives themselves.

Align Initiatives

Having too many initiatives running at once can drain energy and focus. For this reason, prioritization and regular monitoring are essential. By narrowing efforts to those that deliver the most value, you avoid overwhelming people with too much all at once.

Monitoring tools can help you identify what is working, what needs adjustment, and what may no longer serve your goals. This process of organized abandonment allows your team to let go of low-priority work and reclaim time and resources for the projects that truly make an impact (Aleccia, 2011). This abandonment is not random. It is based on data collected through the monitoring process to identify those initiatives with little or no value added.

Alignment is not just about reducing effort—it is about creating coherence and clarity. When you align curriculum, instruction, and student outcomes across teams and grade levels, you create a strong foundation for sustainable growth. Clear goals, data-driven decisions, and collaboration build momentum that not only supports current work but inspires future innovation. By focusing on alignment, you empower educators to move forward with confidence, knowing their efforts are making a meaningful difference.

Align Vision With Change

Leading improvement and innovation is rewarding, but it can also be overwhelming. Waves of new initiatives and constant change can cause fatigue and frustration, especially when urgency feels relentless (Chung, Choi, & Du, 2017). Meaningful change takes time. Educators need patience, support, and opportunities to build capacity. As an advocate for your team and school, you have the power to take a long-term view, modeling and supporting resilience and persistence in the face of challenges.

Keeping the vision of the organization at the forefront can help you ensure that goals align with this common vision. It is important for your team to ask that the vision be regularly revisited with staff. Engage staff in networking and professional dialogue about developments that impact or contribute to the vision. Collaboratively developing strategies to address those developments demonstrates a team's sensitivity to factors that are changing. It allows for alignment of changing marketplace, workplace, work, and worker factors with the current vision of the organization. This facilitates improvement and innovation as the work is implemented.

Align Energy With Areas of Influence

As you and your team monitor for implementation, you can become architects of your school's fate instead of passive reactors. This requires the school-improvement team to identify what is under the control of those working on improvement. It is easier to identify and guide staff in the work when you use your energy on things over which you have some control or influence. This enables team members to engage stakeholders and focus them on the variables with which they can be effective. Stakeholders can proactively take control of these variables rather than just reacting. The nature of their energy in doing this is positive, enlarging, and magnifying. Proactivity allows individuals to focus on and nurture what is under their influence.

Helping people focus on the things over which they have influence is part of the growth mindset that is so important for successful implementation of improvement work, such as focusing on your big rock. Focusing on those things that they can influence will propel educators into a cycle of continuous improvement—continuously imagining and seeking innovative solutions.

Idea Hub: Aligning Efforts Status Check

Make a list of the initiatives or programs currently implemented in your school or building. Consider the following questions.

» Do these programs or initiatives duplicate work, or are they in conflict with each other?

» How does your school currently monitor the implementation of these initiatives and share regular updates?

» Where might you advocate for reducing or eliminating initiatives to help streamline efforts and save time for staff and students?

Embracing Action Research

Action research is an effective way to monitor implementation, align efforts, and make data-driven improvements. This process, which involves planning, acting, observing, and reflecting, allows teams to systematically analyze their efforts and make real-time adjustments. For example, a school-improvement team implementing a new student engagement strategy might conduct action research by tracking engagement levels, identifying barriers, and modifying instructional approaches accordingly. This structured cycle ensures that improvements are intentional, adaptable, and aligned with school goals.

Action research is not just a method—it is a mindset about being curious, reflective, and intentional in your work. When used collaboratively, action research builds a strong foundation for monitoring and continuous improvement (Mertler, 2025), fostering a sense of community and shared ownership of problems and solutions. It encourages teachers to be participants in the research process as opposed to recipients, which promotes critical thinking, self-reflection, and decision-making skills.

Action research bridges the gap between theory and practice, connecting academic research with real-life applications while providing immediate feedback and solutions to improve practices through a cycle of planning, acting, observing, and reflecting. It facilitates the systematic collection of data, allows decisions to be supported by evidence, and encourages experimentation and creative problem solving. This iterative cycle fosters sustainable and long-term improvements rather than temporary fixes, building teachers' capacity for ongoing reflection and adaptation because *adaptation* is just as important as *adoption*.

**Success
Tool Notes:**

There are eight steps to effectively implementing action research. The tool in figure 9.3 can guide your inquiry from problem to practice.

Instructions: Start with a manageable scope—one question, one class, or one unit. Document progress in a notebook, digital journal, or shared team folder. Consider collaborating with a colleague for shared learning and feedback.

Step	Guiding Questions	Notes
1. **Identify the focus.**	What problem or area of practice do I want to improve? Why is it important for student success?	
2. **Define the research question.**	What specific question will guide my inquiry—for example, "How does using graphic organizers impact reading comprehension for fifth-grade students?"	
3. **Review current practices and data.**	What do I already know from student data, observations, or feedback? What gaps or trends do I see?	
4. **Develop an action plan.**	What new strategy or change will I try? What resources or support do I need? What's my timeline?	
5. **Collect evidence.**	What data will I collect (for example, student work, assessments, surveys, or observations)? How will I document it?	
6. **Analyze results.**	What patterns or results do I see in the data? Did the strategy make a difference?	
7. **Reflect and adjust.**	What worked well? What could be improved? How will I refine or scale this practice?	
8. **Share learning.**	How will I share what I learned with colleagues, teams, or stakeholders?	

FIGURE 9.3: Success tool—Action research planning chart.

*Visit **go.SolutionTree.com/schoolimprovement** for a free reproducible version of this figure.*

A high school demonstrated this process in practice. The school identified writing quality as its big rock and formulated a research question: "How does structured peer feedback impact student writing quality?" The school-improvement team partnered with teachers to determine how this pilot would be implemented and introduced the intervention in select classrooms. Teachers and the school-improvement team tracked student progress, gathered feedback, and adjusted the approach as needed. This iterative process allowed for immediate refinement and ensured the strategy was effectively meeting students' needs.

By embedding action research into school-improvement efforts, educators can move beyond intuition and use structured reflection to drive change. This method not only validates effective practices but also builds capacity for ongoing improvement and innovation.

Idea Hub: Action Research to Drive Improvement

Ask yourself the following questions, and then discuss them with your team.

» How does your current improvement process compare to action research?

» How might you embed action research into your efforts?

» How might this shift impact your improvement efforts?

» What are some areas in which you can use action research in your school to inform or validate practices?

Reviewing Examples of Standard 9

To help you use what you have learned in chapter 9, we have included an example of an effective practice and an example of a less effective practice. Comparing these examples will help you determine what to do and what to avoid when applying the work of standard 9.

An Effective Example

For three years, the school-improvement team at Danet STEM Academy had been supporting the school to implement strategies aligned with the state's framework for 21st century skills. The school's big rock was to improve student agency and problem solving across all grade levels through interdisciplinary project-based learning. Recognizing that progress had plateaued after initial enthusiasm, the team decided to focus on monitoring adoption and implementation with greater intentionality.

The team members began by identifying specific adoption indicators they could track, such as the number of interdisciplinary projects conducted per semester, student reflections on problem solving, and evidence of peer collaboration in work products. Using surveys and classroom walkthroughs, they collected data to determine which grade-level teams were fully integrating project-based learning and which were struggling with implementation fidelity.

The team also introduced short-cycle monitoring, where grade-level teams would meet every six weeks to reflect on their data and refine practices. They used a simple implementation checklist to self-assess and visibly identify where support or adjustment was needed. This promoted transparency and shifted the culture from compliance to shared accountability.

To scale and sustain the work, the team launched a teacher-led action research initiative. Teachers selected their own inquiry questions aligned to the school's improvement goals, such as "How does student-led conferencing affect ownership of learning?" or "What is the impact of real-world mentors on STEM engagement?" They documented and presented their findings each quarter at staff meetings and stakeholder sessions, reinforcing both learning and innovation.

By the end of the year, more than 85 percent of staff had engaged in some form of inquiry or data reflection, and student achievement in problem solving showed double-digit gains on district assessments. More importantly, teachers reported increased confidence in their ability to adapt instruction and use data meaningfully. The school's reputation for innovation and collaboration attracted new community partners, and the work gained visibility at the district level as a model for evidence-informed improvement.

A Less Effective Example

A guiding coalition came together at Birdsong Elementary to study how students could learn 21st century skills in kindergarten through sixth grade. Coalition members attended a summer workshop together, which focused on the development of the young brain via cumulative layering of foundational skills influenced by relationships, experiences, and environments. They defined their big rock as nurturing social, emotional, cognitive, and language skills and started to review research and develop a three-year implementation plan. This process began with professional learning for teachers and analysis of factors that would impact implementation.

Informed by their inquiry, coalition members developed a plan for the upcoming school year. They arranged to present it to the full leadership team and curriculum directors for the school system. They shared their learning and their research-based rationales for the plan components, along with the plan itself.

As expected, participants raised questions about time constraints, teacher learning curves, family engagement, and other issues. Coalition members provided answers based on their research of best practices for changes in curriculum, assessment, and instruction. Then, participants asked two questions that their research had not yet explored.

1. "How will we know if this is working in time to make changes or reverse course?"
2. "Who has accountability for this effort, and how will teachers be supported and held accountable?"

Coalition members responded that they had been busy exploring what was needed to install these changes in the instructional core. They had not yet developed monitoring processes or explored accountability. Those attending the presentation commended them on their work to date and asked that they add these two items to their plan and provide an update in two weeks.

> ### Idea Hub: Reflection
>
> Reflect individually on what you learned in this chapter, and record your thoughts. Then use your individual reflections to collaboratively answer the following questions with your team.
>
> » What did Danet STEM Academy do that aligns with the guidance in this chapter?
>
> » What did Birdsong Elementary do that misaligns with the guidance in this chapter?
>
> » What are your and your team's biggest takeaways?
>
> » How will you embrace the work of chapter 9?
>
> » Who will you engage in the work of chapter 9?

Conclusion

In this chapter, we discussed developing adoption indicators before beginning an initiative and using them to check for full integration or use of new practices. We shared the implementation practices checklist to monitor best practices through the implementation stage. Next, we emphasized the importance of aligning efforts and using action research, which enables teams to create coherence and clarity and develop a strong foundation for sustainable growth. We shared the action research planning tool to help guide your research, reflection, and shared learning. By integrating monitoring tools, adoption indicators, and action research, your team will stay agile, responsive, and committed to long-term success.

Chapter 10 focuses on growing the capacity of those who are engaged in big rock solutions and innovations. It shares how to grow and shift ownership when needed and how to sustain progress and results. Although standard 10 is the last of the CSIS standards, it is important at every step toward successful improvement and innovation.

Before moving on to chapter 10, complete the "Standard 9: Do and Avoid Chart" and "Standard 9: Plan-Ahead Chart" reproducibles (pages 186 and 187) with your team to reflect on and process the work you accomplished for standard 9 and plan ahead for next steps.

Standard 9: Do and Avoid Chart

As you move through the standards for improvement, you will find things to do and things to avoid. After reading the effective and less effective practice examples and reflecting on them and the work of standard 9, complete the following do and avoid chart to help you record your thoughts about the work of this standard.

Instructions: Record what you plan to do and avoid. Consider the following questions.

1. How will you introduce your team to the processes introduced in this chapter?
2. How will you determine and communicate adoption indicators for initiatives?
3. How will you advocate for ways to resolve factors that impact adoption and implementation?
4. How will you ensure efforts are aligned across groups and content areas to avoid any negative impacts of working at cross-purposes?
5. How can you use action research to inform efforts?

Do	Avoid

Standard 9: Plan-Ahead Chart

To get a clearer perspective on the next steps, consider your do and avoid chart as you complete the following plan-ahead chart. The work of standard 9 prepares you to monitor accountability and adoption.

Actions	Person or People Responsible	Due Date
Instructions: Use the information from chapter 9 to identify your and your team's next steps to complete each action.		
Develop and check adoption indicators to assess progress, recognize success, adjust course when needed, and build momentum (see figure 9.1, page 176).		
Complete the implementation practices checklist (see figure 9.2, page 179) to monitor best practices, making sure every effort is intentional and aligned.		
Align efforts to ensure resources and focus remain on the most effective strategies.		
Embed action research into your process as an effective way to monitor implementation, align efforts, make data-driven improvements, and encourage teachers to participate in the research process (see figure 9.3, page 182).		

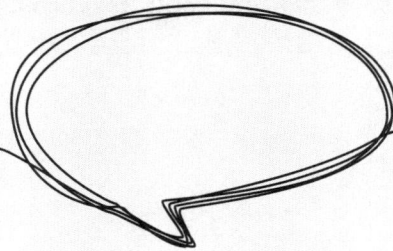

Chapter 10

Standard 10: Implement for Sustainability

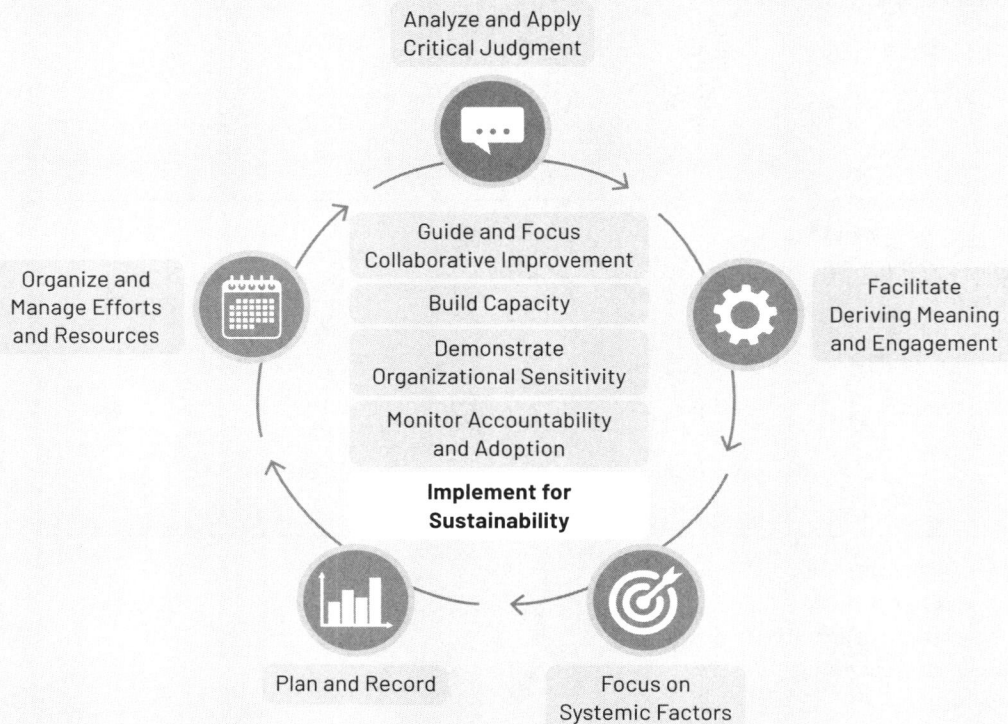

Analyze and Apply
Critical Judgment

Organize and
Manage Efforts
and Resources

Guide and Focus
Collaborative Improvement

Build Capacity

Demonstrate
Organizational Sensitivity

Monitor Accountability
and Adoption

**Implement for
Sustainability**

Facilitate
Deriving Meaning
and Engagement

Plan and Record

Focus on
Systemic Factors

$\mathcal{S}$tandard 10 is about continuing the work of improvement and making a difference in the long term. This is accomplished while preparing others to sustain their gains and continuing to transform teaching and learning to maximize student achievement. Sustainability acts as a guiding principle that integrates improvement, innovation, and implementation, ensuring changes are not short-lived but have a lasting positive impact.

When we researched and validated the CSIS standards (Page & Hale, 2013), we found that if the school-improvement team built the capacity in the building, those doing the work were empowered to own the change. The efforts were sustained even if team members leading or facilitating the change left the building or shifted positions because those doing the work were invested in this part of the culture. The improvement team was able to build educator and staff capacity, apply a systems lens throughout the change process, and put processes and tools in place to support the work. The team members successfully guided others to implement for sustainability, the work of standard 10.

We begin this chapter by focusing on coherence and the importance of a strategic approach to aligning improvement, innovation, and implementation efforts to enhance school effectiveness. You will learn how the stages of implementation defined by the National Implementation Research Network (NIRN) can guide your work to ensure successful implementation (Fixsen, Aijaz, Fixsen, Burks, & Schultes, 2021). By focusing on the stages of implementation for your big rock and ensuring the necessary success drivers are in place, you can increase the odds that you will achieve your shared goals. To help with your school-improvement work, we offer a twelve-step implementation and sustainability checklist to assess and improve your practices. You can use this checklist to see whether you have successfully implemented the best sustainability practices and if any work remains.

In this chapter, we also explain the importance of transferring ownership of the work. Members of the school-improvement team cannot be the only ones owning the work if it is going to be sustained. We share ways to evaluate the work, including the success case method, which combines storytelling with rigorous evaluation methods and principles. We offer the define, promise, deliver, and remind protocol as a guide to target the value you will create, demonstrate your commitment, stay focused on implementation, and keep others informed about your efforts.

Focusing on Coherence

Coherence in school improvement refers to the intentional alignment and integration of goals, strategies, actions, and systems to ensure all efforts work together to support student success. In a coherent system, improvement, innovation, and implementation are not isolated activities—they are interconnected, reinforcing one another to create clarity, reduce fragmentation, and drive sustained progress. When coherence is present, educators understand not only *what* they are doing but also *why* it matters and *how* their work contributes to the broader vision. Fostering coherence helps school-improvement teams avoid the trap of disconnected initiatives and instead build a shared sense of purpose, direction, and momentum.

Schools are complex systems with many interconnected parts that exhibit dynamic behaviors that often cannot be easily understood by analyzing the individual components alone. You must recognize patterns that emerge so people can work collaboratively and accomplish the organization's goals. The individual actions of school-improvement team members collectively influence the results of improvement, innovation, and effective implementation, the last of which promotes organizational alignment (McIlrath & Kotnour, 2002). Aligning these systems, processes, and efforts within a school facilitates success because it ensures good execution and maximizes educator and student success.

Improvement is about focusing on optimizing existing processes, systems, or products. It involves identifying areas for refinement or adjustment to increase efficiency, reduce costs, or improve quality. Improvement aligns with innovation by establishing a foundation of operational efficiency that supports new ideas and ensures that when innovations are implemented, they integrate well with improved, streamlined systems, avoiding disruption.

Innovation introduces new ideas, technologies, or processes to drive growth, adapt to market changes, and differentiate the organization. Innovation aligns with improvement by identifying and filling gaps where traditional methods fall short, fostering a readiness to innovate. Innovation also bridges implementation by converting creative ideas into actionable plans and prototypes.

Implementation translates improvements and innovations into operational realities. This is where planning turns into action, ensuring changes are deployed smoothly and deliver tangible results. Implementation connects back to improvement by monitoring outcomes and adjusting based on real-world performance. Implementation validates innovation through testing and refining ideas in practical settings, ensuring they are feasible and scalable.

Consider the following three key components of mature and aligned efforts and determine whether these are fully adopted and implemented. If not, consider what you will do to achieve them.

1. **Cross-functional teams:** Teams that include members from different content areas who have a variety of experience levels, areas of expertise, backgrounds, and more that encompasses innovation, process improvement, and implementation ensure that ideas are practical and can be deployed effectively.

2. **Feedback systems:** Feedback systems that allow insights into improvement, innovation, and implementation to inform others facilitate progress and success. Monitoring creates feedback cycles. The output of a system cycles back as an input, influencing future outputs. Positive feedback about outputs amplifies changes, making an even greater impact.

3. **Short tasks, monitoring, reassessment, and adaptation:** Dividing tasks into short phases of work and adapting plans after monitoring and reassessment allows for continuous iterations. These processes encourage a cycle of improvement, innovation, and implementation that adapts to feedback and changing conditions.

Aligning improvement, innovation, and implementation creates a balanced and coherent approach in which each reinforces the others, resulting in a sustainable and scalable way to drive progress and help your school and community thrive.

Using the Stages of Implementation

As you have worked through this book and applied the processes, practices, and tools, you have selected improvement solutions or innovations to implement, and you may even be well on the way to implementing them. Now is the time to apply one more lens to your approach—the stages of implementation. NIRN at the University of North Carolina at Chapel Hill defines four key stages of implementation: (1) exploration, (2) installation, (3) initial implementation, and (4) full implementation (Fixsen et al., 2021). Using these stages to reflect on and guide your efforts to address your school's big rock can significantly increase your chances of success.

Research from NIRN has also identified a hallmark of organizations that consistently achieve results from their programs, initiatives, and systems—the intentional formation of an implementation team (Fixsen et al., 2021). An *implementation team* is a dedicated group responsible for actively supporting the use of effective practices, removing barriers to implementation, collecting and using data for decision making, and ensuring the work aligns with the larger vision and improvement goals. All leadership teams and school-improvement teams are involved in implementing what they have planned; however, this implementation team uses research-based practices to advise on high-priority programs, projects, and initiatives (see NIRN's website at https://nirn.fpg.unc.edu). NIRN has found that rather than leaving implementation to chance or adding it as an afterthought, high-performing organizations use these teams to drive, monitor, and sustain change (Fixsen et al., 2021). School districts can develop these teams to support their schools, or schools can develop their own. Building and supporting such a team can transform your improvement efforts from isolated attempts to coordinated, strategic action that endures and evolves over time.

Consider one of the projects you have planned or are planning. Determine which of the following four stages of implementation, defined by NIRN (Fixsen et al., 2021), your project is currently in.

1. **Exploration:** This stage involves preparing for change by identifying the need for change and exploring potential solutions or innovations. The improvement team chooses goals, analyzes the current state of the project, finds gaps in performance, and identifies the factors and causes to address. The team then drafts a plan, identifying who will do what by when.

2. **Installation:** During this stage, plans and infrastructure for the change are put in place. This includes securing resources, developing people, and establishing policies and procedures necessary for implementing and sustaining the change. It also focuses on nurturing communication and leadership support as well as day-to-day performance and progress. As this happens, initial implementation is underway.

3. **Initial implementation:** During this stage, the change is first put into practice. This stage is fragile and awkward because that is the nature of trying something new while trying to move away from old habits. The implementation team must focus on continuous improvement and support. It is essential to celebrate small wins and adjust as needed so those implementing the innovation or initiative feel supported and are resilient in these early steps. Your team must ensure they do not regress to the old ways of doing things (NIRN, 2015).

4. **Full implementation:** During this stage, the practices are fully integrated into the school's operations. Ongoing support and monitoring are required to ensure fidelity to the practices and sustained implementation over time. Sustainability is created when there is long-term commitment and follow-through with the desired practices within the school. This stage involves ensuring best practices become part of the organization's culture and are supported by ongoing resources. In full implementation, the individual ownership needed to begin the work has grown into a collective and powerful organizational ownership that facilitates the consistency and pervasiveness needed to sustain the work.

The Collaborative for Implementation Practice (n.d.) and NIRN provide a planning tool that assists teams in determining where they are in the stages of implementation. (You can find the "Implementation Stages Planning Tool" at www.implementationpractice.org /wp-content/uploads/2021/08/NIRN-CIP-Implementation-Stages-Planning-Tool -fillable-7.29.21.pdf.)

Checking Implementation and Sustainability

If you have effectively used the proven processes and tools provided throughout this book, the conditions for sustainability and success may be taking root or bearing fruit. For sustainability, the school-improvement team or guiding coalition must pay attention to engaging, supporting, and developing those who will perform the work of the school-improvement plan and project plans. Countless schools and organizations have used the implementation and sustainability checklist in figure 10.1 to assess and improve their practices. It can be a useful tool for teams as they look at each project plan and check to see if the best implementation and sustainability practices have been completed and what remains to be done. Use this tool, which aligns with this book's ten standards, to support planning and reflection for your big rock.

Instructions: Review the following steps and determine whether they have been completed. Note the chapters in this book related to each step.

- ☐ 1. Agree on the goal. (See chapters 1 and 2.)
- ☐ 2. Agree on the gaps between the baselines and needed performance and performance factors. (See chapters 1 and 2.)
- ☐ 3. Conduct collaborative analyses and choose suites of solutions to close the gaps. (See chapters 2 and 3.)
- ☐ 4. Develop a plan or plans to launch and implement the suites of solutions and implement the plans collaboratively. (See chapters 4, 5, 6, and 7.)
- ☐ 5. Break down and distribute the work. (See chapter 4.)
- ☐ 6. Achieve engagement, commitment, and critical mass. (See chapters 2, 4, and 6.)
- ☐ 7. Monitor progress, adoption, and leading indicators. (See chapter 9.)
- ☐ 8. Put an oversight structure in place. (See chapter 7.)
- ☐ 9. Sustain attention by measuring and reporting. (See chapters 6, 8, and 9.)
- ☐ 10. Reward adoption and results. (See chapters 9 and 10.)
- ☐ 11. Shift ownership. (See chapters 7, 8, and 10.)
- ☐ 12. Evaluate and tell your story. (See chapter 10.)

FIGURE 10.1: Success tool—Implementation and sustainability checklist.

Visit go.SolutionTree.com/schoolimprovement for a free reproducible version of this figure.

As teams complete this checklist, they gain clarity on the extent to which key implementation and sustainability practices are in place and where focused attention is still needed. This reflection is not just about tracking progress; it is about preparing the conditions for long-term success. When the foundational work outlined in these twelve steps is thoughtfully executed, teams are better positioned to begin the next essential phase: transferring ownership from a small lead group to the people who will continue and sustain the work. Ownership is what ensures the work continues beyond the initial planning and launch. The next section will help you move from driving the work to transferring ownership so that others are empowered and equipped to carry it forward.

··· Idea Hub: Implementation and Sustainability Reflection

Reflect on your team's current practices, school-improvement goals, and project plans you have in place. Then ask yourself the following questions and discuss them with your team.

> » Where is each project or initiative in relation to each stage of implementation?
>
> » Where is each project or initiative based on the twelve-step implementation and sustainability checklist (see figure 10.1, page 193)? What efforts have led the team to being on this step?
>
> » What is one step you and your team might take to help each project or initiative move one step further in your current implementation?

Transferring Ownership

If you have followed the guidance in this book and used the tools provided, your team has focused on empowering teachers, leaders, and other stakeholders to take ownership of your school's improvement efforts. These stakeholders cannot simply buy in; they must truly embrace and lead the change. By involving staff in analyzing data, setting goals, and developing actionable plans, your team fosters a strong sense of shared purpose and accountability. Together, you monitor progress, make necessary adjustments, and celebrate achievements along the way. This collaborative approach builds a culture of collective responsibility and continuous growth, increasing the likelihood of lasting success.

To ensure sustainability, your next step is to intentionally transfer ownership of the work. This includes moving from team-driven implementation to widespread, distributed leadership. The following are specific action steps your team can take to support this transition.

1. **Identify new owners:** Clarify who will be responsible for sustaining each part of the improvement or innovation. This might include department chairs, grade-level leaders, instructional coaches, or committee facilitators.

2. **Create a leadership transition plan:** Document responsibilities, key milestones, and timelines. Share clear expectations with those taking on new roles, and align their responsibilities with school goals.

3. **Facilitate a formal handoff process:** Schedule structured transition meetings to communicate status and share lessons learned, and transfer key documents, tools, and routines. Invite questions, and allow time for joint planning.

4. **Provide training and support:** Offer job-embedded professional learning, mentoring, or shadowing opportunities to ensure new leaders feel equipped and confident in their roles.

5. **Use gradual release of responsibility:** Shift responsibilities over time—first modeling and supporting, then observing and coaching, and finally stepping back while remaining available for consultation.

6. **Embed ownership in structures:** Integrate responsibilities into existing collaborative teams or leadership routines to make ownership visible and ongoing. Celebrate and reinforce leadership behaviors that support sustainability.

7. **Monitor and revisit:** Continue to check in using progress indicators and feedback systems. Adjust support as needed, and celebrate those who step up to sustain and scale the work.

By taking these steps and aligning them with your school's vision and values, you build capacity and commitment among those who will carry the work forward. Transferring ownership is not the end of your improvement journey. It is the beginning of a new phase in which success is no longer dependent on a few individuals but shared across the school community.

Evaluating the Work

Sometimes, school improvement includes outside assistance and support from experts, but it is unsustainable if it is entirely driven from the outside. School leaders, the school-improvement team, and academic coaches must accept their responsibility to facilitate the process, monitor and evaluate, and take corrective actions as needed. Since new projects will inevitably be necessary, distributing leadership, responsibility, and accountability is critical so improvement projects gradually produce daily work routines that result in improved practices and results. It may be tempting to just do an evaluation of the work's progress and impacts for those you are supporting; however, engaging the people doing the work in the evaluation continues to support ownership and implementation. The following are three important items to monitor when evaluating the work.

1. **Gains:** Look at how much has changed from when the work began to specific points in time, such as quarterly or semiannually. Then, celebrate the gains made, and ask, "Is this enough?"

2. **Goal accomplishment:** Compare the gains made to targets or goals set by the team. Then, ask why you are achieving outcomes and what you need to do to sustain the gains made and increase the odds of accomplishing the goals.

3. **Return on investment:** Determine the degree to which the investment of time and resources in a solution or a combination of solutions was worth the effort. Then ask whether the road taken was the best road compared to the gains made and if it is wise to continue down the same road.

The strategies in this list help guide your checking and monitoring. They also help you present data about the school, set targets with the appropriate groups, and lead discussions about how frequently to check on and discuss progress.

Robert Brinkerhoff (2005) developed the success case method for evaluation. It combines storytelling with rigorous evaluation methods and principles. Success cases, written in an engaging case study format, cite solid evidence and document confirmable accounts of what real people experienced using specific tools and methods. These success cases monitor gains, goals, and the return on investment when evaluating results and provide evidence and communicate insights about the following six key questions regarding an initiative.

1. What is really happening (observations, analyses, and recordings of what is occurring in a format that tells the story of success or failure)?
2. What results are being achieved (gains and goal accomplishment)?
3. What is the value of the results (return on investment)?
4. How can it be improved?
5. What supported progress in achieving the needed results?
6. What, if anything, impeded progress and results?

When Deb Page was conducting a study for a state department of education, she used the success case method (Brinkerhoff, 2005) for studying and documenting the practices and results of those who had guided turnaround and sustained improvement in low-performing schools. Those cases revealed patterns that led Judith Hale and Deb Page to conduct the research and analysis that resulted in the codification and validation of the ten standards to which this book aligns and that The Institute for Performance Improvement uses for training and certification.

By identifying areas for growth and celebrating success stories, your team can spotlight achievements that inspire and energize the community while shaping actionable plans to address emerging opportunities. This process transforms data into a story of progress and potential.

Idea Hub: Reflection on Shared Ownership and Evaluation

Ask yourself the following questions, and then discuss them with your team.

» In what ways has your team or school transferred ownership of a change or an initiative to those responsible for implementation?
» What might you do to enhance ownership across all stakeholders involved?
» When does your team come together to identify successes and overall progress on each school-improvement goal and its associated initiatives?
» How is that information communicated and celebrated across the broader school community?

Demonstrating Value

When leading the school improvement process, you must commit to personal growth, which begins with self-assessing your ability to facilitate others in doing the work. This requires determining your progress and results in the work to set goals for continued personal development. The ultimate measure of your effectiveness is evidence that those you guide and support can now do the work unassisted and, ultimately, take ownership. The work of school improvement and innovation gives you the opportunity to add value to your school, educators, students, and community. Consider using the tool in figure 10.2 to implement the define, promise, deliver, and remind protocol and demonstrate the value you have contributed through your big rock and other improvements and innovations.

Success Tool Notes:

Instructions: Review each component of the protocol and describe how you are doing it or will do it. Record your thoughts, reflect on them, and update them as needed. We recommend treating this like a reflection log or journal that you can continually revisit and update.

1. *Define* in advance, in writing, the value you add through the work you do individually and as a team. Be clear and specific about the outcomes, results, and goals you will help those you guide to achieve.

2. *Promise* your defined value both verbally and in writing to those you guide and those who evaluate you by clearly stating that you are committed to their success.

3. *Deliver* what you have promised and more, guiding others to effectively perform to achieve the desired results of the initiatives and to constantly evaluate progress and your effectiveness.

4. *Remind* those you guide and serve of achieved results, goals, and outcomes through regular updates, individual handwritten notes, emails, social media, electronic newsletters, meetings, and other frequent, planned forms of communication. This helps others regard you as a valuable resource and themselves as successful professionals.

FIGURE 10.2: Success tool—Define, promise, deliver, and remind protocol.

*Visit **go.SolutionTree.com/schoolimprovement** for a free reproducible version of this figure.*

Posing reflective questions helps you and your team recognize the value you have created. It supports developing a greater sense of professionalism and efficacy, and extracts meaning from what you share to inform future practice and growth.

Serving as an effective school-improvement professional is an ongoing process. With continuous school-improvement processes, there is always room for growth and learning. By continuously evaluating impacts and results, school or teacher leaders, improvement teams, and the entire school can continue to grow and evolve skills that not only support school improvement as they comply with expectations but also help true school transformation meet the needs of their students and communities.

Idea Hub: Define, Promise, Deliver, and Remind Protocol

Ask yourself the following questions, and then discuss them with your team.

» Take time to reflect on each phase of the define, promise, deliver, and remind protocol. Consider the unique value you bring to your team and school-improvement initiatives. How have you demonstrated your commitment to this work in meaningful ways?

» Reflect on the impact of your efforts. How do you measure progress and know that your contributions have made a difference?

» Finally, think about how often you remind your team members of your unwavering support and willingness to partner with them throughout these efforts. These reflections will strengthen your skill set and inspire others to stay focused on shared goals.

Reviewing Examples of Standard 10

To help you use what you have learned in chapter 10, we have included an example of an effective practice and an example of a less effective practice. Comparing these examples will help you determine what to do and what to avoid when applying the work of standard 10.

An Effective Example

Two years ago, the Esperanza School District developed its next-generation learning blueprint with a focus on equipping and supporting all students and educators to succeed and thrive in an ever-changing and interconnected world. Internally, it stated its goal as "to nurture a hopeful, resilient, and future-ready culture aligned with a shared vision of learning, increasing clarity, coherence, and collaboration." Through community, family, employer, student, and educator input, the district developed a graduate profile outlining the academic and nonacademic competencies students would need for future success. It created an aligned educator profile and widely communicated both to stakeholders.

As the district crafted a five-year strategic plan, each school renamed its school-improvement team the *school-improvement and innovation team*. Each team then developed its own school-specific next-generation learning blueprint, identifying a big rock challenge to address, grounded in student needs and aligned with district goals. The teams created these blueprints using the define, promise, deliver, and remind protocol to focus their efforts on value creation, visible commitments, disciplined execution, and consistent communication.

This year's districtwide summer learning conference featured structured sessions in which each school's team shared its progress, identifying which stage of implementation it was in using the NIRN framework. Esperanza Middle School, for example, had moved from installation to full implementation of its inspired to achieve framework, which promoted students' development in the four Cs: (1) critical thinking, (2) communication, (3) collaboration, and (4) curiosity.

The team presentation modeled distributed leadership and sustainability practices. Team members defined their goals, promised their roles in guiding change, shared progress data and leading indicators, and used evidence from staff and student interviews to demonstrate adoption of new routines. They shared how they used the twelve-step implementation and sustainability checklist to track progress and distribute responsibilities across departments. As part of transferring ownership, they had trained grade-level leads and group facilitators to monitor and support the work using a gradual release model with embedded coaching.

The team also included a success case story to illustrate how these changes positively impacted student learning and educator practice. The team members collaboratively evaluated and reflected on the year's work and invited stakeholder feedback through the school's website, where they posted their recorded presentation and a call for participation in upcoming initiatives.

Their session closed with a clear action plan for the coming year, including a preplanning kickoff session in which all staff would commit to modeling and growing the four Cs in their daily routines. They ended with a reflection on the culture shift underway, noting a deepening sense of shared purpose and ownership—evidence that sustainability had begun to take root.

A Less Effective Example

At Harmony Junior High, a school in the Esperanza School District, the school-improvement team developed a next-generation learning blueprint aligned with the district's vision. However, while the school's blueprint included ambitious goals—such as building student agency and integrating project-based learning—implementation faltered due to limited coherence, planning, and ownership.

The team initially developed its plan with minimal involvement from staff outside the leadership group. Teachers were informed of the plan during a faculty meeting but were not engaged in identifying the big rock or shaping the strategy. Although the school documented goals and actions, it did not use the define, promise, deliver, and remind protocol, and many faculty members remained unclear about what the initiative aimed to accomplish or how it aligned with their daily work.

The team made some progress on installing new strategies, like student-led conferences and interdisciplinary projects, but it lacked clear monitoring systems or implementation support structures. It did not assess its stage of implementation in using the NIRN framework and, as a result, jumped ahead to full implementation activities without first securing resources, training, and leadership support—key elements in the installation stage.

Because responsibilities remained centralized among a few team members, there was no transfer of ownership. When two key leaders left midyear, momentum stalled. New team members had no formal transition or training, and project updates ceased. Without clear documentation or shared leadership routines, much of the work had to be restarted the following year.

The team members did not use the twelve-step implementation and sustainability checklist to guide or evaluate their efforts, and they had not collected data to determine gains, goal achievement, or return on investment. At the summer conference, the team gave a general update with limited evidence of progress, no clear sustainability strategy, and no plan to build educator capacity. The culture remained one of compliance rather than commitment, and few educators felt a sense of ownership of or connection to the school's strategic direction.

While the vision was promising, the lack of coherence, distributed leadership, and structured implementation practices meant the initiative was not yet on a path to sustainability.

> **Idea Hub:** Reflection
>
> Reflect individually on what you learned in this chapter, and record your thoughts. Then use your individual reflections to collaboratively answer the following questions with your team.
>
> » What did Esperanza Middle School do that aligns with the guidance in this chapter?
>
> » What did Harmony Junior High do that misaligns with the guidance in this chapter?
>
> » What are your and your team's biggest takeaways?
>
> » How will you embrace the work of chapter 10?
>
> » Who will you engage in the work of chapter 10?

Conclusion

Standard 10 emphasizes the essential final phase of the school-improvement journey: ensuring sustainability and long-term success. By this point, your school has likely implemented improvement and innovation plans. The focus now must shift from managing the work to sustaining the gains, transferring ownership, and evaluating impact.

Throughout this chapter, we explored how to align improvement, innovation, and implementation for coherence; how to apply the stages of implementation to deepen adoption; and how to assess progress using structured tools like the implementation and sustainability checklist (see figure 10.1, page 193). We examined how high-performing schools and districts use implementation teams of trained educators who can advise on implementing all types of plans. We focused on how to support the work and distribute leadership so success is not dependent on a few individuals but becomes part of the school's culture. We also introduced concrete steps for transferring ownership and evaluating the work in ways that promote accountability and build internal capacity.

Across this book, we have guided you through a practical, research-based process grounded in the ten CSIS standards. Each chapter builds your capacity to reach the ultimate goal: creating sustainable systems and a culture of shared responsibility for student and educator success. Implementation has been a thread throughout, from setting SMART+IE goals and choosing improvement solutions to executing project plans and measuring results. Now, with the full framework in place, your school is positioned not just to improve but to thrive.

The journey of school improvement is ongoing. But with the right people, processes, and purpose in place, your team has everything it needs to create and sustain lasting change—for educators, for students, and for your community. We wish you great success!

As you conclude your journey through the school-improvement process, complete the "Standard 10: Do and Avoid Chart" and "Standard 10: Plan-Ahead Chart" reproducibles (pages 201 and 202) with your team to reflect on and process the work you accomplished for standard 10 and plan ahead for next steps.

Standard 10: Do and Avoid Chart

As you move through the standards for improvement, you will find things to do and things to avoid. After reading the effective and less effective practice examples and reflecting on them and the work of standard 10, complete the following do and avoid chart to help you record your thoughts about the work of this standard.

Instructions: Record what you plan to do and avoid. Consider the following questions.

1. How will you introduce your team to the processes introduced in this chapter?
2. How can you help your team develop a cohesive strategic focus on aligning implementation, innovation, and improvement?
3. Why are the stages of implementation important to review?
4. How can the implementation and sustainability checklist (see figure 10.1, page 193) help your team?
5. How will your team ensure that ownership of the work is transferred to other stakeholders who can sustain the work?
6. How can your team use the success case method to evaluate the work?
7. What other tools can you use to evaluate the work?
8. How can your team use the define, promise, deliver, and remind protocol to focus on the value you will create and keep others informed about your efforts?

Do	Avoid

Standard 10: Plan-Ahead Chart

To get a clearer perspective on the next steps, consider your do and avoid chart as you complete the following plan-ahead chart. The work of standard 10 prepares you to achieve sustainability.

Actions	Person or People Responsible	Due Date
Instructions: Use the information from chapter 10 to identify your and your team's next steps to complete each action.		
Focus on coherence to check alignment and integration of goals, strategies, actions, and systems and to ensure all efforts work together to support student success. (Consider the three key components of mature and aligned efforts on page 191.)		
Explore the stages of implementation (see page 192) to increase your chances of success. (Use the Collaborative for Implementation Practice and NIRN resource "Implementation Stages Planning Tool"; Collaborative for Implementation Practice, n.d.).		
Transfer ownership to sustain the work. (Use the suggested actions on pages 194–195.)		
Evaluate the work to celebrate successes and take any corrective action needed to achieve goals. (Consider gains, goal accomplishments, and return on investment on page 195.)		
Use the define, promise, deliver, and remind protocol (see figure 10.2, page 197) to demonstrate your value in meeting goals.		

Epilogue

As we reach the end of this exploration into improvement, innovation, and implementation, it is important to reflect on one simple truth: Progress does not happen by accident. It is the result of deliberate action, a willingness to embrace uncertainty, and the resilience to push forward when the path is unclear. It requires a culture of exploration. Throughout this journey, we explored how improvement is about finding opportunities for growth. Innovation is about daring to reimagine what is possible, and implementation is the bridge that brings ideas to life. Together, these elements form the foundation of meaningful change for improvement.

School improvement is not a new challenge. Yet, too often, these efforts falter or fail (Backstrom, 2019). Projects outlined in school-improvement plans can stall without sufficient buy-in and true ownership from those tasked with bringing them to life. Collaborative school improvement is pivotal in supporting these efforts by clearing barriers and fostering an environment of empowerment. When projects are launched prematurely—without first engaging educators and leaders in determining the work and communicating its purpose—the results can be false starts and confusion. Pauses may turn into full stops, requiring revisions or leading to abandonment altogether. This phenomenon, often called *improvement whiplash*, can leave those involved feeling demotivated and disconnected, jeopardizing implementation.

The most groundbreaking transformations often begin with a single step. Whether it is refining a process, adopting a new mindset, or implementing a bold idea, remember that even a small change can ripple outward into larger impacts. Progress thrives in environments where creativity and experimentation are valued over fear of failure. Let your curiosity guide you, and encourage those around you to think differently, take calculated risks, and learn from outcomes—both successes and setbacks.

Successful improvement work requires balance, patience, and urgency. Innovation requires a sense of urgency, but it also demands patience. You must balance patience and urgency.

Balance the drive to act quickly with the discipline to iterate, refine, and adapt your ideas over time. No matter the magnitude of the challenges your school faces, you have an important decision to make. You can choose to "do the best you can" without using proven strategies, or you can choose to "achieve the best you can" by applying disciplined and intentional processes. Discipline in this context is about not rigidity but focus—a systematic and systemic approach to managing resources, aligning efforts, and creating environments where growth thrives. It is about building momentum through thoughtful strategies, consistent monitoring, and collaborative teamwork. A disciplined approach ensures improvement is not just intentional but sustainable, leading to long-lasting, meaningful change.

The work of improvement is about hope. It is about belief in the power of educators to transform schools, no matter the challenges. It is about resilience—the ability to adapt, persevere, and lead, even when the path forward is unclear. While this work may not always be easy, it is always worth it because it makes a lasting positive difference for students, teachers, and the entire school and community.

At their core, improvement, innovation, and implementation are about people. Whether you are addressing student or teacher needs, supporting a team, or transforming a school, empathy and collaboration are essential for success. Just remember that progress is a journey, not a destination. The work of improvement, innovation, and implementation never truly ends. What works today may need to evolve tomorrow. Stay open to change, and view each challenge as an opportunity to learn and grow.

As you conclude this book, take a moment to envision what is next for you. What steps can you take to turn your aspirations into reality? How can you inspire others to join you on this journey of transformation? Our hope is that this book has equipped you with the tools, strategies, and inspiration to lead with confidence and clarity. Remember: The tools, frameworks, and insights shared here are just the beginning. True impact comes when you apply what you have learned, share your successes, and continue to push the boundaries of what is possible. When you commit to applying what you have learned with consistency and intention, you will see results that are both successful and sustainable. Together, your team can create a brighter future for your school—one where every educator, student, and community member thrives. Stay hopeful, stay resilient, and know that your work matters.

As you move forward, remember that every small improvement, bold innovation, and well-executed plan contributes to a greater collective impact. The path is never without obstacles, but each challenge is a stepping stone toward meaningful change. Now, go forward boldly. The future is shaped by those who dare to improve, innovate, and implement. Let you be one of these people.

References and Resources

Aleccia, V. A. (2011). Taming the crammed curriculum: Selective abandonment as a strategy in professional learning communities. *Northwest Journal of Teacher Education, 9*(1), 89–93. https://doi.org/10.15760/nwjte.2011.9.1.8

American Psychological Association. (n.d.). *Resilience.* Accessed at www.apa.org/topics/resilience on July 30, 2025.

Armstrong, A. J., Holmes, C. M., & Henning, D. (2020). A changing world, again. How appreciative inquiry can guide our growth. *Social Sciences and Humanities Open, 2*(1), Article 100038. https://doi.org/10.1016/j.ssaho.2020.100038

Azorín, C., & Fullan, M. (2022). Leading new, deeper forms of collaborative cultures: Questions and pathways. *Journal of Educational Change, 23*(3/4), 131–143. https://doi.org/10.1007/s10833-021-09448-w

Backstrom, B. (2019, July). *School turnaround efforts: What's been tried, why those efforts failed, and what to do now.* Rockefeller Institute of Government. Accessed at https://files.eric.ed.gov/fulltext/ED605669.pdf on March 18, 2025.

Battelle for Kids. (n.d.). *A future-ready vision for every student.* Accessed at www.battelleforkids.org/portrait-of-a-graduate on March 18, 2025.

Binder, C. (1998). The Six Boxes™: A descendent of Gilbert's behavioral engineering model. *Performance Improvement, 37*(6), 48–52.

Brinkerhoff, R. O. (2005). The success case method: A strategic evaluation approach to increasing the value and effect of training. *Advances in Developing Human Resources, 7*(1), 86–101. https://doi.org/10.1177/1523422304272172

Brinkerhoff, R. O. (2017, February 9). *Promote learning transfer, accelerate strategy execution.* Chief Learning Officer. Accessed at www.chieflearningofficer.com/2017/02/09/37372 on March 18, 2025.

Card, A. J. (2017). The problem with "5 whys." *BMJ Quality and Safety*, *26*(8), 671–677. https://doi.org/10.1136/bmjqs-2016-005849

Chuang, S. (2021). The applications of constructivist learning theory and social learning theory on adult continuous development. *Performance Improvement*, *60*(3), 6–14. https://doi.org/10.1002/pfi.21963

Chung, G. H., Choi, J. N., & Du, J. (2017). Tired of innovations? Learned helplessness and fatigue in the context of continuous streams of innovation implementation. *Journal of Organizational Behavior*, *38*(7), 1130–1148. https://doi.org/10.1002/job.2191

Collaborative for Implementation Practice. (n.d.). *Implementation stages planning tool.* National Implementation Research Network. Accessed at www.implementationpractice.org/wp-content/uploads/2021/08/NIRN-CIP-Implementation-Stages-Planning-Tool-fillable-7.29.21.pdf on August 13, 2025.

Cook, E., & Black, P. (2020). Effective implementation and evaluation of trauma-informed schools. In E. Rossen (Ed.), *Supporting and educating traumatized students: A guide for school-based professionals* (2nd ed., pp. 373–395). Oxford University Press.

Cordeiro, P. (2021, August 19). School culture: A key aspect of positive and successful schools [Blog post]. *Global Ed Leadership*. Accessed at https://globaledleadership.org/2021/08/19/school-culture-a-key-aspect-of-positive-and-successful-schools on August 12, 2025.

Costa, A. L., & Kallick, B. (Eds.). (2008). *Learning and leading with habits of mind: 16 essential characteristics for success.* ASCD.

Costa, A. L., & Kallick, B. (Eds.). (2009). *Habits of mind across the curriculum: Practical and creative strategies for teachers.* ASCD.

Coyle, D. (2018). *The culture code: The secrets of highly successful groups.* Random House.

Delbecq, A. L., Van de Ven, A. H., & Gustafson, D. H. (1975). *Group techniques for program planning: A guide to nominal group and Delphi processes.* Foresman.

DeMatthews, D. E., & Wang, Y. (2023). How can principals lead the school improvement planning process? Reducing biases in shared decision making. *The Clearing House: A Journal of Educational Strategies, Issues and Ideas*, *96*(2), 43–51. https://doi.org/10.1080/00098655.2022.2163971

Dirksen, J. (2024). *Talk to the elephant: Design learning for behavior change.* Pearson.

DuFour, R., DuFour, R., Eaker, R., Many, T. W., Mattos, M., & Muhammad, A. (2024). *Learning by doing: A handbook for Professional Learning Communities at Work* (4th ed.). Solution Tree Press.

Dweck, C. S. (2006). *Mindset: The new psychology of success.* Random House.

Eaker, R., & Marzano, R. J. (Eds.). (2020). *Professional Learning Communities at Work and High Reliability Schools: Cultures of continuous learning.* Solution Tree Press.

Elegbeleye, O. S. (2005). School supervision and performance enhancement devices at the local education authority level. *The Anthropologist, 7*(3), 177–183.

Fischer, R. L. (2008). *In God we trust, all others bring data: Assessing the state of outcomes measurement for faith-based and community-based programming.* Office of the Assistant Secretary for Planning and Evaluation. Accessed at https://aspe.hhs.gov/sites/default/files/private/pdf/200221/Fischer.pdf on March 18, 2025.

Fixsen, A. A. M., Aijaz, M., Fixsen, D. L., Burks, E., & Schultes, M.-T. (2021). *Implementation frameworks: An analysis.* Active Implementation Research Network. Accessed at https://whale-accordion-cssw.squarespace.com/s/AIRN-AFixsen-Frameworks Analysis-2021.pdf on March 18, 2025.

Fixsen, D. L., & Blase, K. A. (2020). Active implementation frameworks. In P. Nilsen & S. A. Birken (Eds.), *Handbook on implementation science* (pp. 62–87). Elgar.

Fournies, F. F. (2000). *Coaching for improved work performance* (Revised ed.). McGraw Hill.

Gallagher, M. W. (2018). Introduction to the science of hope. In M. W. Gallagher & S. J. Lopez (Eds.), *The Oxford handbook of hope* (pp. 3–7). Oxford Library of Psychology.

Gallo, C. (2019, July 15). The art of persuasion hasn't changed in 2,000 years. *Harvard Business Review.* Accessed at https://hbr.org/2019/07/the-art-of-persuasion-hasnt-changed-in-2000-years on July 31, 2025.

Gallup. (2019a, October 22). *Engagement and hope positively influence student outcomes: Key findings from Gallup's student poll analysis in Texas.* Author. Accessed at www.gallup.com/education/267740/engagement-hope-positively-influence-student-outcomes.aspx on August 12, 2025.

Gallup. (2019b, May 22). *Positive relationships between student engagement and hope and student behavior.* Author. Accessed at www.gallup.com/education/257732/positive-relationships-student-engagement-hope-student-behavior.aspx on August 21, 2025.

García-Martínez, I., Montenegro-Rueda, M., Molina-Fernández, E., & Fernández-Batanero, J. M. (2021). Mapping teacher collaboration for school success. *School Effectiveness and School Improvement, 32*(4), 631–649. https://doi.org/10.1080/09243453.2021.1925700

Ghani, B., Hyder, S. I., Yoo, S., & Han, H. (2023). Does employee engagement promote innovation? The facilitators of innovative workplace behavior via mediation and moderation. *Heliyon, 9*(11), Article e21817. https://doi.org/10.1016/j.heliyon.2023.e21817

Gilbert, T. F. (2007). *Human competence: Engineering worthy performance.* Pfeiffer.

Gladwell, M. (2000). *The tipping point: How little things can make a big difference.* Little, Brown.

Grant, A., Haider, Z., & Raufuss, A. (2023, February 24). *Black swans, gray rhinos, and silver linings: Anticipating geopolitical risks (and openings).* McKinsey & Company. Accessed at www.mckinsey.com/capabilities/risk-and-resilience/our-insights/black-swans-gray-rhinos-and-silver-linings-anticipating-geopolitical-risks-and-openings on March 18, 2025.

Gross, J., & Vostroknutov, A. (2022). Why do people follow social norms? *Current Opinion in Psychology, 44*, 1–6.

Guttena, R. K. (2024, September 6). *"Appreciative inquiry," a powerful tool for teachers to engage students in the classroom* [Blog post]. Accessed at https://blog.efmdglobal.org/2024/09/06/appreciative-inquiry-a-powerful-tool-for-teachers-to-engage-students-in-the-classroom on March 18, 2025.

Hale, J. (2012). *Performance-based certification: How to design a valid, defensible, cost-effective program* (2nd ed.). Pfeiffer.

Hale, J., Page, D., & Quigg, J. (2024). *The school improvement specialist field guide: Proven processes and tools for school improvement coaches* (2nd ed.). The Institute for Performance Improvement.

Hampton Roads International Society for Performance Improvement. (n.d.). *What is HPI?* Accessed at www.hrispi.org/general-5 on July 31, 2025.

Hancock, J. (n.d.). *5 whys: Getting to the root of a problem quickly.* Accessed at www.mindtools.com/a3mi00v/5-whys on March 18, 2025.

Hasso Plattner Institute of Design. (n.d.). *Empathy fieldguide.* Author. Accessed at https://hci.stanford.edu/courses/cs147/2024/au/readings/FIELDGUIDE-Screen-DTBC-March-2015-V2.pdf on March 18, 2025.

Heath, C., & Heath, D. (2007). *Made to stick: Why some ideas survive and others die.* Random House.

Herrmann, Z. (2019). Cooperate or collaborate? *Educational Leadership, 76*(9), 68–72.

Hiatt, J. M. (2006). *ADKAR: A model for change in business, government and our community.* Prosci Learning Center.

Huck, C., & Zhang, J. (2021). Effects of the COVID-19 pandemic on K–12 education: A systematic literature review. *New Waves: Educational Research and Development, 24*(1), 53–84.

Joiner, B. L. (1985). The key role of statisticians in the transformation of North American industry. *The American Statistician, 39*(3), 224–227.

Kizart, C. C. (2025). *Beyond implicit and explicit bias: Strategies for healing the root causes of inequity in education.* Solution Tree Press.

Kotter, J. P. (2018). *Leading change* (2nd ed.). Harvard Business Review Press.

Kotter International. (n.d.). *The 8 steps for leading change.* Accessed at www.kotterinc.com/methodology/8-steps on March 18, 2025.

Kythreotis, A., Pashiardis, P., & Kyriakides, L. (2010). The influence of school leadership styles and culture on students' achievement in Cyprus primary schools. *Journal of Educational Administration, 48*(2), 218–240.

LaMorte, W. W. (2022). *Diffusion of innovation theory.* Boston University School of Public Health. Accessed at https://databoom.us/wp-content/uploads/2025/02/Diffusion-of-Innovation-Theory.pdf on March 18, 2025.

Lau, W. W. F., & Yuen, A. H. K. (2019). A meta-analysis of the effectiveness of STEM professional development for K–12 teachers on teacher self-efficacy and student achievement. *Educational Research Review, 26*, 43–57.

Learning Forward. (n.d.). *Professional learning definition*. Accessed at https://learningforward.org /about/professional-learning-definition on March 18, 2025.

Lewin, K. (1958). Group decision and social change. In E. E. Maccoby, T. M. Newcomb, & E. L. Hartley (Eds.), *Readings in social psychology* (pp. 197–211). Holt, Rinehart & Winston.

Maldonado, G., & Greenland, S. (2002). Estimating causal effects. *International Journal of Epidemiology, 31*(2), 422–429. https://doi.org/10.1093/intjepid/31.2.422

McIlrath, B., & Kotnour, T. (2002). *Process alignment for strategic implementation*. Industrial Engineering and Management Systems. Accessed at https://citeseerx.ist.psu.edu /document?repid=rep1&type=pdf&doi=010f80bf420b7d623cf987e5727a0f05748 67620 on March 18, 2025.

Mertler, C. A. (2025). *Action research: Improving schools and empowering educators* (7th ed.). SAGE.

Meyer, A., Hartung-Beck, V., Gronostaj, A., Krüger, S., & Richter, D. (2023). How can principal leadership practices promote teacher collaboration and organizational change? A longitudinal multiple case study of three school improvement initiatives. *Journal of Educational Change, 24*(4), 425–455. https://doi.org/10.1007/s10833-022-09451-9

Mifsud, D. (2024). A systematic review of school distributed leadership: Exploring research purposes, concepts and approaches in the field between 2010 and 2022. *Journal of Educational Administration and History, 56*(2), 154–179. https://doi.org/10.1080/002206 20.2022.2158181

Muhammad, A. (2024). *The way forward: PLC at Work and the bright future of education*. Solution Tree Press.

National Implementation Research Network. (2015). *Implementation stages overview*. Frank Porter Graham Child Development Institute. Accessed at https://implementation.fpg.unc .edu/wp-content/uploads/Implementation-Stages-Overview.pdf on March 18, 2025.

Nauman, S., Bhatti, S. H., Imam, H., & Khan, M. S. (2021). How servant leadership drives project team performance through collaborative culture and knowledge sharing. *Project Management Journal, 53*(1), 17–32. https://doi.org/10.1177/87569728211037777

Okes, D. (2019). *Root cause analysis: The core of the problem solving and corrective action* (2nd ed.). ASQ Quality Press.

Page, D., & Hale, J. (2013). *The school improvement specialist field guide*. Corwin Press.

Peart, N. (2020, November 6). The most important ways companies can improve work-life balance. *Forbes*. Accessed at www.forbes.com/sites/nataliapeart/2020/11/06/the-most -important-ways-companies-can-improve-work-life-balance on March 18, 2025.

Pierson, R. (2013, May). *Every kid needs a champion* [Video file]. TED Talks. Accessed at www.ted.com/talks/rita_pierson_every_kid_needs_a_champion on March 18, 2025.

Pojasek, R. B. (2000). Asking "why?" five times. *Environmental Quality Management, 10*(1), 79–84.

Raikar, S. P. (n.d.). Black swan event. *Britannica*. Accessed at www.britannica.com/topic/black -swan-event on March 18, 2025.

Raja, S., & Stein, S. L. (2014). Work-life balance: History, costs, and budgeting for balance. *Clinics in Colon and Rectal Surgery, 27*(2), 71–74.

Ramachandran, K. K., & Karthick, K. K. (2019). Gantt chart: An important tool of management. *International Journal of Innovative Technology and Exploring Engineering, 8*(7), 2278–3075.

Rogers, E. M. (1962). *Diffusion of innovations*. Free Press.

Rothwell, W. J. (2005). *Beyond training and development: The groundbreaking classic on human performance enhancement* (2nd ed.). AMACOM.

Rothwell, W. J. (2015). *Effective succession planning: Ensuring leadership continuity and building talent from within* (5th ed.). AMACOM.

Shackleton-Jones, N. (2023). *How people learn: A new model of learning and cognition to improve performance and education* (2nd ed.). Kogan Page.

Shank, P. (2017). *Write and organize for deeper learning: 28 evidence-based and easy-to-apply tactics that will make your instruction better for learning*. Learning Peaks.

Shank, P. (2025). *Practice and feedback for deeper learning: 26 evidence-based and easy-to-apply tactics that promote deeper learning and application*. Learning Peaks LLC.

Sinek, S. (2009a, September). How great leaders inspire action [Video file]. TED Talks. Accessed at www.ted.com/talks/simon_sinek_how_great_leaders_inspire_action on March 18, 2025.

Sinek, S. (2009b). *Start with why: How great leaders inspire everyone to take action*. Penguin.

Snyder, C. R. (2002). Hope theory: Rainbows in the mind. *Psychological Inquiry, 13*(4), 249–275. https://doi.org/10.1207/S15327965PLI1304_01

Stolovitch, H. D., & Keeps, E. J. (Eds.). (1999). *Handbook of human performance technology: Improving individual and organizational performance worldwide* (2nd ed.). Jossey-Bass /Pfeiffer.

Suárez-Barraza, M. F., & Rodríguez-González, F. G. (2019). Cornerstone root causes through the analysis of the Ishikawa diagram, is it possible to find them? A first research approach. *International Journal of Quality and Service Sciences, 11*(2), 302–316. http://dx.doi.org /10.1108/IJQSS-12-2017-0113

Thalheimer, W. (2018). *The learning-transfer evaluation model: Sending messages to enable learning effectiveness*. Accessed at www.worklearning.com/wp-content/uploads/2018/02/Thalheimer -The-Learning-Transfer-Evaluation-Model-Report-for-LTEM-v11.pdf on September 3, 2025.

Tharp, B. M. (2009). *Defining "culture" and "organizational culture": From anthropology to the office*. Haworth. Accessed at www.thercfgroup.com/files/resources/Defining-Culture-and -Organizationa-Culture_5.pdf on March 18, 2025.

Toropova, A., Myrberg, E., & Johansson, S. (2021). Teacher job satisfaction: The importance of school working conditions and teacher characteristics. *Educational Review, 73*(1), 71–97. http://dx.doi.org/10.1080/00131911.2019.1705247

Torres, D. G. (2019). Distributed leadership, professional collaboration, and teachers' job satisfaction in U.S. schools. *Teaching and Teacher Education, 79*, 111–123. https://doi.org/10.1016/j.tate.2018.12.001

Travers, M. (2024, August 30). What Hanumankind's "Big Dawgs" teaches us about hidden bias—by a psychologist. *Forbes.* Accessed at www.forbes.com/sites/traversmark/2024/08/30/what-hanumankinds-big-dawgs-teaches-us-about-hidden-bias-by-a-psychologist on August 29, 2025.

Turner, N. S. (2023). *Simply instructional coaching: Questions asked and answered from the field* (Revised ed.). Solution Tree Press.

U.S. Department of the Army. (1993, September). *A leader's guide to after-action reviews* (TC 25-20). Author. Accessed at www.hsdl.org/c/view?docid=775082 on July 30, 2025.

Van Driel, J. H., Borko, H., & Osborne, J. (2023). A meta-analysis of the effects of STEM professional development on teacher and student outcomes. *Frontiers in Education, 8,* Article 1086392.

Van Tiem, D. M., Moseley, J. L., & Dessinger, J. C. (2012). *Fundamentals of performance improvement: Optimizing results through people, process, and organizations* (3rd ed.). Wiley.

Waters, R. D., & Farwell, T. M. (2022). Shaping tomorrow's industry leaders by incorporating inclusivity into campaign planning curriculum: Student reactions to the SMART+IE mindset in strategic communication efforts. *Journal of Public Relations Education, 8*(4), 183–239.

The W. Edwards Deming Institute. (n.d.). *The PDSA cycle.* Accessed at https://deming.org/explore/pdsa on March 18, 2025.

Whitmer, J. (2020, April 27). *Don't believe the lies* [Blog post]. Accessed at https://jennwhitmer.com/blog/dont-believe-the-lies on March 18, 2025.

Wile, D. (2012). Why doers do: 15 years wiser. *Performance Improvement, 51*(6), 14–18. https://doi.org/10.1002/pfi.21273

Wilson, M. (2016). Becoming data and information rich in education. *BU Journal of Graduate Studies in Education, 8*(1), 5–9.

Wilson, S. M. (2013). Professional development for science teachers. *Science, 340*(6130), 310–313.

Woods, R. (n.d.). *Module 2: Identifying priorities and creating SMART goals* [PowerPoint slides]. Georgia Department of Education. Accessed at https://inspire.gadoe.org/user-files/a7671053-7a45-4f76-a611-0af6ac510756.pdf on July 6, 2025.

XPLANE. (2023, March 9). *How to engage people and bring your strategy to life* [Blog post]. Accessed at https://xplane.com/how-to-engage-people-and-bring-your-strategy-to-life on March 18, 2025.

Yao, L., Chu, Z., Li, S., Li, Y., Gao, J., & Zhang, A. (2021). A survey on causal inference. *ACM Transactions on Knowledge Discovery From Data, 15*(5), Article 74. https://doi.org/10.48550/arXiv.2002.02770

Index

H

habits of mind, 153, 155

Hale, J., 2, 41, 116, 196

hope

    school culture and, 153

    success tool for hope and resilience
        assessment, 154–155

human performance improvement
    (HPI), 6–7, 11–12

human performance technology (HPT), 6

I

if-then consequences, 161, 162

if-then decisions, 101.
    See also decision making

implementation

    implementation teams, 191.
        See also teams

    monitoring, 178–179

    school-improvement efforts and, 2

implementing for sustainability standard

    about, 189–190

    Certified School Improvement Specialist
        (CSIS) standards, 2, 8, 188

    checking implementation and
        sustainability, 193–194

    conclusion, 200

    demonstrating value, 196–197

    evaluating the work, 195–196

    focusing on coherence, 190–191

    reproducibles for, 201–202

    reviewing examples of the
        standard, 198–199

    transferring ownership, 194–195

    using the stages of
        implementation, 191–192

implicit bias, 157. *See also* bias

improvement whiplash, 203

inclusive dialogue, 127

induction, focusing on, 142

influence

    crafting inner and outer
        circles of, 116–117

    energy, aligning with areas of
        influence, 180–181

    identifying circles of, 116–120

    identifying individuals who have
        influence and where, 122–124

    influencers and best approaches for
        interacting, 124

    leveraging outer circles of, 121–122

    success tool for influence planner, 123

    widening your circles of, 120–124

initial implementation stage, 191, 192.
    See also stages of implementation

innovation

    focusing on coherence and, 190

    school-improvement efforts and, 2

inquiry charts, success tool for, 51

installation stage, 191, 192.
    See also stages of implementation

instructional practices and professional
    learning, 140

interviews

    success tool for empathy interview
        protocol, 46–47

    success tool for interview theme
        definition process, 48

introduction

V

W

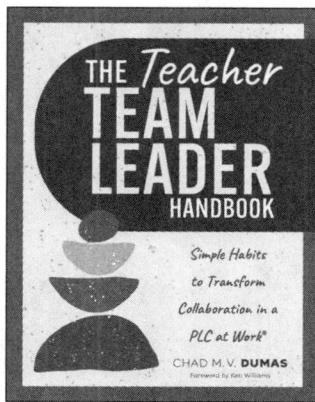

The Teacher Team Leader Handbook
Chad M. V. Dumas

Education expert and award-winning researcher Chad M. V. Dumas provides teacher team leaders with clarity on their role and approach, accompanied by actions that help teams get going, gain momentum, overcome obstacles, and refine skills that maximize their effectiveness in professional learning communities.

BKG210

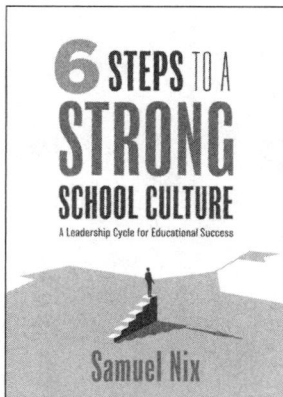

Six Steps to a Strong School Culture
Samuel Nix

Principals can use Samuel Nix's field-tested resource to become leaders of learning and establish a school culture of accountability and student improvement. Learn how the six steps in the leadership cycle apply to every strategic-planning and decision-making scenario.

BKG188

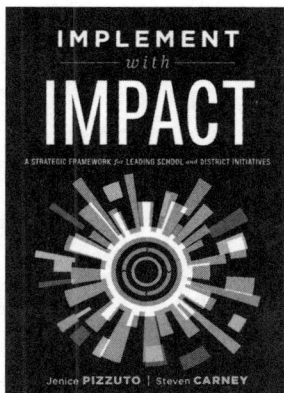

Implement With IMPACT
Jenice Pizzuto and Steven Carney

Learn how to build an implementation team that will bridge the implementation gap and prevent the adopt-and-abandon cycle that often comes with change. The IMPACT framework provides distinct stages and human- and learning-centered design elements to help you achieve quick, tangible wins and sustainable, scalable results.

BKG093

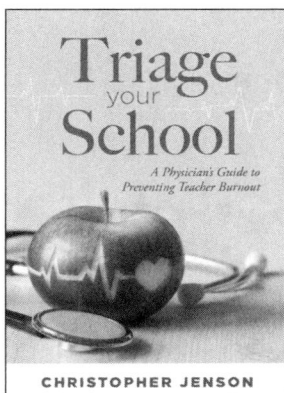

Triage Your School
Christopher Jenson

Triage Your School offers school leaders insight into why attempts to resolve educator burnout often fail and presents meaningful solutions. Engage in your work with a new perspective. Apply operational changes and practical strategies from leading healthcare settings to prevent teachers from leaving the profession.

BKG137

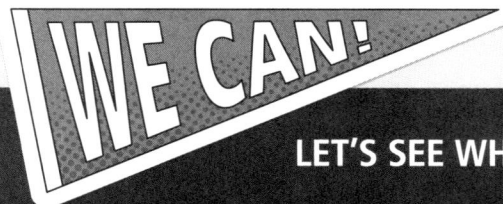